"Nicki Scully and Linda Star Wolf have brilliantly mapped out the step by step initiations we all go through in life. *Shamanic Mysteries of Egypt* is very profound and I think will provide help to all during these changing times."

SANDRA INGERMAN, AUTHOR OF
SOUL RETRIEVAL AND *MEDICINE FOR THE EARTH*

"*Shamanic Mysteries of Egypt* opens a new and magical window into the eternal world of pharaonic Egypt and its gods. Its special quality lies in the fact that it is written with an open heart and a searching soul, very much in the manner of an initiated scribe of this ancient land."

ROBERT G. BAUVAL, AUTHOR OF
THE ORION MYSTERY AND *THE EGYPT CODE*

"Scully and Star Wolf have tapped into the mythic field of ancient Egypt, cradle of civilization. I wholeheartedly recommend using this book as a guide for a most profound shamanic voyage up the Nile. It is an amazing adventure you won't want to miss."

JUSTINE WILLIS TOMS AND MICHAEL TOMS, COFOUNDERS OF
NEW DIMENSIONS BROADCASTING NETWORK AND COAUTHORS OF
TRUE WORK: DOING WHAT YOU LOVE AND LOVING WHAT YOU DO

"Scully and Star Wolf know Egypt, and their book is a guide to the emotional, living *experience* of Egypt; what Egypt means and how to *feel* it. It's scholarship of the heart, rather than of the mind. Very interesting! Useful, too."

JOHN ANTHONY WEST,
AUTHOR OF *SERPENT IN THE SKY*

"More than any other book, *Shamanic Mysteries of Egypt* answers why so many people, now and throughout the ages, have been called to Egypt. These journeys reach into the depths of your being to empower your unique soul purpose. Discover how the awakened heart-mind consciousness transmitted through these initiatory experiences is essential for the healing of our planet."

MARY K. GREER,
AUTHOR OF *TAROT FOR YOUR SELF*

"Nicki Scully and Linda Star Wolf are part of a movement we might call taking the Gods seriously. This book shows us how the *neteru* can be both the genuine deities of the Ancient Egyptians and a powerful force in our own lives."

RACHEL POLLACK, AUTHOR OF
SEVENTY-EIGHT DEGREES OF WISDOM

"These refreshingly direct methods of meditation and ritual reveal where true magic and mystery meet, in the sacred chamber of the heart of the soul. Like Isis providing the missing piece to Osiris, this book brings back the heart to the process of understanding and exploring the mysteries of Egypt."

DETRACI REGULA, AUTHOR OF
THE MYSTERIES OF ISIS

"This brilliant integration of the Egyptian mysteries, Jungian individuation, and the Tarot causes the reader to be initiated by the *neteru*—all of the aspects of nature. *Shamanic Mysteries of Egypt* is a great book for those who are entirely new to these mysteries, and it is a deep pool of wisdom for those already familiar with them. This book unlocks the hidden keys of ancient wisdom for the modern world."

BARBARA HAND CLOW, AUTHOR OF
THE MIND CHRONICLES AND *THE MAYAN CODE*

SHAMANIC MYSTERIES
OF EGYPT

AWAKENING THE HEALING
POWER OF THE HEART

Nicki Scully
and
Linda Star Wolf

Illustrated by Kris Waldherr

Bear & Company
Rochester, Vermont

Bear & Company
One Park Street
Rochester, Vermont 05767
www.BearandCompanyBooks.com

Bear & Company is a division of Inner Traditions International

Library of Congress Cataloging-in-Publication Data
Scully, Nicki, 1943–
  Shamanic mysteries of Egypt : awakening the healing power of the heart / Nicki Scully
and Linda Star Wolf ; illustrated by Kris Waldherr.
      p. cm.
  Includes bibliographical references and index.
  ISBN-13: 978-1-59143-068-1 (pbk.)
  ISBN-10: 1-59143-068-2 (pbk.)
  1. Shamanism—Miscellanea. 2. Gods, Egyptian—Miscellanea. I. Wolf, Linda Star.
II. Title.
  BF1622.E3S38 2007
  299'.93—dc22

                                                                              2006103162

Excerpts from *Awakening Osiris* by Normandi Ellis reprinted by permission of Phanes
Press, an imprint of Red Wheel/Weiser, Newburyport, Massachusetts, and San Francisco, California.

Lyrics to *Brokedown Palace* by Robert Hunter, copyright Ice Nine Publishing Company. Used by permission.

To contact illustrator Kris Waldherr go to www.artandwords.com.

Printed and bound in Canada by Webcom

10 9 8 7 6 5 4 3 2 1

Text design and layout by Jon Desautels
This book was typeset in Sabon with OptiCivet as the display typeface

THIS BOOK IS DEDICATED TO
THE INTREPID SHAMANIC SOULS WILLING TO ENTER INTO THESE MYSTERIES
IN ORDER TO AWAKEN THE HEALING POWER OF THEIR HEARTS.

CONTENTS

PART II ❧ THE SECOND GREAT ROUND

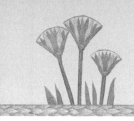

ACKNOWLEDGMENTS

THERE ARE MANY magical and generous kindred spirits in this realm and in the *neter* world who lovingly supported and guided us throughout the birthing of this book.

Thank you Anubis and Thoth, and all the neteru of Shamanic Egypt for your constant presence, both in vision and voice as you led us through unchartered waters into the depths of our souls, and the heart of Egypt. We have waited many lifetimes to come together at this perfect moment. Thank you for the resounding message, "It's Not Too Late!"

We are deeply grateful to the wonderful staff at Inner Traditions • Bear & Company, especially Jeanie Levitan, Peri Champine, and our stellar project editor, Laura Schlivek, for your exquisite care and expertise that added so much to the clarity and quality of this book. Thanks also to Victoria Sant'Ambrogio for her perceptive and sensitive line edit of the manuscript. And thank you Kris Waldherr for magically translating our vision into the gorgeous illustrations that grace this book.

To Mohamed Nazmy for setting up the magic, Emil Shaker, our passionate and knowledgeable Egyptologist, and Hatem Ali and Akram Farouk for taking such good care of us all—thank you for being our faithful, caring guides on our shamanic journeys through our beloved Egypt. We honor and thank all the participants in the "As One" Egypt groups who came together this past year and contributed greatly in the birth of these sacred rites, and especially our co-leaders, Brad Collins and Anyaa McAndrew, and Imsara and Patricia Bowers.

We send special thanks to Normandi Ellis for your inspiration and wealth of wisdom, and the magical words of "remembering" in your exquisite book *Awakening Osiris*.

✺ FROM NICKI

It took the support of a tremendous number of people to assist and hold space for me during the creation of this book. I send immeasurable gratitude to my husband, Mark Hallert, for the deep love that we share, your focused attention to this project, for watching my back, and for keeping the home fires burning. To Liisa Korpella for the numerous ways you've supported me both at home and in Egypt. For Linda Oliver who kept the office running smoothly in spite of my lengthy absences, both at home and abroad.

Gloria Taylor Brown and Charla Hermann, my soul sisters who, each in your time read every word and made your comments known—I am so grateful for your friendship and support. Thank you Anita Bermont and Steve Harter for your attention to detail and your endurance listening to and commenting on the final edit. To Tree for tending the garden and typing the bibliography. To Joan Porter for a soft place to land and keep it all together during hard times. To Robert and Michele Bauval for opening your home, your hearts, and your library to me in Egypt. To Marwan El-Azzouni for showing me the wonders of secrets hidden in the desert. For Sherry Littlefield for taking care of Mark (and me) when Mark's knee was replaced during the pressure-filled editing rewrites. To Kaydee Hallert for filling in while I (and my office staff) journeyed to Egypt. To Mary Greer and deTraci Regula for reading and critiquing the first draft. And to all those who have helped me over the years to bring in the teachings and initiations that laid the foundation for the work in this book, thank you. You know who you are!

✺ FROM STAR WOLF

Thank you to my beloved husband and best friend, Brad Collins, for holding the fort with our home and businesses, for rubbing my feet, feeding my body, making me laugh, loving me, believing in this work and encouraging me to open up to let my biggest self come forth into the world, and for helping me to not be afraid of being "Too Much." To my grandmothers, Mammy Jones and Ovie Finley, and cousin Margaret Jean Moore for teaching me about dreams, magic, and Tarot. To my parents, Richard Finley and Sue Finley, for your loving support on all levels, for teaching me about Edgar Cayce, and for being proud of me. For my son, Casey Piscitelli, and his family, Shelley, Aidan, and Cian for their inspiration. And to Grandmother Twylah Nitsch for leading me back to my spirit clan, and inner voice and magic.

Deep gratitude to my friends: Windraven for holding space for me to ground after countless hours of visioning and channeling, and for the others on the healing team that kept me together in Egypt—Barb Westover, Kathy Paxson, and Brenda Todd. To Ruby for your unending support and keeping a vigilant, caring eye on our business and community affairs. To Kathy Morrison, Sarah Jane Fridy, and the rest of the Isis Cove community. To Kathy Paxson, Anne Kenan, Susahn Smith, and Buzz Gibbs for helping me to remember a very important part of my soul's purpose. Thank you Anyaa McAndrew for believing in the "work" and me. Thank you to all my dedicated Venus Rising students and soul friends who have journeyed with me to awaken the "*shaman within*" over these many years.

We both wish to honor and thank the immense spirit of Egypt herself, her land and the generous spirited people who always embrace us with warmth and welcome us home. And finally we thank you, the readers, for choosing to join us on this spiritual adventure.

Nicki Scully (Blue Eagle)

and

Linda Star Wolf

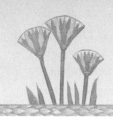

PREFACE
THE ROADRUNNER AND WILY COYOTE

WHEN THE CONCEPT of this book first came to us, Star Wolf and I reminded each other that if you want something done, give it to a busy person. We laughed heartily as we studied our calendars and tried to find the hours a day that would be needed to make it happen in the brief months we were promised. To set the context for our partnership, we traveled two similar yet very different roads that converged at the altar of the Egyptian Mysteries in the summer of 2002.

Star Wolf and I first met through email. We can't remember who saw whose newsletter first, but we both knew we were destined to meet. She recalls that when she saw my newsletter she felt that she could have written it. I contacted her to see about using her Shamanic Center in Marin County, and it just so happened that Star Wolf and her husband Brad were teaching in Portland the following weekend. I invited them to stop by for the night. They thought I was either very gracious or a nutcase, but they decided to take a chance.

Smitten by our garden, they decided to check me out further by joining Normandi Ellis and me two weeks later for our seventh annual Egyptian Mysteries retreat. Our subject that year was "Becoming the Oracle," a mind-bending, reality-stretching new map that carried us into some previously uncharted waters. The gifts of prophecy and the potential for oracular medicine poured through our tentative yet open minds, and into the participants. In Star Wolf's case it was a set-up: the torrent of visions that burst through her prepared and open heart awakened her already committed soul to a new level of purpose, and she was able to claim the stellar gift of prophecy that had been awaiting the auspicious moment for its birth.

We each went on with our lives, and it was Star Wolf who felt the call to co-lead a group to Egypt with my company, Shamanic Journeys, Ltd., and me. As the founder and creator of the form, Shamanic Breathwork, she had a strong base to draw from; between us, forty-two participants came together in October, 2005, to become the "As One" group, one of the most deeply connected and joyful groups in either of our experience.

In 1978, I had traveled to Egypt with the rock band The Grateful Dead, when they played three concerts in front of the Sphinx under a full moon. Those two weeks of pure magic changed the course of my life, yet the gift of prophecy was not mine, and it has been an ongoing surprise as I discovered, mostly in retrospect, how deep my connection was and continues to be to that land and the pantheon that speaks through its enduring monuments. It would be years before I understood that it was the ancient voice of these ancestors that also spoke within my DNA.

Although my relationship with the pantheon and the Egyptian Mysteries deepened and expanded during the course of leading thirty-plus groups, the tour with Star Wolf catalyzed a major shift. On the flight to Cairo, I was reading *Shamanic Wisdom in the Pyramid Texts* by Jeremy Naydler, and had the revelation that the Sed Festival rites described in these texts were returning, and that we would be presenting some version of these rites of renewal during our pilgrimage. When Star Wolf arrived in Cairo a couple of days later, she confirmed my insight when she told me of a dream she'd had a few nights before. Anubis came to her in the night and took her through an experience that I recognized as the first major initiation in the work, which was to happen at Sakkara where the Sed festivals had taken place during the Old Kingdom. This synchronistic magic was compounded when I discovered that my dear friend and mentor Mohamed Nazmy, the Egyptian land agent who makes all our dreams come true, had already planned a special private entry for us into the step pyramid at Sakkara, a rare (almost unheard of) privilege that would allow us to perform this rite in a manner that would add considerably to its potency.

Star Wolf became ill almost as soon as she arrived in Cairo. In spite of her growing difficulty breathing, and at my urging, we soon discovered that she had a direct and clear channel to Thoth, my primary teacher and the architect of this and my previous work. Although Star Wolf was physically impaired throughout the trip, our co-leaders Anyaa McAndrew and Brad Collins (Star Wolf's husband) were tireless in their support; thus, along with a number of participating priestess/healers, we managed to keep her together and get her to most of the temples as we traveled throughout Egypt. Each night we would meet and Star Wolf would download the next set of instructions and images, which because of my intimate relationship with Egypt, I was able to translate into the new/old instructions for the required rituals of initiation. While Star Wolf reclined on her bed in a semitrance state of meditation, we would enter into a place of the heart/mind and trust. There was always a deep space of reverence and a mixture of the sacred and profane while we moved ahead and trusted the process. Thoth, my teacher, the Egyptian god of wisdom and communication, became her oracle and spoke the powerful mystery teachings that we soon realized were meant for us personally as well as for the world.

Although Star Wolf had channeled before, this was the first time she gave herself over fully to the process without reservation. Her debilitation created an altered state of consciousness, so that while the sacred voice of Thoth spoke through her, and while she was engaged in the ceremonies and rituals at the temples, she felt no distress and could breathe easily; at those times the symptoms of her illness magically disappeared. It was not until a few days after we returned home from Egypt that she actually emerged from the mysterious illness.

As a consequence of her shamanic death, Star Wolf experienced the rebirth that prepared her vessel for the even deeper work of bringing in this book—for which our journey to Egypt became a preview of the coming attraction. Through the birth of the ancient sacred heart rituals in Egypt, a connection was forged between Star Wolf and myself that included the Egyptian pantheon. With the sacred trust that resulted from this powerful heart/mind bond, I was able to place my faith in the truth of her ability to bring in something altogether new and magical. I went with my inner knowing and released my attachment to all previously conceived dogma and rituals from my past experience and knowledge of Egypt. Although Star Wolf's familiarity with Egypt's myths and pantheon was quite limited when we began this work, she perceived with absolute clarity and conveyed with meticulous articulation detailed descriptions of instructions, symbols, and even attire that she had never seen before. It was my heartfelt joy to translate her vision into this book that is the map to these Shamanic Mysteries of Egypt.

One night on the Nile when the co-leaders and I were especially concerned for Star Wolf, the four of us snuggled together on her bed to bolster her while preparing for the next day's ritual. Through our large cabin window, we could clearly view the ageless beauty along the river's edge as we drifted past. A loud and persistent message suddenly burst through Star Wolf with absolute clarity: *"It's not too late! There is still hope, there is still time."* As the tears flowed from us, our doubts and pessimism for the tragic situations of the world were washed away in the knowing that we are *not too late*. That message has sustained us, and has continued to uphold us as we created space for this work to enter in its fullness.

By February, it was clear that Thoth wanted us to write a "small" book in order to awaken these rites more fully into human consciousness. I was already engaged in writing two other books, and did not see how I could include another major project. Thoth promised that it would be mercurially quick, and assured us that although it would streak through our lives like a comet, what we would learn would assist in everything else that we were doing. That this book would be an expression from the heart of Anubis added further incentive, and we agreed to go for it.

We began the work on Valentine's Day and once again I was amazed at the clarity and precision with which Star Wolf perceived complex Egyptian cosmology and theology, along with details such as the shapes of crowns and symbols to which she had no previous exposure. This unique talent continued throughout our collaboration. The first round was completed on Easter Sunday. In between, we spent two to three hours most mornings on the phone, Star Wolf visioning and I scribing at the computer. I held the space for her to birth these heart/mind mystery teachings as the true shaman she is. Then I wrote, crafted, and added context to her visions with my research, knowledge, and experience until the manuscript was completed.

It was apparent from the beginning of our collaboration that Star Wolf, in part due to her long-time connection to the Wolf Clan, is identified with Anubis (Jackal deity) energy, while I have always had a strong connection with Thoth (Ibis deity). While experiencing my own journey through these rites in Egypt I received my *ren*—my sacred spirit name— Blue Eagle. We knew we were the bird and the canine, and sometimes during the chaotic birthing of our work we felt like a Roadrunner cartoon, especially during the bringing in of the second round.

While the first round was accomplished over the phone, the second round transpired while at least one of us was in motion—one or both of us in a car, or on a boat, or in the air, or even out walking. We started working on it while she was home in North Carolina and I was on our cruise ship on the Nile. After I returned from Egypt, we planned to spend four days together so that we could make some quick progress. We thought it was a bit peculiar that we were directed to use the only time we had together during the entire process to drive all the way to California to visit friends. For me it was not a new concept, as my husband Mark Hallert and I have always done our best visioning work while he drives and I scribe. Because it was the first time Star Wolf attempted to drive and vision at the same time, Thoth explained how the movement through the element air enhanced and sped up the visioning process. . . . During our return trip, with only a few pages left in the entire book, we were winding our way past Mount Shasta and up the Siskyou Pass into Oregon. As we were told to journey our readers to the highest point in their area, be it a rooftop or a mountain, we crested the pass where a sign read, "HIGHEST POINT ON I-5." We barely had time to giggle and complete the final instruction when we passed a bright yellow eighteen wheeler, on the side of which was painted a red crested roadrunner wearing a smirking grin and dragging wily coyote in chains, his tongue lolling from his mouth. We had just been told that the exercise ended with a sound, and our laughter rang throughout both Oregon and California!

It is our hope that the joy and passion, the pathos and humor, and the depth of our commitment infuse these pages and inspire the growth, excitement, and transformation that has so deeply touched and enriched our lives. We offer it to you at this time with heartfelt devotion and gratitude to Anubis, Thoth, and the entire family of Egyptian neteru. May these journeys unite your heart, mind, soul, and spirit so that we can all achieve our destiny as divine humans.

NICKI SCULLY
(BLUE EAGLE)

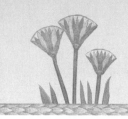

INTRODUCTION

AS WE TRANSIT from the age of Piscean energy to the Aquarian age, we can already discern the advent of fundamental paradigm shifts. During the last several thousand years, mainstream traditions have required intercession with most all forms of expressed divinity, or God. Most people have looked outside of themselves for the savior, the teacher, the messiah, and even for their own personal well-being. We are entering a time when people are searching for a way to stretch the envelope. Many of the fundamental traditions are splintering and disintegrating from within, as institutionalized power structures age and fall. The old ways are not working, and we are being driven to find what is real and true, and what will carry us forward. An inevitable result of this search for solutions will bring us into the intrinsic power of our time: we will become aware of our own divine nature, and the authority and power that are the essence of all awake and aware beings.

The renewal of the healing power of the heart is the result of the sacred marriage between the heart and the mind. This renewal is the reflection of the evolution of divinity as it mirrors the awakening of consciousness in humans. The purpose of this book is to return certain of the ancient mysteries of Egypt to today's world to help human beings embrace and step into their divine nature.

As a species, we are but adolescents in the human experiment, and in the changeable way of all adolescence, we try to remain children at the same time we are striving to become adults in our young, godlike evolvement. We are the young gods. The gods of Egypt are the old gods.

In Egypt, the gods are called *neteru; neter* is the male word for god, *netert* the female. The origins of the word moved from the Coptic Christian *netjer* to the Greek *netcher* and into English as *nature.** True to their meaning, the neteru describe the myriad attributes of nature portrayed as the diverse aspects of the One God, as seen by ancient Egyptians. By whatever names they are called, the family of the neteru of Egypt dwell within and without humans. It is our intention to familiarize our readers with members of the ancient spiritual family that has overseen the human experiment and assists in our evolution and awakening, whether or not we are aware of their presence in our lives. We will show how their essences are woven inextricably into our very DNA, as prominently as that of our ancestors. When we connect with them through the rites of passage described in this book, we have the opportunity to know ourselves more fully and take a more active role in co-creating a healthful, joyful, and wondrous future.

The energies and archetypes expressed through this work are here to break through the veils that have always separated the gods from most human beings. They are here to help us, to assist us on our evolutionary journey. They are here to help us raise our consciousness. This has always been so. Although the neteru have emerged in very dynamic and powerful ways in individual conscious awareness throughout time, they are coming together in a large collective way at this moment, for it is time, and enough individuals are now at a place of consciousness to receive their guidance.

Although the rituals presented here are closely connected to the ancient ways they were practiced, their current expression is based in modern-day, Aquarian understanding. We cannot strictly adhere to old fundamentalist ways or even to the venerable shamanic and mystical religious traditions. The vibrant magic of alchemy as it was lived in the

---

*Normandi Ellis, *Dreams of Isis: A Woman's Spiritual Sojourn* (Wheaton, Ill.: Quest Books, 1995).

ancient traditions of Egypt requires renewal and revitalization, with a fresh interpretation. It is necessary for all things to continue to evolve, including the gods and the rituals. These rituals constitute a unique, fresh expression that is built upon the essence of the old in the same way that the foundations of the ancient temples were built upon those from previous dynasties. We are not trying to replicate the exact details of the past ritual ceremonies; our purpose is to transform and evolve those rituals and ceremonies so that they are accessible and relevant in today's world.

EXOTERIC VERSUS ESOTERIC

All religions and spiritual belief systems are presented in both exoteric and esoteric ways. *Exoteric* is that which is openly displayed—what is seen, written, shown, easily grasped by the mind and intellect. This outer doctrine is available for all adherents and would-be followers and is put forward to help people to make sense of things in their daily lives in a somewhat simple way. People can wrap their minds around exoteric ideas in order to give themselves a spiritual path to walk, with more or less clear guidelines.

The exoteric path usually includes a hierarchy. There is the priesthood or clergy whose members hold various degrees of importance, usually leading up to a venerated master or leader such as the pope or Dalai Llama, an imam or a tribal medicine chief. The congregation, the parish, the individuals who follow that leader agree to conform to the tradition and follow the letter of its law as interpreted by their leader. Over time, this hierarchical organization usually results in fundamentalist ideology and dogma. Fundamentals themselves are important; consider, for example, the fundamentals in mathematics and English as well as in religion. When taken to the extreme, however, fundamentalism can become rigidly stuck and even destructive or dangerous.

There are clear distinctions between exoteric and esoteric knowledge. Esoteric traditions are much more closely related to the mysteries. In the past, these were meant only for the select few who had access to the secret, initiatory knowledge that was held tightly for the exclusive inner priesthood. An uncorrupted person still in tune with his or her divinity would have held that knowledge with integrity and impeccability.

The esoteric spiritual paths hold the energy of the Great Mystery, that ineffable source behind anything that can be seen, written, or articulated. The people who have been most involved in the esoteric have been the mystics, saints, shamans, and prophets. Many times they have been identified as crazy, extremist, or shams, because the mystics tend to think outside of the box. They must feel their way into mysteries, as the mystical path is not charted. True esoteric spiritualism is more about passion than zeal.

In recent times, many of the world's great religions have been locked into the ways of the past, perhaps holding on to secrecy too tightly, slow to change with the evolving spiritual needs of humanity. When people cannot feel the passion behind a particular ritual, spiritual path, or religion, that religion will soon lose its power and dry up. We may liken it to a beautiful lake, the source of which you cannot see because it is fed by an underground spring. If you didn't have the constant flow of that invisible, underground surge of fresh waters coming in, the lake would stagnate and eventually evaporate. Religions and spiritual paths have the same requirements to sustain their viability. If the vital knowledge and access to source is not shared with the common people, the rituals dry up and the branch that fosters them is doomed.

Although a present-day alignment with the esoteric mystical/shamanic traditions of ancient Egypt might seem limiting in its scope and relevance, it is not. The rituals of the heart/mind that we are bringing forth are actually intended for all kinds of people, from all walks of life, regardless of their religious or nonreligious paths. These rites will renew the heart and return heart-centered perspective to the lives of all who pass through the portals within. These passages respond to the deep need of all people at this time for a merging of the heart and mind. It is akin to a mass soul retrieval for all who are able to give themselves fully to the experience accessible through performing these rites.

A MESSAGE OF HOPE

For many, Egyptian cosmology evokes mystery and an intuitive feeling of resonance and connection. For others it has been a subject that brings up fear and intimidation. A good example is the common reaction to the *Egyptian Book of the Dead,* which might be more accurately called *Cycles of Transformation* or *Cycles of Change.* What many don't know is that this book is also referred to as the *Book of Coming Forth by Day.* Misunderstanding is the principle barrier between humans and the ancient gods with their message of hope and eternal life, which has been blocked from most people's awareness. It's ironic that fundamentalist religious advocates do not honor the ancient shamanic traditions that are at the source of most religious truths. These perennial wisdom teachings permeate all religious cultures in ways we are still discovering. Although there are aspects of the creation that are dark in nature or of the shadow world, the concepts of punishment and of the Underworld as a fearful place were misrepresentations, some of which we hope will be corrected as a result of this work. Our purpose here is to return to the heart rituals of ancient Egypt, which were not only about the physical heart, but also about the energy of the heart chakra center—an energy of love and wisdom, and intelligence. The Egyptian word for heart is *ab,* which is also the word for conscience, and for desire. *Ab ba* the heart-soul is the seat of consciousness, and is the relationship formed between spiritual will and the power of love. When we apply our deepest heart's desire to conscious alignment with the desire of a higher will, or god, transformation happens and we can change our destinies.*

The fundamentalist branches of subsequent religions have interpreted the images of many of the neteru as evil or demonic, which is not accurate. In the world of creation, all the vital energies of the negative and positive that are flying around and coming together to create life and physical form, and the myriad images that we receive, are neither good nor bad, they are simply energies. They describe the internal processes that create or dismantle our life. For example, you might dream of a skeleton, and if you have a fear of death or have seen movies where the skeleton is foreboding or evil, you might miss the point: that perhaps your psyche is telling you to come back to the bones, or your foundation. Or the skeleton might signify a shamanic death experience, which

---

*Normandi Ellis, *Dreams of Isis* (Wheaton, Ill.: Quest Books, 1995), chapter 9.

means you are ready for renewal, to put on new skin, or to see things from a different perspective.

Many people are afraid of such images as snakes, spiders, and bats. And yet, since earliest times, in the temples and in the indigenous cultures, the snake has often been a symbol of regeneration and healing. The spider has been a symbol of wisdom and writing and weaving. And the bat has long been the symbol of inner knowing and intuition, a keeper of magic and mystery, which are the things we perceive with our inner radar—it can't see and must rely instead on its knowing, and its acute sensitivity.

The qualities that all three of these animals and symbols represent are those considered to be the more feminine qualities and closer to the yin, or earth, energies. We have been separated from those energies in our culture for hundreds, if not thousands, of years. They have been perceived as negative and even evil, when perhaps they are simply the other half of who and what we all are.

The rituals herein renew in us the intelligent heart, which is also the intuitive and discerning heart. Therefore we, as initiates, must be able to embrace not only our outer awareness but also our inner knowing. We must hold within ourselves both the yin and the yang—both the divine feminine and the masculine. Individuals who are willing to embrace both of those energies will be more able to receive and grasp the deeper meaning accessible through the rites offered here.

A spiritual pilgrimage to Egypt stimulates reflection on the deeper meaning of life. Bold statements are impressed on the great monuments and temples of that great civilization, still standing, vibrant and alive, throbbing with their initial intention to inform us and awaken our memory to who we actually are. There is strong evidence that most modern religions, and perhaps humanity itself, have roots connecting them with the ancient beings portrayed upon those aged, venerable walls.

History traces the rise and fall of empires through what is left behind, and there is legendary support for several far older than Egypt. Whether their demise came from cosmic or planetary relationships and the instability of their times, natural disasters, or cataclysms created by humans (or other species) is open for debate. It isn't too much of a stretch to hypothesize that whenever human civilizations have reached a pinnacle of power to the point of being able to affect the climate on the planet, it may have been disastrous. When humans reach the ability to affect nature to such a degree that, whether intentionally or unintentionally, they begin to control the weather, then humans have stepped into the role of gods.

To recognize and acknowledge our divinity may well be appropriate, even necessary, in order to meet our current challenges. However, if we are children of the gods and have that divine right and heritage, we must begin to assume the full responsibility for what our inherited position means.

Consciousness is awakening around the ability of humans to affect nature; but awareness alone is not enough to make positive change. People have to care. We have to move beyond apathy. Instilled in us are the maternal and paternal instincts to care for our children so that the races will continue; yet we must also care about our creations: the things we make that influence civilization and impact the earth. Through our science, technology, and genetics, we have come to the next stage of godhood. To be fully human is to care about other beings—to become fully divine is to care about and take responsibility for all our creations, all that we are manifesting and destroying. In spite of, or perhaps because of the wars, the natural disasters, the endless suffering, and the social chaos, humans are beginning to awaken, and some are already fully awake. The problem is that there are not enough awake beings who feel they can make a difference or who have fully owned their power.

In our current shamanic Egyptian Mysteries work, the neteru of Egypt are urging us to open our hearts and reconnect with our divine origins. If we understand that we are the sons and daughters of gods and that deep within us we possess divine power, we also realize we are still fledglings. As a species on the planet, humans are young. We are behaving much like teenagers who can't wait to drive the car, yet are not yet ready for the responsibility required.

But think: a helpless infant, in just a couple of years, learns to walk, feed itself, use language to communicate, and use its hands to build things. Is it such a stretch to realize that human beings can, in a relatively short period of time, step into their enlightenment and their divinity?

We've been trained to believe that we lack the skills to confront or change the megalithic power of those who are running the governments, corporations, and other institutions that affect planetary affairs; yet that is not the case. How ridiculous is it to feel that we could not change things, when everything around us shows what we've already done? How much more powerful do we have to be, if we can change the very face of the planet—with roads, with tunnels through mountains, underwater transportation, heavy planes that can fly, boats that weigh thousands of tons and yet glide across the water—rearranging and transforming Earth's resources in unprecedented ways? Even the weather itself is defenseless against our creations!

So what can we do? All power comes from the same source and we can choose how to use it. We need only to rechannel our energy and power. It is not a matter of getting more; it is a matter of redirecting. Our energy must no longer pass through the first three chakras only: it must be driven by more than the urge to survive, the urge to procreate, the urge to exude power, and the urge to control. It must move into the heart/mind so that the energies of our higher (conscious) selves can join the energies of our lower (unconscious) selves and create an embodied, impassioned, and wise way of being and acting.

When we merge the heart with the higher mind we experience the sacred marriage between spirit and humans, and the shift from ego agenda to soul purpose is born. When we open fully and connect to the resulting heart/mind—when we can think and feel and know from that place—we can make the shift at a concrete physical level. There is great power in every awakened soul, and nothing human can defeat the power that is unleashed when enough souls are awakened.

The gods of ancient Egypt are calling out to us. It is time to remember the neteru and build a relationship with them. It's time to bring them out of the mist and fog of the distant past and the faraway land. We are a rainbow bridge to bring consciousness of these ancient ones into the present and allow their intelligence to inform our future. We have a destiny to reestablish, renew, and reawaken our heart/minds, and can do so through our relationship with these ancestors. In so doing, we are not only remembering our family; we are re-membering ourselves.

THE SACRED NETERU OF
SHAMANIC EGYPT

The neteru are the deities of Egypt who express the principles of creation through a rich zoomorphic pantheon, developed over thousands of years of observation and interaction with nature. Throughout history, starting long before the myths were written, stories were handed down that over time morphed into the complex, overlapping, and sometimes confusing relationships between the principles of nature and the creation and sustenance of life.

Although the Egyptians understood the Divine Creator as the one Universal Power, the pantheon of Egypt is huge, in part because ancient Egyptian wisdom found God, and the myriad aspects of God, in nature. These deities embody the multitude of forms found in the natural world and have many, many names. Because the gods often merge with one another, and spirit is recognized to exist in all things, there is no definitive count. In this book, we will introduce twenty-six major principles, one by one, as they appear to perform their respective functions in these rites, according to the principles they represent, and in the order in which they presented themselves to us.

Regarding the gods: they are us, we are them, and yet we are separate from them. All the different neteru are aspects of the One, and all are contained within the others. All future generations of children, even the newest kids on the block of evolution, contain within them the ancestors, just as the seeds of all future generations reside within the ancestors. The mighty oak tree and all future acorns live within its seeds. When our perceptions come by way of the holographic paradigm and the original image is fractured, all fragments contain the entire original within them. Cell division works the same way. Even though each cell in our body contains DNA and has the potential to express the entire encyclopedia of our history and potential, we are individual, separate sparks of all that came before, including the neteru, the great deities that still live within as well as all around us.

Although the gods live in the invisible world of spirit and the ethers, they show up in the physical world through us, their children. Throughout time we are all evolving, and in the great span of eternity, we humans are but adolescent children, struggling through our adolescent challenges. Yet the gods are getting older even as we are, and they grow and accumulate wisdom as they observe us growing in our own stages of development.

When we become aware and as we develop, we become extensions of these beings. We become their hands and feet and eyes and senses in the world. We actually are one body. Just as there are invisible yet vital elements within our physical form—from the molecules and bacteria to the bones and organs that are hidden within our skin, to the space between the atoms—it takes all of it to complete a whole being.

We exist in physical form and are aware of the auric and energy fields that extend beyond the parameters of our body. Yet do we consider that our spirit encapsulates who we are? We tend to think of ourselves as vessels for spirit; yet we live in a field of spirit, and spirit is striving to enter the cells of our bodies so that it is both within and without. It is when spirit inhabits flesh that we begin to comprehend and experience immortality—and when the gods get to experience mortality.

We, the authors, hope that the rituals, initiations, meditations, and ceremonies presented by each of these shamanic archetypes will be perceived with the heart as well as the mind, and that the dynamic forces that are the deities will catalyze tangible physical experiences that awaken cellular memory.

Each chapter will describe and bring forth in depth the stories and characteristics associated with each deity. There is also a Glossary of the Gods at the back of the book that you can refer to in order to learn more about who they are and how they have been perceived throughout history. Now, though, it is important to first speak briefly about Anubis, the Egyptian shaman priest who brings us these sacred heart rituals of ancient Egypt.

ANUBIS, THE SHAMAN PRIEST

Anubis, the guardian between the worlds of spirit and matter—above and below—is the great shaman priest of ancient Egypt. He is our staunch ally, and is ready to help us change our perspective and die to the belief that we have no purpose and no power to transform things on this planet. It is he who leads us through the sacred heart rituals of ancient Egypt in order to help us discover our divinity and learn to perceive and act from our heart/mind. Anubis guides and guards us through these new/ancient rituals of transformation.

At the onset of this work, it was Anubis who appeared first. He stood tall, with tears in the corners of his eyes, offering us a pink rose quartz heart.

Anubis is most commonly known as the dark jackal, associated with and guardian of the Underworld and sometimes called the Opener of the Way. This title is usually taken to mean the opener of the way at death, but Anubis is also the opener of the way of the heart. This great being has a huge, compassionate heart. Although this book is primarily sourced in Anubis's role as the divine heart surgeon (traditional Egyptologists call him the Divine Embalmer) and as the high priest of the sacred heart rituals, it is Thoth's intelligence that speaks through Anubis. Thoth is the god of wisdom, language, communications, and sciences and was considered to be the highest representation of mind to ancient Egyptians. *Shamanic Mysteries of Egypt* is our expression of an alchemical convergence between Anubis, the heart, and Thoth, the mind, which creates the illumined heart/mind.

The Greeks recognized this blend as the combination of Hermes and Anubis and called him Hermanubis. In Roman times he was pictured as a man with a jackal or dog's head holding the caduceus, sometimes with a crocodile at his feet (much like Kuan Yin, the Oriental goddess of compassion and mercy, and her dragon).

Some people believe that all canines have evolved from the original wolf. Anubis carries the ancient wolf energy and is the predecessor of the modern-day wolf, known totemically as a wisdom teacher and guide.

Although there are various accounts of Anubis's origins, we understand that his mother was Nephthys and his father Osiris. Anubis was born in circumstances designed to set him up with a number of important parental influences, through which he absorbed the dark side from Nephthys and Set, and the light from Osiris and Isis. Beyond that, Thoth was like an uncle. Osiris and Nephthys were his biological parents, Set was his shadow father, and Isis and Thoth were his spiritual parents and teachers, and he inherited attributes from all of them.

Anubis has the intuition of his mother Nephthys, and the vision of his adoptive mother and teacher, Isis. He has the keen sensitivities of the jackal, and the ability to guard equally in both the dark and the light; he knows all the pathways that lead from the darkness back into the light. Anubis stands in between the worlds of light and dark as the gateway between ego and soul; he has an energy similar to Christ consciousness. And like Christ, Anubis has also functioned in certain situations as the scapegoat.

The concept of the sacrificial goat, or scapegoat, is very old. In ancient Jewish tradition, the goat was sent out into the desert, bearing all the sins and burdens of the people of the village on its back. Occasionally it returned, but usually it was expected to die in the desert. If the village offered up a scapegoat, then God would be appeased and would forgive the sins of the people. Later, in Christianity, it was Jesus who became the Lamb of God and was nailed to the cross to carry the sins and burdens of the people. Anubis was left out in the desert by his mother at birth. Perhaps that is why he also became known as the guardian of miscarried, aborted, and abandoned children.

The similarities between Jesus and Anubis continue with regard to their parentage. Osiris, Anubis's father, was a powerful energy akin to the Holy Spirit that impregnated Mary. Although Mary was Jesus' biological mother, she did not have the authoritative parental relationship of jurisdiction over him, even when he was a child.

Anubis is like Jesus in another way. He has the courage, strength, and most of all the compassion to walk with people through the valley of the shadow of death. The walkers between the worlds—hospice workers, psychopomps, shamans, and others who help guide people in their death passages—have the kind of empathy and big-hearted love bequeathed by Anubis.

In this work, we see Anubis emerging from the bittersweet role he has played throughout history and in the people's minds. His work has kept him in the womblike cave or sacred heart space, where precious, essential mysteries live, yet have been unutterable. His domain required a deep, nonemotional connection within the heart—private, and sacred. To speak of it would have been blasphemy. Although Anubis will continue holding that space for people, now is the auspicious moment—in the ongoing process of human and planetary evolution—for more of these mysteries to be brought out into the light of day.

It is also time for Anubis to be brought into the light and acknowledged for who he is, the shamanic high priest of the sacred heart rituals, a great being with a huge, compassionate heart, closely aligned with Kuan Yin, Christ, and all of the ancient bodhisattvas of compassion.

While Thoth's wisdom expresses the overarching energy of these Great Mysteries, Anubis is clearly the psychopomp and shamanic priest. He is the heart surgeon who presides over these rituals and teaches us how to perform them. Because he is more physical and related to the divine human, Anubis carries the grounded energies of an Earth shaman and knows the magic that alchemically transforms and awakens the healing power of the heart.

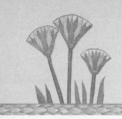

HOW TO USE THIS BOOK

"Do not believe in any traditions just because they have been valid for long years in many countries. Do not believe in something just because many people constantly repeat it. Accept nothing just because someone else has said it, because it is based upon the authority of a wise man, or because it is written in the holy writings. Do not believe in anything just because it seems probable. Do not believe in the fantasies and visions, which you consider to be given by God. Believe nothing just because the authority of a teacher or priest stands behind it. Believe in that which you have perceived to be right through a lengthy examination of your own, in that which lets itself be reconciled with your own good and that of others."

GAUTAMA BUDDHA

OUR PURPOSE IN writing *Shamanic Mysteries of Egypt* is to offer you, our readers, an opportunity to awaken the healing power of the heart through these new iterations of ancient rituals—to reclaim your divinity while maintaining your humanity. As you follow this journey of transformation you will shape-shift into the initiate and embrace your potential to transform your world by healing yourself and expanding your awareness. As you reclaim your internal connection to the guiding principles of Egypt, the visions and experiences you receive will provide wisdom, renew your sacred purpose, and become a living reality as well as a message of hope for the world.

The rites given in this book comprise two great rounds on the human evolutionary spiral, plus four chapters that describe and activate the sacred archetypes of the elements. It is best to move through the chapters in consecutive order, from beginning to end when first encountering this process. Taking these rites in chronological order the first time through is imperative if you want to receive the maximum benefit and full potential they have to offer. So as you take your first swoop through the loop, take your time and savor the lessons and experience of each ritual, meditation, or initiation. Once the rounds have been completed and integrated, chapters can be revisited as needed or the book can serve as a divination tool. Initiates will find that they intuitively open to the chapter that is relevant to their current situations and enquiries.

It is helpful to read each entire chapter, including the initiation, ritual, or meditation before actually doing the journey. With practice, you can experience these unique and powerful initiations while reading them. Alternatively, you can tape the initiation text or have someone else read it aloud. Music can enhance the rituals, and can be used as a background for the initiatory experience. Both live and recorded music can be quite beneficial. Circles who wish to come together to follow this path can work in community, taking turns at reading the journeys so that everyone gets the experience. While it would be best for people to have the opportunity to go through these rituals in a guided way, it is important for readers to be able to work alone when necessary. In order to relish the deep transformational changes offered by these initiations, initiates will want to give themselves appropriate time to integrate each experience.

It's helpful to create a journal in which to record your experiences, as journaling is a very important part of the process of integrating this work. It is best to dedicate a special journal for following your progress with these rites. Make entries immediately after each journey to keep track of your experiences, feelings, and the magic that happens surrounding you as you continue to move forward.

Regardless of how you approach the journeys and rituals in this book, it is important to engage all possible modes of perception. Sight is the most common way we experience guided visualizations but seeing images in the mind's eye is by no means the only way to access these rituals. For our purposes here, kinesthetic sensitivity—or feeling—is equally important. Our feeling sense can be enhanced through practice and attention, as can our other inner senses. Seeing, feeling, hearing, smelling, knowing—all combine to enhance our visionary experience. Imagination also plays a key role, and can get us into the flow of the experience when we think we are not quite "there." If guided visioning is new or difficult for you, take some time to practice and discover your unique way of "seeing" by spending some time in meditation. Perhaps you will want to practice the invocation meditation that appears prior to the first initiation—The Dove—on page 23.

We have not taken a linear or intellectual approach to these initiations; rather we invite you to join us on an experiential journey. When you read the introduction to each rite, which gives you the context in which the journey takes place, it is important to know that the contextual explanations are simply a container for the experience. They are not meant to create a box of limitations that could serve to distance you from a truly mystical experience. If, while reading the descriptions, you experience some confusion or lack of clarity, don't become discouraged. When you move into the journey itself the path will become more apparent, and each repetition provides an opportunity for further clarity. In addition, you can refer to the Glossary of the Gods and the Glossary of Terms at the end of the book to become better acquainted with the Egyptian pantheon and any unfamiliar Egyptian words. Your own deepest memories and knowledge are embedded within your DNA and are activated through the esoteric experiences that these rites provide.

Attention is the coin of the realms—it is what we "pay." Gratitude and appreciation are the most powerful expressions of attention. When we receive help and guidance from these deities, it is always appropriate to reciprocate with gratitude; you can sprinkle it liberally throughout, and offer it also at the end of each process.

After completing the rounds, the initiate can practice various aspects of these rites at different times. When someone is going through crisis or tragedy, a caring circle of friends may choose to come together and practice the appropriate rituals, which can be modified to suit the occasion and the people for whom they are given. This work is designed to become universal, for its principles are translatable to and harmonious with other cultural or spiritual paths.

Ideally, you could travel to Egypt with one of the authors and be guided through the journeys. Or you can consult *Shamanic Mysteries of Egypt* as a spiritual guidebook to the deep experience of the temples themselves. It is our intention to continue offering seminars and retreats, as well as pilgrimages to Egypt, during which we will observe these rites and explore new levels of these mysteries.

The true alchemy of this journey is the sacred marriage between the heart and the mind. It is this sacred union that conceives the initiatory experience and results in the expansion of consciousness and the embodiment of spirit. The rituals will be much more productive if they are felt body experiences. You will miss the embodiment of these potentially powerful rituals if you allow yourself to go through the guided imageries in an intellectual way only. The mind must merge with the heart to maximize each meditation or ritual. In order to receive the full body experience, you must allow the import of each ritual to pass through the heart. Otherwise, your journey will be no more than an intellectual concept; not the transformative experience that it could be.

To create a viable shamanic spiritual path, readers can integrate many of these rituals as practices to give more depth and meaning to their lives, and in order to help themselves and others. Such practices can be translated into healing for oneself or for another, or incorporated into meditation forms and other rites of passage. They are imbued with the essence of Egypt, and their vitality depends upon the spontaneous permutations and translations that keep them vital and alive.

As more and more people turn toward alternative and individualized spiritual paths, there will be more circles that share a common essence or theme. These groups are not to be confused with cults because none of them will have a single charismatic leader. Here lies one of the differences between the Piscean age and the Aquarian age. The Piscean age, out of which we are currently transitioning, is very much about a circle that is guided in a hierarchical way with a teacher at the helm who offers the ultimate in wisdom or salvation. This codependency-driven era is passing; we no longer feel the need to give our power to someone or something outside of ourselves. Although the metaphor of the shepherd and the sheep was appropriate because the shepherd needed to take care of and protect the sheep, the portal we have passed between the ages asks us to give up the old patriarchy with its outer authority, so the old metaphors no longer serve.

Readers are encouraged to spiral back through these rites again and again. Each time you will discover a new level of understanding and experience. You will build deeper and more intimate relationships with the neteru as they continue to reveal their many attributes and secrets.

This book has the powerful goal not only of awakening the healing power of the heart but also of renewing the shamanic Egyptian Mysteries to help guide us into the new age or *aeon*. These rituals of the heart will lead individuals to find the powerful spirit of Egypt within themselves.

PART I

THE FIRST GREAT ROUND

"May my heart increase. May it open wide as sky, enough
to hold the breadth of god. May it shape itself into crystal.
May a light shine on the hidden things that a man might
know himself, his colors, songs and days. May the eight gods
whisper secrets. May a man grow great enough to inhabit
his own heart. May he walk in it on long roads winding past
lotus pools and flowers. May his heart be wide enough to hold
the hearts of others. May those he loves link hands, a chain
of forever. May his heart and arms and legs be strong and
his strength be used for dancing and sowing fields, holding
his wife and uplifting their children. May his heart become
an altar unto god. May all that passes through be offered to
heaven. May the life which touches him, turn again to life. My
heart is a field above which the sun rolls. Never-ending beat,
beat, beat. May the will of the great heart infuse the body.
May the rains come followed by sun, and the green leaves
clinging to the vine that bend themselves toward light."

NORMANDI ELLIS, *AWAKENING OSIRIS:
THE EGYPTIAN BOOK OF THE DEAD*

0
THE DOVE
INITIATE
Innocence/Trust

ALL WHO CROSS the threshold of these mysteries are responding to an ancient call. Deep inside, you always knew this time would come, and that you would be required to leave your doubts, your intellectual skepticism, behind in order to fathom these mysteries.

THE CALLING . . .

To enter into these rites each person must return to the beginner's mind and the innocence and purity of the white Dove. In the form of the Dove, you will carry an olive branch to the neteru as an offering, thanking them for their help as you move through this process of initiation and transformation.

The Dove transcends history and culture as a universal symbol of peace and innocence. The olive tree is sacred to the goddess Athena, the Greek goddess of wisdom, and its branches are a symbol of peace throughout the world.

Today visitors to Egypt often awaken to the sounds of doves cooing outside their windows. Each night at sunset in the temple of Luxor, numerous doves settle onto the capitals atop the many, many giant pillars that surround the central courtyard at the heart of the temple.

While Star Wolf and I were working with the publishers to determine the title and subtitle of this book, a magical synchronicity occurred. My friend Charla Hermann had a vision and saw the subtitle clearly. I stepped onto the deck in my backyard to write down the suggested words, "awakening the healing power of the heart," when I heard a slight rustling sound above. I looked up and saw about forty doves flying over me, a stunning sight. I had never before seen doves around my home and was assured that we had found the right words at last.

By choosing to participate in the rituals that follow, you are embarking on a shamanic journey through inner Egypt. Although one should not have preconceived ideas or expectations, it must be remembered that it is the nature of the shamanic experience to disintegrate the old way and reintegrate anew. The Shamanic principles of death and rebirth, and dismemberment and re-memberment, are basic precepts in ancient Egypt, and easy to recognize as expressed in the myth of Osiris and Isis. (See the Glossary of the Gods on page 191 for more information.)

The first introduction to these rites calls for an invocation that begins with your intention to enter into Egypt, and to tap into the immense love and life force energy that abides in the vast caverns of her heart.

This first passage must be entered with the energy of innocence and trust, the beginner's mind where, like the Fool in the tarot, you stand at the precipice, willing to step over the edge into the unknown. When you cross the threshold with humility and reverence and from a meditative, heart-centered perspective, you will transform into the dove and enter the state of mind that is Egypt within. This requires preparation: at the beginning of each ritual, you will start with a meditation. This first one sets the scene and will be reiterated to some degree as you begin each subsequent ritual.

As part of the preparation for becoming the dove, take a few moments to learn and practice the following breathing technique. Using the "heart" breath in this sacred manner will feed and nourish you, alter your consciousness, and help transport you into the heart of Egypt.

This is a shamanic tool that we will use throughout this book each time we journey.

⚝ THE HEART BREATH

[*In order to fly it is important to be connected to the earth. Either sit or lie down and make sure you have a felt, body sense of being connected to the earth, the ground of your being. Ground and center and focus on your heart.*]

Once you feel grounded and centered, look within and find the eternal flame that lives within your heart center. As you bring your heart flame into focus in whatever way you perceive it, feed it with love. Love is the fuel, and as you pour love upon your heart flame, it grows. It brightens and intensifies. See, feel, and perceive with as many senses as you can apply. . . .

Now inhale as though you are pulling a breath up from deep within the earth. While you intend the movement of your breath, focus on it and feel the breath move up through your body to the level of your heart center. . . .

Let the breath mingle for a moment with your inner heart flame . . . then exhale with the intention of sending your breath out from your heart center, throughout your body, and into the world.

Breathe in that way for a few breaths. . . .

Bring your attention to the sky above you, and inhale your breath in from above, as though you are pulling it down from the sky. Feel it flow into your body through your crown as you draw it down to the level of your heart, again allowing it to mingle for a moment with the flame in your heart center. . . . Now exhale with the intention of sending your breath out through your heart center and into the world.

Do this breath several times. . . .

Draw the breath from the earth and sky simultaneously, and experience the two breaths coalesce at your heart flame for a moment before you exhale them out into the world once again. . . .

Continue to breathe in this manner—in from above and below at the same time, gathering in your heart, and expressing out into the world as love.

As the intelligence and power of the spirit that flows through you from breathing in this way further feeds your heart flame, you may feel subtle surges of energy as well as warmth radiating through your entire being. Notice how this heart breath functions like bellows to increase the power and light that radiates from your heart flame. It is this inner radiance that will light the way for the journeys and rites that are to come.

Once you have felt the resonance, the sense of connection with Earth and sky within, relax your breathing and ground and center, knowing that you are fully supported as you enter into the shamanic mysteries of Egypt.*

Once you've practiced this simple breathing technique and gone through your first journey, it will become natural to slide back into the heart breath each time. By the time you have completed the first round, you will comprehend its value in your life, and heart breathing will become a natural process easy to practice and utilize. Using the breath in this way will help you learn how to journey shamanically in and out of various dimensions and levels of awareness and consciousness.

It is also helpful to prepare sacred space within which to enter these rites. The purpose of an altar is to create an intersection point between your physical world and the spirit world. A candle and smudge or incense placed upon a special cloth is sufficient; however, you can elaborate upon your altar as feels appropriate. Luscious fruits and flowers are always inviting to the spirits. An image, fetish, or statue of the deity that you are working with is also a welcoming touch, although not necessary. This first initiation should be embarked upon in a quiet, private place, for you will be entering the cave of your own heart.

◈ OPENING MEDITATION

[*Close your eyes, and take a moment to ground and center yourself. . . . Find the eternal flame that dwells within your heart center. As you bring your heart flame into focus, feed it with love. . . . As you continue to pour love upon your flame, experience it grow and intensify. As you look within, tune out the outer world and notice how your heart flame radiates outward, filling you with warmth and light. . . .*]

---

*For further information and uses for the heart breath, see Nicki Scully, *Alchemical Healing* (Rochester, Vt.: Bear & Company, 2003).

Begin to breathe the heart breath, starting by inhaling the power and intelligence of the earth, breathing it up from the central core of the earth, up through all the layers within the earth and up through your body, up into your heart. . . . Let the power of Earth mingle with the love you are pouring into your heart, then exhale the resulting radiant love out in every direction from your heart. . . . Take several earth breaths. . . .

Once the power of the earth is engaged, add the sky breath, drawing down the power of the heavenly bodies and the intelligence of the cosmos, as you inhale from the heart of the universe down through your crown, pulling the energy down into your heart from above. . . . Notice how that power, intelligence, and energy mingles with the power from the earth and the love you continue to pour into your heart flame. . . . As you exhale, it is a more intense, powerful light that radiates out in every direction. . . .

Your heart begins to open as you continue to breathe Earth and Sky simultaneously. . . .

Bask in the glow of your expanded heart radiance. . . . As the light that you are emitting brightens further, it attracts the attention of the neteru and other spirit guides and intelligent beings in the universe. Invite the spirit guides, totem allies, plant spirit helpers, or other higher powers that are sacred to you to support you and witness your entry into these rites of passage. . . .

Your heart opens as you continue to breathe the heart breath. As your heart flame expands yet further, invite the deepest memories within the heart of your being to awaken as you invoke Inner Egypt. . . .

Continue to breathe into your heart until you have built a warm fire of gentle desire to hear the calling within you. Listen for the call from the Great Mystery, from that which is hidden. . . .

You will find yourself in a very private place near the edge of a remote cliff overlooking a great canyon, facing the huge orange ball that is the setting sun in the west. Listen closely. . . . Listen to your heart, which has drawn you to this place. Listen. . . .

Although you may not see him, you can sense the presence of Anubis, the shaman priest, standing by your side.

Listen. Your intuitive self can hear an inner calling. It is the voice of the invisible mysterious goddess Nephthys. Listen, you can hear her calling you. . . .

Nephthys speaks: *I am she who is veiled from you and whom you will soon come to know. I am calling you to come to the edge and to look out over your world, as you know it, to reflect on all the things in your present life that distract you, or that you wish to change. Bring them to the altar of your heart flame. Bring all of this and lay it upon the altar of your heart. For as your world is now, know that it will change. And soon, it will be only a memory as you embark upon these shamanic mysteries of ancient Egypt. . . .* [Pause.]

Take a deep breath. . . . When you are ready, step off the cliff and let go. . . . As you begin to fall, continue to breathe deeply, exhaling your spirit into the void, calling out to all things sacred and holy to uplift you and to guide you through the surrounding vortex and into mighty Egypt, alive and available deep within the DNA of your own being.

Allow yourself to trust the process and to become innocent. . . . Move into the unknowing with an open heart. . . .

As you fall through the abyss, feel yourself becoming a white dove. . . . Your wings stretch to catch your fall, and you find yourself gliding smoothly through a tunneled vortex. . . . [Pause.]

As you begin to emerge out of the vortex and into the light, look below and see the landscape of Egypt, with its vast and blazing desert and the lushness around the silver snake that is the Nile. You can see temples here and there, and pyramids. There are many villages, mostly along the Nile, and verdant fields crisscrossed with irrigation channels, all connected to the Nile. Even from this perspective flying above Egypt, you can feel the life and vitality emanating from the fertile land below. As your vision of Egypt clarifies, your ancient heart memory returns and you feel nourished by all the powerful elements that are rushing into your consciousness simultaneously. . . . [Pause.]

Your memory begins to stir. . . . As you soar above this ancient land in your dove form you are reminded of a bittersweet memory, a poignant moment of coming home. Receive whatever messages emerge from this moment of remembering. These can be images, colors, sounds, or glyphs. You may have sensations and feelings, inner knowing, or whatever experience comes to you. . . . [Pause.]

Your perspective shifts as you recognize this potent opportunity for your soul's journey. You find yourself moving from your ego's awareness to your soul's consciousness. . . . [*Long pause.*]

When you have familiarized yourself with this new level of perception and feel that this experience is complete you have reached the end of the first journey. As you begin to come back to your outer awareness and ordinary consciousness, be aware that part of you remains in Egypt. Feel your return journey as you are lifted back on gentle warm currents of the winds, back to conscious awareness of your physical body. Enter into your human form once again and return to the altar from which you began your journey. . . . Take a deep breath. Inhale through the small of your back and fill your belly with air, then exhale through your tailbone into the ground to make a solid reconnection with the earth. Take a moment to acknowledge and thank the spirit beings that responded to your invitation to witness and hold space for you as you enter and continue through these rites of passage. . . .

It is important to ground and center every time you return from a journey. Make sure that you are centered in your physical form before opening your eyes.

You are now prepared to cross the next threshold and take a further step into the heart rituals of ancient Egypt. For each subsequent journey, rekindle the heart flame and breathe the heart breath to open your heart as you prepare to meet the next of the great neteru of Egypt. You will be directed to become the innocent dove once again, with the olive branch of peace held in your beak. Each time, you will make this offering to the ancient ones, while you open the floodgates of your heart to receive the majesty of these powerful beings.

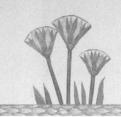

1

NEKHBET-MOTHER-MUT
ALCHEMIST
Wisdom Keeper/Grand Mother

NEKHBET-MOTHER-MUT (pronounced similar to moot) is the overseer, the wise old magician crone who brings all the elements together in preparation for the shamanic journeys that make up these mysteries. Beautiful relief sculptures and paintings of Nekhbet-Mother-Mut in her vulture aspect appear on the lintels of temples in Egypt so that you can look up and see her flying above as you enter the sacred places. In her vulture aspect, she soars above us, watching for the perfect moment that is ripe for the transformation offered by these rituals. She will fly over us throughout these rites as we ride the silver snake of the Nile winding its way through Egypt. Nekhbet-Mother-Mut is closely aligned with the voices of both Thoth and Anubis, as both speak through her. Nephthys, Isis, and Nekhbet-Mother-Mut are three in one: the virgin/mother/crone aspects of the divine feminine.

In this work, it is Nekhbet-Mother-Mut who holds the caduceus,* the staff of power and balance generally associated with Thoth and Hermes. For the alchemist, the caduceus is the key to healing. The rod of this staff is the spine and the two snakes that twine up and around it are the spiraling DNA chains. This staff of balance and power represents

---

*For more information on the caduceus and a Caduceus Empowerment initiation, see chapter 14 of Nicki Scully's *Alchemical Healing* (Rochester, Vt.: Bear & Company, 2003).

the kundalini, or life force, energy. The magician/alchemist who wields the caduceus comprehends this energy and knows how to use it to create life and death—and to achieve transformation.

In preparation for the journey you are about to take, it helps to know what will be required of you, the path you will follow, and whom you will meet along the way. This preview can free your thinking mind from distractions, so that you enter the journey with your whole self.

To connect with Nekhbet-Mother-Mut, you must first acknowledge Anubis, the facilitator of these rites whose acquaintance you made in the Introduction and whose image is central to the cover of this book. It is he who leads you to the precipice. Once you have committed yourself to the process, you will pass through the energies of Ma'at, the goddess of balance and truth, and of Thoth, the god of wisdom. Both will be nearly invisible during this first journey, yet you can be assured that they are at constant attention to your progress, holding you in balance, encouraging you and helping you to open into the light in the heart of Egypt.

As the wise and venerable grand dame of shamanic Egypt, Nekhbet-Mother-Mut weaves and blends the ingredients that result in our alchemical transformation. As the Grand Mother, she is so ancient that all who come after her contain her within themselves, for she is a very old ancestor. We require her approval in order to proceed into these mysteries. When you, the initiate, come to Nekhbet-Mother-Mut in innocence and trust as the dove, you will offer an olive branch of peace. This honoring is similar to the tobacco offerings made to Native American elders. When you make your offering to the alchemist, she will take you to Nephthys—the veiled sister of Isis who represents the virgin, in its original meaning as the whole woman unto herself. It is Nephthys, the High Priestess, who enters the dark void within to bring back insight and vision. When your heart is open and prepared, Nephthys comes in to connect you to your intuitive nature, that part of yourself that will be able to see clearly in the darkness. Nephthys is related to the Owl, and both carry the ability to see in the dark and to know how to transform any situation or thing.

Soon after, you will encounter her twin sister, Isis, the great Earth mother who in the tarot would be called the Empress. Nephthys and Isis are acknowledged at this stage because they function intimately with

Nekhbet-Mother-Mut to assist you through this alchemical process. Once you have arrived and made your offering to the great alchemist, the teachings can begin.

🌿 JOURNEY TO ENTER THE MYSTERIES

[Prepare sacred space and ground and center yourself. Follow the instructions from the first meditation and journey in chapter 0, The Dove. Kindle the heart flame and feed it with love. . . . Take a number of heart breaths to open your heart and build a strong heart flame. . . . Set your intention to respond to the call and enter these mysteries.]

In the light of your expanded, radiant heart flame, perceive yourself standing upon the threshold once again as you respond to the ancient call. Deep inside you always knew this time would come.

Breathe deeply of the heart breath. . . . As your heart opens further, embrace the beginner's mind. This journey requires you to trust where your heart is leading you.

As your heart glow increases with your breath and your love, you can see Anubis in the light of your heart's radiance, standing tall in his jackal-headed man form, wearing a golden kilt and facing a glorious sunset. Join him and find that you are standing on the edge of a cliff above a vast canyon, facing the purple and red tinged sunset in the west. Allow your perception to clarify as you spend a moment or two contemplating the call to which you are responding. Any distractions disappear as you focus on your intention. You know that a mysterious adventure awaits you, and you may feel the sensation of anticipation, the butterfly twinges that often portend powerful transformations.

The space before you is vast, like the Grand Canyon. This is the cavernous heart of Egypt. You are tapping into the huge heart and love and life force energy of ancient Egypt. There is an incredible feeling of awe accessible here in the face of such depth, grandeur, and beauty. Look down into the vast void below. The swirling energies are compelling. With absolute trust, step off the cliff. . . .

Fall in a downward spiral through the canyon. The spiral turns into a kind of tunnel, a vortex. . . . Become the white dove once again as you enter and fly through the caverns of the heart. Feel the last rays of the golden sun warmly touching your wings, creating a shimmering light all around your body.

Your heart beats rapidly from the excitement of going into the unknown, yet you know that in making this journey, you are coming home. Although you may feel fragile and vulnerable, you are at peace as you fly with trust and innocence.

In your beak you carry the olive branch as a sacred offering to those who came before, to the ancestors of ancient Egypt, to the deities, the ones most high, the bright shining ones of antiquity.

As you glide through the vortex, you see an opening and begin to move toward it. Purifying the heart allows you to enter into this place, so you continue to breathe the heart breath, to keep your heart open. You are keenly aware of your offering to the gods of Egypt, the olive branch that you hold within your beak.

Through the swirling energy of the vortex you get a glimpse of radiant Ma'at, the winged goddess of truth and balance. She is the one who guards the mysteries of the heart. Your perception of her may not be strong at this time, as she upholds this part of the work as an apparition. She will become a more visible entity later in these mysteries.

For now, know that she sees that you are a seeker of truth and have come to renew your heart. She gives you an almost imperceptible nod of recognition and acknowledges your intention.

As you move through the open portal of the heart, notice that your perception alters and Thoth, the illumined architect of wisdom, is also present, though he, too, is barely visible. There is a tangible shift as you move from ego into the heart/mind of your soul's journey and open to the mystery so that it may be revealed within your own being.

There, hovering in midair with wings outstretched in her magnificent vulture form, is the ancient grand dame of Egypt, Nekhbet-Mother-Mut. She holds in her sharp golden talons a caduceus with two intertwined serpents spiraling upward around the central staff.

Nekhbet-Mother-Mut is majestically regal in her appearance and commands respect as she observes your approach with her watchful eye. Long, multicolored feathers grace her huge extended wings that point downward to the silver serpent called the Nile below. She fixes her eyes upon you with the same piercing gaze that Isis uses to see clearly into the heart of any matter.

Nekhbet-Mother-Mut welcomes you in your white dove form with a nod of her head. . . .

You offer her the olive branch, which she accepts.

This time you are invited to land and enter the cave of your own heart, which is within the heart of Egypt. . . .

Nekhbet speaks: *"It is because you are pure of heart and are willing to follow your heart that you have been allowed to safely fly through this vortex and return to the ancient heart rituals of Egypt. You are like the Fool in the tarot, who has innocently begun this journey with a certain naiveté and trust. It takes a Fool, with beginner's mind, to enter into the unknown. You also have a great courageous heart. If you did not, you would never have taken the first step off the cliff.*

"I, Nekhbet-Mother-Mut, will be your guide as we fly together up the silver snake. My wings will turn from a rainbow of colors to the dark wings of the vulture as you proceed upon your path and undergo alchemical transformations of shamanic death and rebirth.

"Along with Isis and many other aspects of myself, we shall rebuild the human and spiritualize matter itself.

"As a rainbow bridge, Nekhbet-Mother-Mut, I am the wise old woman/crone of Egypt. As the maiden/medial/priestess I appear with dark wings and shape-shift into Nephthys whom some refer to as the Veiled Isis. And as Mother Isis kneeling with one knee upon the precious earth, with her brilliant multicolored wings spread wide and lifting upward toward the heavens, I embody the mother of us all. I am Nekhbet-Mother-Mut, Isis, Nephthys, and more. I am three in one and all that came before. I am the alchemist who will be your guide into the shamanic mysteries of Egypt."

Continue to sit in the cave of your heart and listen for further messages, teachings, or instructions from Nekhbet-Mother-Mut as she prepares you to ride on the back of the silver snake that is the life force of Egypt, the Nile River. . . . [*Long pause.*]

When you have received this first teaching, take flight again and fly through and beyond time and space to an ancient wisdom, not only of the mind, but also of the heart, while opening yourself further to this mystery. Allow any remaining distractions to fade away now. There is only this place in the giant heart of Egypt. It is as high as the great pyramids, as vast as the desert, and as deep as the Red Sea.

In this place, there is a memory that belongs to you. It holds the key that will unlock the cellular DNA deep within your memory. Take some time to remember. . . . [*Long pause.*]

Once you have received your teaching, place it in your heart. Your journey is coming to a close. Feel yourself begin to return as you are once again lifted back on gentle warm currents of the winds, back to the conscious awareness of your physical body in its human form. Connect again to your breath. Send it down to the earth, your feet, your hands, and your body. Ground and center; feel your body connected to the earth. Take a deep breath and slowly open your eyes, returning to your outer reality. A noticeable shift has occurred within your inner being. Offer your gratitude to Nekhbet-Mother-Mut and the neteru of Egypt who have been supporting you thus far.

Whether you are making this journey through Egypt, or in the mystery school, or on your own, do your best to leave your heart open for the duration of the time you are on the journey. You are now ready to take the next initiation in these mysteries.

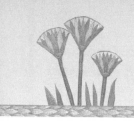

2
NEPHTHYS
THE HIGH PRIESTESS
Intuition/Mystery

NEPHTHYS STANDS IN the shadows so that she can be known without fully revealing herself in physical form because it is not her function to do so. Although Nephthys is an important deity unto herself, there are many images of her on the temple walls standing half obscured behind her sister Isis. Rather than being in the shadow of her sister, she *is* the shadow. She is the mysterious, veiled aspect of the goddess. She is associated with the occult and hidden mysteries—that which cannot be seen and the secrets that are hidden. These are the secrets that must be kept in order to safeguard the ancient mysteries and rituals.

SURRENDERING
THE HEART

The time has come upon the planet for these mysteries to be revealed; however, they will remain concealed from those who do not have the eyes to see nor the ears to hear, for they are hidden in the heart. As you open and surrender into your deepest heart/mind knowing you will gain the insights and inherent powers that reside in the depths of the heart. Thus, these mysteries are protected from the uninitiated, yet available to true seekers who are willing to undergo their own shamanic death and renewal.

Nephthys and Anubis worked together to help Isis find the missing parts of her murdered husband, Osiris, so that they could re-member him. It makes sense that Anubis would use his keen sensitivities—his sharp ears, acute sense of smell, and discriminating eyesight. Nephthys made use of her strong intuition and was able to connect directly to the secret knowledge and formulas as needed. Whenever they found a part of Osiris, Isis ordered that a temple be erected in honor of that part of her husband. Thus Nephthys and Anubis played vital roles in the re-membering and resurrection of Osiris. In these rites, as on our trips to Egypt, we go from monument to monument renewing the lost pieces of ourselves.

As you prepare for your journey, Nephthys appears in the shadows with long olive-shaped eyes and olive complexion. Her eyes are rimmed with dark kohl, like Cleopatra's. Circling her head is a headband with a cobra coiled around it. The eyes of this cobra are lapis blue to represent the third eye, and it springs forth from Nephthys's third eye. The color of the band is silver to depict the more lunar aspect of this deity. She wears gossamer silk pants like those a belly dancer would wear, and silver and gold and copper bangles dangle from her waist. Serpents are also wrapped around each arm, and she holds their heads between her fingers. Around her neck is an ornate necklace that is the tree of life, with many different branches lying against her hair, neck, and skin. The top that she wears is a belly dancer's bodice, sky blue trimmed with silver.

She begins to dance in a very snakelike, sensuous way as if in a trance. Her dance is mesmerizing and tantalizing to all who see her there in the shadows, and she conjures up the willingness to follow her wherever she goes. There is a way in which she helps initiates follow their heart's longing for something more than what they can see in their concrete, ordinary reality. Hers is the promise that there is something more to be known and experienced, something more fulfilling to the soul.

After a period of dancing, Nephthys begins to give voice to melancholic and enchanting notes and tones. Some might say this is the sound of wind blowing, and others say no, it is the songbird outside the window. Still others would say, no, it is the mighty ocean surf pounding against cliffs. Whatever the initiate needs to hear in order to be guided deeper into the unknown, Nephthys will provide.

Although she is the birth mother of Anubis, in truth, Nephthys remains the Virgin. Although she steps forth to reveal secrets to initiates that are ready to receive them, she remains the veiled and nebulous aspect of the divine feminine.

Nephthys is also the one who knows the right combinations of nectar and poison. She knows the right mixture of those alchemical elements to combine, to create the elixir that moves you into the appropriate altered state for the work at hand. She is a master of shamanic methods to expand consciousness—snake venom, mushrooms, breathwork, sacred plant medicine—all of the myriad things that bring a person into trance or altered states of consciousness, which open us up to other worlds. She's the one who says, "You're more than who you think you are. Follow me. I will take you to my son Anubis . . . ."

ANUBIS AND THE SED FESTIVAL RITES

One of the most important titles that Anubis carries is that of the Opener of the Way. Some depictions show him leaning over the bier of pharaoh, preparing his body for immortality. Although conventional Egyptology calls him the Divine Embalmer and considers these rituals to have been based in funerary beliefs and performed primarily as funerary rites, there is mounting evidence that they were practiced as shamanic renewal rites for the living pharaoh. Over time, these esoteric, secret rites were also offered to the high priests and certain nobility.

According to Jeremy Naydler, during the Sed festival rites, "The king was thus engaged in a ritual communion with the spirits of the land of Egypt. The underlying purpose of this was to reach across to the more subtle spirit world that upholds and vitalizes the physical world, in order to ensure a beneficent connection with it and an unhampered flow of energies from it into the physical."*

---

*See Jeremy Naydler's *Shamanic Wisdom in the Pyramid Texts: The Mystical Tradition of Ancient Egypt* (Rochester, Vt.: Inner Traditions, 2005), 85.

It is the role of a shaman to travel between the worlds in order to bring back power or healing for his or her community. To gain such access, the shaman must have mastered death—through illness, dreams, visions, and/or sacred initiatory rites—and have gained experiential understanding of his or her own immortality. As in traditional views of shamanism, the pharaoh underwent these rites not only for his personal rejuvenation, but also for the rejuvenation of the entire country of Egypt and her people.

Naydler goes on to say, "The central rite of the Sed festival needs to be understood in this context of the king's harmonizing the relationship between the invisible and visible worlds for the benefit of the whole country . . . crossing the threshold between worlds in order to stand in direct relationship to the normally hidden spiritual powers."*

According to Naydler, the Sed festival, which was supposed to be held at thirty-year intervals in each pharaoh's reign, was enacted to renew the power of the pharaoh. In actuality, it was held much more often, and the evidence that it included rites similar to the one that follows is plainly written in the Pyramid Texts, most specifically as translated from the walls inside the burial chamber, antechambers, and corridors of the pyramid of Unas.

This new incarnation of the ancient rites has the same objective; however, it is meant to reach *all* initiates who are ready to journey to discover their own divinity, and have shown the appropriate intention and purity of thought, mind, and action.

The following ritual is a new iteration of the renewal rites, one of the highest and most potent initiations of ancient Egypt, and no less relevant today. Perhaps, because of the urgency of our planetary situation, it may be even more important now, as it prepares initiates to take the next step in the process of co-creating our future with the great ones who initially created the human experiment—the deities of Egypt.

In order for the heart to be fully renewed, it must be surgically removed and placed in a safe place where it undergoes a powerful alchemical transformation. The body must be cleared and purified at every level in preparation to receive the renewed heart, which will be

*Naydler, *Shamanic Wisdom in the Pyramid Texts,* 85.

returned to the body later on in the progression of the rites. All energetic systems are revitalized in the process. It's like taking a car in for a thorough tune-up, taking the carburetor out and cleaning everything, changing the oil, and so forth. It's a complete overhaul.

You can only enter such a rite with a fully open heart and from a place of deep trust. To allow others to hold your heart in their hands, either figuratively or literally, while they prepare you for death and rebirth is an initiation of great consequence.

Anubis and his mother, Nephthys, officiate in this ceremony. To complete this, you must literally put your life, your heart, into Anubis's hands. In so doing, you will open yourself to be cleansed of the pain and suffering lodged throughout your body. This is an extremely intimate experience that you should consider carefully. Do not attempt to take this initiation unless you are willing to commit to completing the entire first round. Once you have completed the entire process, you can come back to any of the rites whenever called to or as needed.

🪷 JOURNEY FOR THE SURRENDER OF THE HEART

[*Start by creating sacred space and meditating on your intention to prepare once again to enter the heart of Egypt. Kindle the eternal flame within your heart center, and begin breathing the heart breath. . . . Feed your heart flame with love and breathe deeply of the earth and sky as you prepare to enter the heart of Egypt. As you continue to breathe the heart breath and meditate on your journey, become the dove once again, carrying the olive branch, and fly over the land. . . .*]

Magically Anubis and Nephthys appear, and lead you to the ancient and mysterious temple complex at Sakkara. Return to your human form and stand in the vast courtyard square, in front of and facing the age-old step pyramid. . . .

Anubis asks if you are truly willing to surrender your heart as Nephthys looks on. . . .

If you agree, humbly step forward and offer the olive branch to Nephthys and Anubis. . . . Anubis and Nephthys lead you into a small entrance at the base of the pyramid. . . . Follow them through a dark passageway that leads into the interior of the pyramid then turns sharply downward. When you have descended almost thirty meters beneath the pyramid, the path ends abruptly and you enter into a chamber in which there is a sarcophagus.

Anubis hands you a cup filled with an elixir that has a strange though not unpleasant fragrance. As you hold the cup in your hands, allow your intention to be infused into the medicine. . . . [*Pause.*] When you take it to your lips, first breathe in its fragrance and feel the vapors enter your body. Then taste the brew, and be sure to swallow it physically. . . . [*Pause.*]

As it enters your body, feel the soothing comfort it brings to you as you relax. Any remnants of fear will vanish. . . . [*Pause.*]

Nephthys stands beside Anubis as he, in his most gentle and loving way, reassures you that it's okay to die. They help you into the sarcophagus.

With tender, loving care, Anubis makes an incision and very meticulously severs your heart from each artery and vein that connects it to your body and to the extensive vascular system that keeps your blood flowing. This is not painful. . . . [*Long pause.*]

Your heart becomes suspended in time, but you feel no fear as Anubis holds your heart in his capable and loving hands, and brings it up to the huge golden ankh he is wearing around his neck. The energy from the ankh is palpable as it purifies the heart from all its pain and suffering. . . .

Anubis speaks these magic words, "Now you are blessed, oh heart, with eternal life."

He carefully hands the heart to Nephthys, who with equal care places it in a beautiful alabaster jar filled with nectar that emits a fragrance similar to plumeria. The nectar was created by the gods to restore the heart and take away its burdens. All of the pain and sorrow of your past stories are removed, all of the grief and death, and all the parts of your heart that hurt are relieved.

There is an image of the scarab god Khepera sculpted in relief upon the surface of the canopic jar. He's a large scarab beetle with big arms wrapped around the jar, as if he is holding the heart inside.

While gazing at Khepera, Nephthys begins to chant and sing sacred words in an ancient tongue. She chants a special invocation that is accompanied by dance movements. She is chanting and dancing with the great cobra that is curled around her arm. Although it is a venomous snake, it does not bite her. You become aware that during this activity by Nephthys, the snake is milked of its venom. Nephthys pours the venom into the canopic jar, where it blends with the other fragrant nectars and essences.

Nephthys uses three feathers—ostrich, peacock, and hawk—as she chants over the vessel. Now she adds essential oils of sandalwood and lavender, lemon and myrrh. All of these oils are placed into the vessel while Anubis prepares to anoint the body. The heart continues to hold the soul while it is kept alive, suspended between worlds, beyond time and space, protected in its canopic jar. It also holds the lifetime essences of all the incarnations of the initiate.

While Nephthys chants and dances, Anubis anoints the body with the oils and very carefully removes each organ that is left in the body, without detaching it. He cleanses, bathes, and anoints each, and lastly he cleanses the intestines. . . . [*Long pause.*]

When the organs have been returned to their places, he purifies the body and begins to prepare it to be the vessel for the heart/mind, the higher heart self that is the returned and renewed heart. While the heart continues to undergo its alchemical transformation in the canopic jar, the body must be cleared of all the old hurts and pain, and the disappointments and suffering that has been embedded in the cells, tissues, blood, and bones. Then all the energy fields are cleared and the chakras are once again opened. . . . [*Long pause.*]

When Anubis and Nephthys have completed their work, Anubis lays his hand upon your shoulder, signaling that it is time to rise. He assures you that your heart will be safe while you go through the initiatory processes necessary to complete preparations for your renewed heart. Anubis and Nephthys help you up.

As you feel your way into yourself and your body, it seems as though there is more space inside you. You are still deeply relaxed, yet your senses are heightened. . . . As the three of you walk the path back through the pyramid and out into the bright sunlight, you might notice that your visionary capacities, both inner and outer, have increased and become clearer. . . .

Thank Anubis and Nephthys, and Nekhbet-Mother-Mut as well. She is circling above the Sakkara complex, radiant and golden in the sun, and preparing to take you south for the next phase of your passage.

Take all the time you need to ground and center, and open your eyes when you are ready.

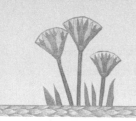

3
ISIS
HOLY QUEEN/MOTHER OF US ALL
Embodied Manifestation of Love

ISIS SPEAKS: *"I know the mysteries of life and death. I know the mysteries of immortality. I know the mysteries of taking creation apart and putting it all back together again. I know all the gods by their first names. I call them forth when it is time for their part. I call forth Set and Wadjet. I call forth Osiris and Ptah. I call forth Sobek and Horus and Sekhmet. I call forth Khepera. I call forth Sothis, Khonsu, and Ra. I call forth the divine couple, Geb and Nut. I call forth the hidden one, Nephthys, and my grandmother, Nekhbet-Mother-Mut.*

"I work closely with the craftsman Khnum and with the Sphinx, who is the satellite receiver for the transmission of information onto Earth. I call forth Bast when it is time to birth. I call forth Hathor when it is time to unify. I call forth Ma'at when it is time to balance and to measure. I call forth Thoth when it is time to illuminate. I call forth Anubis when it is time to open, to heal and renew the heart. I call forth each and every being. I stand with my wings brilliantly glistening in the heat of the noonday sun. I call forth the powers of the waters from the Nile. I call forth the energies and power of Earth, and the great pyramids. I call forth the scorching red-hot desert and the burning sting of the scorpion, which initiates human beings and takes them into the eye of the Ibis. Look heavenward as the great Ibis flies toward the rising sun and becomes the fiery phoenix of transformation and rebirth."

Isis knows how to take us apart and put us back together in an elevated form. She knows the mysteries of life, death, and immortality. She is like the symphony conductor who directs all the gods and elements. The combinations of the elements in their archetypal expressions are the principles that we call the deities, or neteru of Egypt. She invokes these gods when it is time for their unique contributions to the alchemical process that will ultimately raise us into our divinity. She calls them forth and dances between them; they surround and weave and walk between, and together they create the magic that coalesces into the alchemical gold of spiritualized matter. From her heart pours immense power and love, radiant golden light bursting forth and flowing into people, into nature, into the world. She is the mother of us all, the unseen force within that continuously urges us toward light and love.

With the laser vision and clarity of Wadjet's eye, Isis penetrates the heart of any matter. She is the part of us that sees with the single eye with absolute clarity, compassion, and love. Like Hathor, she can find forgiveness for the worst sin or greatest mistake that any of us could ever commit.

Although she comprehends the need for duality and the resultant opposing forces required for creation to happen in our physical realm, she sees beyond duality, for she loves all that she has created and brought into form. How can she not stand behind us, her children, and support us in our evolutionary process?

As our mother, Isis is so deeply connected to us that she is encoded within our DNA, and it is she who we are expressing when we make the choice to grow and change and when we embark on the shamanic path of death, renewal, and rebirth. It is her song, singing in our blood and our soul, that inspires us to move forward in consciousness. Our faith in her voice, her song, and the promise of her presence within enables us to willingly surrender and die to the old, knowing that we will be renewed. It is the voice of Isis that we hear in all of nature, in every tree, in every flower, in every animal, and in every human. It is the responsibility of Isis—as the one who remembers how to die and be reborn—to rebuild the new human that each of us is becoming.

Isis maintains a deep connection to the physical earth and the preservation and renewal of life. As the archetypal mother of us all, she holds the maiden Nephthys within her. It is Isis's love and commitment to rebirth that gives her the regenerative magic and power to create the rebuilt human.

Although she fully embodies the divine feminine on earth, Isis worships the sun and embraces her more solar, masculine, yang side, which provides her with the energy needed to penetrate matter with her laser gaze. Isis sees things from above and below, and from within and without.

In the renewal of the heart mysteries, the energies of Thoth and Anubis combine to create the intelligent heart/mind wisdom. Isis is then responsible for putting it all together. She takes all of the information that the gods have planted in the DNA through sound, and calls in the spirit of Neith, the great-grandmother spider, to help her weave all the parts she has gathered together, as the ram's-headed god Khnum makes the physical form. She knows the exact way to rewire the DNA throughout the clay form of the human and to weave the ancestral lineage into the expanded molecules through the breath. With her rainbow wings she unites the upper chakras with the lower ones, Heaven with Earth, and spirit with flesh.

Although Isis comes from the stars, she loves Earth. She loves the creations of Earth and the human beings themselves. She is a great geneticist, both in physical and spiritual realms, engaged in the function of spiritualizing matter. She weaves the souls of humans into their physical form and reorganizes the parts so that they can be infused with what is commonly thought of as the energy of Christ, or Buddha, or, less commonly considered but true, the new Horus. Although this energy is not gender specific, it tends to be associated with masculine forms. Yet it is Isis who infuses the renewed heart with the power of light in the form of *sekhem,* the phallic, yang, powerful energy that, when directed creatively, manifests as consciousness in the world. In our culture, this would be considered a masculine function, for in order to bring the heart energy into its full power, it must be expanded with light and infused through conscious direction.

Isis seeks to bring the heart energy into consciousness so that its power can be raised in its light form. As we will learn later on from Ma'at, higher consciousness is full of light. It is this energy that she weaves into the DNA. This is where the combination of the *ka,* the etheric subtle body that connects us to our ancestral lineage, and the *ba,* the soul, becomes elevated in the new human. The infusion of consciousness allows us to release old story lines, while expanding awareness around cellular memory. Building upon the legacies of ancestral experience, the ka holds the essence of what is needed from the past, but expands it forward in the soul's journey. The ba uses the knowledge of the ancestors to make new meaning and purpose for the soul's lessons and journeys. This translates into a type of marriage between the past, the present, and the future. As we progress through this first great round, our goal is to develop the *akh,* the illumined heart/mind that is the result of that marriage. We are literally creating the energies and planting the seeds for the ancestral lineages of future generations.

As you continue with this process, know that Isis, in her role as sacred midwife and mother, is present at every instance of death, whether psychological, physical, or shamanic. She holds us and is there with us, and we are never alone.

✾ CHAKRA BALANCING ATTUNEMENT

Introduction

Imagine Isis standing with her sister Nephthys on a high-prowed Egyptian boat. They are almost one being. Isis is emerging out of Nephthys, who is wearing a white veil with gold trim. It feels as though Isis is moving from the High Priestess into the Empress or Queen Mother energy. We have not encountered Isis directly until now, yet she has been working with all the neteru. She has been the Veiled Isis, Nephthys, the nebulous one. She has been dealing primarily with the mysteries that are hidden within these archetypes. But that part of her job is nearly finished, and it is time for her to come out of Nephthys and bring forth the aspect of her we associate with the Empress in the tarot: the embodiment of higher love and wisdom.

Envision Isis walking through a pastoral scene at the edge of a lagoon not far from the Nile. She is fully embodied, earthy, with bare feet and brown legs. She appears here as a beautiful, fertile woman of around thirty years.

Isis is the Nile—Isis is fertility. As you view the scene with shamanic eyes, you can sense Anubis by her side. It is obvious that he adores her and she him. Thoth also travels with them in his Hermit form, tall and carrying a long staff and wearing a long beard. As they journey to the temple together, you could be looking at a mother, her son, and a grand-father or uncle. They are very familial in that way and it is apparent that they love and respect one another.

Isis prefers to be outside in nature. Here she is found beside water, with one wing pointing up to the heavens, and the other pointing to the earth, on one bent knee, in full sun. There is a beautiful body of water behind her, with palm trees and animals—oxen, goats, and donkeys—designating her connection to the lushness of Earth. Isis lives close to the people of the land, and does not dwell in the temple. There are grapevines and olives and corn growing on the hillsides and fields around her. Egrets glide over the water. She not only conveys, she *is* the absolute embodi-ment of the beauty of Egypt—the fertile, vibrant life of the fields along the Nile. She is Queen, and represents embodied connection to sacred Earth.

With her left knee placed reverently on the ground and her left wing pointed to earth, Isis honors the sacredness of Earth. Her right wing, as it points upward, honors the grandeur of Heaven. She is paying hom-age to the sacredness of both with her body and her spirit, and in so doing she is seeking to end separation and isolation consciousness. This is something that must be realized in the physical body of the human as well as in our conscious mind. In this stance, Isis is the rainbow bridge.

If you are in Egypt, find a village away from cities or a quiet place close to the Nile in which to create this simple ritual. If you are at home, find a place in nature, even a city park, to instigate this connection.

Attunement
[*Prepare sacred space. Focus on your heart flame and kindle it with love. Breathe the heart breath, feeling the powers of Heaven and Earth meet-ing within your heart. In its glow, invoke inner Egypt. . . . Find yourself again flying above the land of Egypt. . . .*]

Once again become the dove and fly into nature, to a place alongside the river or by a body of water where you will not be disturbed. The dove lands gently on the shore. As you land, revert back to your human form and place the olive branch upon the earth. Kneel on your left knee, with your right foot flat on the ground. Stretch the right side of your body, extending your right hand and fingers toward the sky, while you angle the left side of your body downward, pointing your left hand to the earth. Notice as you are reaching to both Heaven and Earth, there is a rainbow connection made between the two. You have rainbow wings extending from each arm. Feel the connection like a rainbow between Earth and sky. Begin running the energy, pulling it from the knee and hand on the earth up through the body diagonally, passing it up through the heart.

This is where the auric fields are created that will surround and be woven through the rebuilt human that is being crafted by Khnum. You must pull energy up through the earth, up through your body and out your hand toward the sun. In doing so, your lower and upper chakras become united in a seamless channel.

It is necessary to work with the breath—inhale as you pull the energy upward from the heart of the earth. . . . Exhale as it shoots upward to the sky.

Once you feel a strong current coming up from the earth and through your body, pay attention to how the energy is simultaneously going the opposite direction. Use your breath to enhance the flow of energy. Feel yourself becoming Isis as energy radiates down from the sun, entering through your fingertips, while at the same time it moves diagonally back through your her heart, and down through your feet into the earth. . . .

Notice how the energies of above and below meet and connect within you, as if you are a lightning rod. As Isis, you become the connecting bridge, bringing together what might appear to be opposites, uniting Heaven and Earth. Working with Isis in this way, you become more comfortable with moving beyond *either, or* to the far more inclusive *and.*

As you run the energy from one direction, it is the **AND,** and from the other direction, it is the **DNA.** You are actually rebuilding the human by bringing in higher consciousness, love, and wisdom, and infusing it into the genetic code of the DNA. When we reverse the direction, we are expressing it back. When we conduct the energies both ways, we get both stories, and we've moved to the inclusive reality of the great AND of higher consciousness that does not get caught in duality. Here, all things are truly one.

Be sure to ground and center yourself in this new expanded awareness before you fully return to your more ordinary reality. With practice, you will be better able to hold this new perspective as you move through your ordinary life. . . .

Take a moment to give thanks for this attunement, the connection with the life-force energy, and the love of the great mother Isis who is always with you. . . .

4
KHNUM
MASTER CRAFTSMAN
Creator of Form/Organizing Principle

NOW THAT YOUR heart is sealed safely in its canopic jar, percolating and undergoing the various stages of its alchemical process of transformation and renewal, we head south, to where the ancient Egyptians considered the source of the Nile to be, in Aswan. There, on Elephantine Island, is one of the most sacred sites in Upper Egypt. Before the recent dams were built in the last century, cataracts tumbled through an exquisite pass and the river split to surround an island on which layers upon layers of temples mark the home of the god Khnum. During the Old Kingdom, in the time of the Pharaoh Djoser, there was a drought so severe that Djoser sent his most trusted high priest, Imhotep, south to the source of the Nile to find out what was causing the drought, and what could be done. Imhotep found the temple in ruins, and brought back instructions to Djoser to build a new temple dedicated to the god with the ram's head, Khnum*—and so another layer was added, the remains of which are still in evidence today.

Nekhbet-Mother-Mut, the great alchemist who stands between the worlds of shamanic Egypt and our own, comes to us now as Isis, as it is the energy of Isis that is required for rebuilding the human. She ushers you down the Nile, which is both the silver snake of Egypt and

---

*Normandi Ellis, *Feasts of Light* (Wheaton, Ill.: Quest Books, 1999), 3.

the kundalini snake within your own spine. The gestation that began in Sakkara continues at the island temple where Isis oversees the work of Khnum, as the body is prepared and renewed with the ka of the initiate. Khnum carries out this part of the transformation, for he is the great craftsman, the creator god who fashions the bodies of all the creatures of Earth on his potter's wheel.

Khnum has the head of a ram, with large, thick ram's horns curled like DNA spirals extending outward. His rotund human body is dark colored with a tremendous presence and a lumbering heaviness like the huge boulders that surround Elephantine Island, yet his hands have the long graceful fingers of a fine artist. His ram's face is furry and dark brown with a big nose and chocolate eyes. He sits at his stone bench in the garden, constantly rebuilding the bodies for the hearts of the beings of Earth. His is the grounding energy, and his responsibility is with the foundation principle. It is up to Khnum to organize the form and build the body around it. He puts things back together in a sequential way, reordering, reorganizing, rebuilding in this shamanic dimension, so that we may be reassembled as new human beings.

Khnum uses a mortar and pestle to grind down what appears to be an off-white limestone substance. To this he adds various essences— hummingbird nectar and herbs from his garden, with flower essences mixed with water from the Nile. It turns into a thick, gray color with a sweet fragrance reminiscent of the Garden of Eden, with birds chirping and bees buzzing all around.

For this work, Khnum functions with Isis as a geneticist facilitating DNA repair. As he creates the new body, he encodes it with higher energies and new programming. The energy is informed shamanically by nature: the pollen and nectars, the flower essences and Nile water, and the whitish powder. Isis oversees the process, as the primal matter, the basic earth, the clay with which the new being is created, is being prepared.

The ritual that accomplishes this crucial organizing component of the alchemy is thus facilitated by Khnum and perceived by the initiate through Isis's eyes. This first part of rebuilding the human includes the creation of the clay and sculpting of the new body and the ka, after which he weaves them together so that your relationship with your ka becomes conscious.

KA

Ka is the expanded awareness that begins to infuse the physicality of the human. It is woven around the cells within the human form. The ka vibrates at a slightly higher frequency than matter, but its frequency is close enough that it can connect with matter and permeate it. Ka lifts matter itself to a higher frequency, and with that expansion, more information and greater consciousness is available to the human once the ka is connected.

Conscious awareness comes in gradations: whereas insight is below awareness, consciousness is above awareness. Consciousness is ka, and ka is consciousness. All consciousness comes from the ancestors, and the ancestors come in many different forms.

The original ancestors are the deities themselves. They are prisms of pure consciousness through which different aspects are illuminated; the god that emerges from the one source depends on which particular aspect of consciousness is being revealed. When you breathe deeply, you activate the energy field from your own cellular memory, which is very compact, like a microchip. The ka equates to the collective soul of humanity. As it is activated and the cells expand, this collective soul awakens to the memory of that huge body of wisdom, consciousness, and knowledge that lives inside all humans.

We—human beings on Earth at this point in time—are ready to awaken that memory. The new body is being created so that this new awareness of DNA will allow the ka to expand throughout the new human. It's like a consciousness replacement that opens up a more collective connection, through which we become complete and can perceive as global humans. We begin thinking beyond our own little physical selves, and become connected to the And/All, which is the gods awakened within us—the ka. That's what the ka is, awakened gods inside the human being!

When humans become conscious that they live in the embrace of their ka, they become conscious of their immortality. Humans consciously infused with ka during their lifetime become able to co-create with the forces of nature, the neteru.

In ancient Egypt, it was thought that the ka was the source of the vital force energy of the deceased. The tomb was called *per ka,* the place of the person's etheric double, or their ka. It was the ka that linked a person, animal, or other being to his or her ancestral group in the spirit world as a source of power, vitality, sustenance, and growth.

Only the pharaoh could be united with his or her ka during life, and he was said to have held that connection for all the people of the land. In order to do that, he maintained consciousness of his ka, and contained it within himself, and as an adept he was able to retain consciousness after death. (Commoners, on the other hand, were said to be assimilated by their ka at death.) Statues of pharaoh's ka were placed within the tomb, the arms bent at the elbows and the hands up and facing out to receive the offerings that fed that which the deceased had become. Ancient Egyptian art shows Khnum creating the king and his ka on his potter's wheel, as a distinct and independent being.*

Although in times of old, full consciousness of ka was the exclusive domain of pharaoh, over time it seeped into the priesthood and nobility, and eventually into esoteric wisdom reserved for initiates. At this time the knowledge of ka and its infusion into our consciousness has been reawakened and is becoming accessible to ordinary people, and it is being expressed in many ways. Reiki, Shaktipad, Deeksha, Alchemical Healing, Shamanic Breathwork, and others are fast becoming mainstream examples of transformative methods used to awaken ka. They also illustrate how one person can transfer ka energy to another.

In the previous chapter, Isis showed you how you can step into your role as a bridge, or even a lightning rod, for carrying the vital force energy between spirit and matter. In the following initiation, as Khnum creates your renewed body in order to prepare it to receive your new heart, your molecules will be expanded, and space made for the infusion and weaving of ka into the matrix of your being. When you as the initiate function as Isis showed in the last chapter, as the rainbow bridge between Heaven and Earth, you are positioned for a reciprocal, even "mythical" relationship between the world of spirit and the physical world of matter.

Khnum is painstaking about combining elements to get the perfect consistency in the clay. Each person has a different role in life,

---

*See Jeremy Naydler's *Temple of the Cosmos: The Ancient Egyptian Experience of the Sacred* (Rochester, Vt.: Inner Traditions, 1996), 195.

and a distinctive purpose. Consequently, each person must come back together in his or her own unique way and own unique body.

The canopic jar that contains your heart has been safely brought to Khnum's temple/studio. During the ritual at Sakkara, Nephthys put into the jar certain substances including cobra venom, which eats away and dissolves the heart matter. This is similar to what happens to the caterpillar while it is in the chrysalis; it must disintegrate before it can be rebuilt as a butterfly. While the old disintegrates, the new heart is gestating in the jar.

The alchemists of old used canopic jars; the new genetic scientists prefer petri dishes. Either way, the essence of the person, the DNA within the original heart, is placed in the alchemical vessel to be transformed. Thus, through alchemy, it becomes a heart without worry. Although we are not discounting any wounds or pain from the past, they are no longer contained in it. This process is about healing the heart. The old heart, with whatever discolorations, scars, and disease it might have developed, is transformed into a new heart, full and vibrant and of rich, pulsing red and purple colors. This renewed heart does not carry the heaviness of the old heart.

This vibrant, red heart is bigger than the old one, yet it is very light, as light as the feather of Ma'at. It holds no malice or judgment toward anyone or anything. When this heart goes into the rebuilt human, it will not experience the limitations of the old wounds that plagued it. There will be no victim consciousness in this new heart. Beautiful, golden energy radiates out around it. Although it is a thick and juicy, even sexy Venus heart, it is a light heart, and the person in whom it beats will be a lighthearted being.

Part of the work of creating the new body that will house this transformed heart involves your being able to ground into it. For this we need the assistance of the god Sobek, the crocodile god.

Sobek is the part of the old Earth, the old consciousness and the old reptilian brain. Even though we are creating the new human in a renewal and rebirth chamber here, we must carry forth Sobek's energy with us because he is part of the actual building blocks of the DNA. You must always have a platform upon which to stand in order to take the next step to higher ground. Sobek has been thought of by some as boundary and limitation and something to be discarded, but without him you would lose the connection with what has been valuable in the past. He is still viable today as the overseer of the autonomic functions, such as the rhythms of eating and breathing, and metabolic activity. He takes care of those functions for us so that we are freed from thinking about them and can move into higher consciousness.

There is a heaviness that is felt around this, which has to do with the relationships between Khnum, Elephantine Island, the crocodile's tail, and gravity. They are all connected. The pull of the earth and our own core connection to the earth is required: gravity is required in order to build the ka.

The whole point of the renewal of the heart is to help create the spiritualization of matter, in order to illumine or enlighten the human being. This is the central tenet of alchemy as well. When matter is infused thus with consciousness, the molecules within the matter speed up. Spirit enters the body on the breath—you breathe in spirit, you breathe in energy—and the molecules are stimulated. This is the essence of what is meant by spiritualizing matter. When a strong connection, or gravitational pull to the earth, is held while simultaneously infusing matter with spirit, the matter, in this instance the heart in the jar, expands, becoming bigger and brighter. This results in healing the whole heart of its wounds and its heaviness. It becomes lighter; it lets more light in and also weighs less. The expansion of matter doesn't make it weigh more, even though it is bigger.

As the energy expands and the heart grows and the molecules become spaced further apart, there is a huge expansion of the human being itself. There is now space for the ka to live, in between the molecules inside the human. The ka body is woven in between the molecules. The human form becomes like a helium balloon that would lift off if we didn't have the crocodile tail to hold us down and ground our connection to the earth.

As the mortar/clay is being imbued with spirit, it expands so that crocodile tail and ka are woven in between the molecules and cells and atoms of the body. Sobek helps Khnum with the mixing and mortaring as he creates the ancient tail of the ancestors on the potter's wheel.

As we reflect upon this new body that is being created, it is important to remember that Nekhbet-Mother-Mut is in all the deities participating in this work—she is the alchemist who works with and through all of the gods. When you understand that she is the great-grandmother of the neteru of Egypt, the one who came before, and that all who have come since come from her, you will have a better comprehension of the true nature of ka.

For instance, if you look at this new heart as a child form of yourself, then you can see that within the child is not only you, but all the ancestors behind you—and also all your descendents to come. In the same way, the acorn holds not only all the oaks that preceded it, but also the majestic tree it will become and all its progeny. When you look at pictures, symbols, and hieroglyphs that represent the deities participating in these rites, remember that the archetypal guiding forces have within them all the ones that appeared prior. They are like the next child of each successive deity represented.

Mythology is often confusing, especially that of a lengthy civilization such as Egypt's. The gods appear and reappear in the different stories, often exchanging names and functions; yet all are true. It is only the judging mind that puts them in linear sequence. If shamanic beings were bound to a linear perspective in other realms, miracles would not be possible. What makes miracles and magic possible is that we are coming from a place outside of our ordinary, limited reality. The myths are always changing not just because their stories are handed from person to person, but also because the gods are infinitely creative beings.

It is now time for a meditation, during which you must ground and prepare yourself to receive the new organizing field that will be the foundation of your renewed body, and that will prepare you to receive the new heart. This meditation is the beginning of the life force energy coming back into and moving once again through the renewed, rebuilt human.

✳ RENEWAL MEDITATION/INITIATION

[*Prepare your sacred space. Start by grounding and centering, and focus on your heart flame. Pour love upon your flame and add the earth part of the heart breath (the sky breath will be added later for the ka activation), drawing deeply from the heart of the earth. . . .]*

As the flame brightens with your love, you will see yourself in its light flying as the dove above the silver snake of the Nile, under the protective rainbow wings of Nekhbet-Mother-Mut in her Isis form. Isis brings you to Elephantine Island and the temple of Khnum. When you land in the garden that is nestled beside the temple, resume your human form and Isis, in her goddess form, leads you into Khnum's studio, a three-sided sand-colored structure. Inside the studio there is a rough-hewn wooden table across the entire back of the building, which serves as an altar. Among the sacred objects on the altar are four canopic jars, two on either side of a central platform. There are candles and flowers and delicious fruits on the altar. You know that Khnum's studio is a sacred Earth temple and that here your heart will be honored and respected as sacred.

Respectfully step into the studio where Khnum is preparing the clay and mortar that will be used to create your new body. As he looks up from his work, offer him the olive branch. . . .

Isis then places the canopic jar with the carved scarab surrounding it on the platform at the center of the altar and asks him to renew your body, your ka, and your heart. . . .

It is important to maintain deep, grounded breathing throughout this process. Bring your breath down into the lower part of your body in order to ground and connect to the earth and the multiple sacred layers beneath the temple upon which you stand. . . . [*Pause.*]

You are invited to step onto the potter's wheel. Do so with full attention, and look into the eyes of Khnum, in which you can perceive the deep love and care he has for his responsibility, and for you. . . .

As you stand on the wheel, feel yourself being adjusted, moved to the absolute center of the wheel.

Khnum is looking at you. Notice that he sees you clearly. This relaxes you and strengthens your confidence. You are comforted, knowing that Khnum is a master, a vigilant and skilled craftsman.

The wheel begins to turn. You may sense a spinning motion, but you soon realize that because you are in the center, there is no dizziness, only expanded awareness. . . .

Once up to speed, feel Khnum's adept hands building your new body, starting from the feet and working up. He works with tender, loving care, sculpting your new body from the clay he has so carefully prepared. . . .

Welcome each part of your new body as it is shaped into form. . . . [*Pause.*]

When he reaches your first chakra center, focus on the earth as you breathe deeply and evenly. The first chakra holds the energy of survival, and of fight-or-flight responses. It is very important for you to be grounded while this is happening. . . .

Khnum moves up through your entire body, fashioning the vessel that will hold the new heart, and the new ka. . . . [*Pause.*]

You can now begin to envision this new body, as if you opened a coloring book and saw the two-dimensional outline of the form, like a vessel waiting to be filled. . . .

As you take your next breath, pulling the power and intelligence up from the heart of the earth, perceive a sensation where your tail would be if you had one. . . . Extend your consciousness deep into the earth. . . .

Visualize Sobek, the crocodile god of Egypt in whatever way your inner perception allows. He appears with a red rose in his mouth, conveying to you that he is not dangerous in this form at this time.

Let yourself go deeper and deeper with your attention and your breath, aware of the different layers that you pass on your way downward as you focus into the earth. When you near the center of the earth and can feel the heat of the molten flow that surrounds its core, begin to pull up the energy from that core. . . . It rises up through all the layers, the rocks and minerals, the water and different strata, and up through the earthen crust and the roots and plants. . . . It rises up through your tail and into your tailbone, and the whole first chakra area fills with molten lava life force energy pulsing into your first chakra, like a heartbeat in the lower part of the body. This is the first part of the reorganization process.

As you stay focused, this tail grows quickly into a long and heavy crocodile tail replete with scales. Continue to breathe with and from your deep connection to the earth. This breath is very grounding, and you can feel it pulling some of your conscious awareness down into the lower part of your body and into the earth. This crocodile tail, though becoming part of you, has a mind of its own, and you feel how it extends from your tailbone down into the earth. Being grounded in this way helps you call forth the powers of strength and the aggressive energies that are necessary for survival on this planet. You require this ancient, primal energy in order to take care of yourself. (It is reminiscent of dinosaur energy, or perhaps even dragon or griffin energy. . . .)

In the first chakra lives the oldest wisdom of the ancestors, and their memory of creation and of early life on earth, and all it has taken to get you to this point. This is what forms the foundation, so that you know you have a platform to stand on. You have inner authority and grounded connection. You can see where you are going if you can see where you've come from.

The first chakra holds the reminder that grounding is required for the next quantum leap in consciousness. With your tail penetrating the earth, vortexes of energy circle around, expand, and surround the auric field. . . .

While Khnum is carefully sculpting on his wheel and as the energies continue to rise up through the newly created body, Nephthys whispers in Khnum's ear the perfect combinations of the ingredients that he is mixing together to create the sweetness of the new human, and Isis stands with her watchful eye as overseer of the process.

Allow and experience the energy as it rises up through every chakra center, opening and clearing and filling as it goes. . . . [*Long pause.*]

When the life force has filled the entire body that Khnum has just created, having moved up through the chakra system as the kundalini energy, Khnum stands back to survey his work.

The spinning stops. . . . Stand tall in your new form, and feel the vitality within. . . .

When you are ready to fully claim this renewed body, Isis will usher you off the wheel. Take your first step as a choice to move forward on your path, and on this journey of initiation. . . . Notice how it feels to move forward in a body that is infused with light.

Isis congratulates you, and you thank her, and Khnum, Nephthys, and Sobek, for their parts in rebuilding your new body.

✣ KA ACTIVATION

Now it is time to activate the ka. Breathe the heart breath. . . . Hold your hands out to either side with your palms facing forward. Bend your elbows at a 90 degree angle so that your fingers point up. Hold this position while you receive the ka activation. As you add the stellar breath to the earth breath and deeply inhale the energies of earth and sky, your body begins to fill with the ka energy; it is as if it was already there, dormant. As you bring your ka and your body together with your breath, notice that you are a receptacle for a huge volume of energy that is woven into the fabric of your new body. It has always been there, waiting to be activated.

As you continue to breathe deeply, the energy that flows into your hands joins with the energy that comes up through the earth and up through your tail. . . .

Feel the kundalini unwind and move up through your sexual center and your belly. You can feel it as a cosmic womb deep within you prepares to receive germination. . . .

As the ka activates, it begins to spin in small spirals, pushing the molecules that hold your body together further apart. You might sense a lightness of being as higher consciousness opens your physical self. You are also aware of the expansion in your emotional and mental selves, but you feel it most powerfully in the physical. It feels as though the cells themselves plump up, become fatter, and begin to unwind. As they unwind like a reverse spiral, they open up at this cellular level, allowing spirit to enter. The activation of the ka body enables the spiritualization of the matter that makes up your body. You have literally expanded and opened so that consciousness can more fully reside within. . . . [*Pause.*]

Take a moment to direct the flow of energy that is moving through you so that it comes out of your hands. . . . When you have done this, you can then direct the energy so that it flows back into your ka. This act of reciprocal generosity and gratitude is a way to feed and nourish the ka that feeds and nourishes you. It also instigates the flow outward, so that you can from now on use this infinite life-force connection for healing yourself and others. . . .

When you feel complete in this activation, relax your breathing and return to your everyday surroundings with your newly expanded and lightened body. Be sure to ground and center and offer gratitude to Khnum, Mut, and the other neteru who facilitated this renewal and activation. . . .

It is important to take some time to integrate this initiation before continuing on this path of transformation. It is also helpful to enter your experience into your journal.

Now that you have completed this ka activation, you will find that the life-force energy from your ka is available to direct in many ways. As the intensity generated from this initiation abates, the capacity to move a higher volume of energy through yourself as a conduit may appear to ebb. Do not be discouraged, for as you assimilate to this new level, more and higher frequencies of energy will be available to you in your renewed body and consciousness. Knowing that you are now consciously interacting with the energies and power of your ancestors, you will be able to ignite the ka energy with your intention as you breath the heart breath. You can then direct it through your hands into parts of yourself or into others who are weak or diseased, into your food, your garden, and so forth. When you direct this energy, it is important to remember that it is not coming from your personal stores, for that would cause you to become depleted. This vital life-force energy is huge, comes from an infinite source, and will move through you and out to wherever it is directed, at any distance. If you want to direct it to someone who is on the other side of the world, simply invoke that person's name, or the situation to which you wish to connect, and intend the current of energy into being. You will feel it flow through you and out from your hands to wherever you intend. The more you share, the more it flows through you, and you are nourished and renewed when you use it.

Remember to feed your ka. . . .

5
THE SPHINX
DIVINE MESSENGER
Earth Altar/Cosmic Library

THE SPHINX IS the messenger from the stars, the walker between the worlds. He/she is androgynous and has to do with the organization and structure of matter and how it is informed.

In classical tarot the Sphinx is the Hierophant, the one who guides the initiate into knowledge of the sacred. Here he/she is a hermaphrodite, functioning as an Earth altar, the conduit for stellar energies as they come from spirit, from the gods. (For the sake of simplicity, we will refer to the sphinx as *he* throughout this chapter.) As the divine messenger the Sphinx stands firmly on the earth, grounded and solid, as he downloads information from the spirit or cosmic realms. In other words, he is a medium.

The Sphinx has a strong ka through which he receives messages and then speaks of what he has heard. This star navigator is in touch with higher intelligence, yet is still very connected to humans and can speak the words of spirit in layman's terms.

Because the Sphinx is built with the grounding energies of Khnum, when people go to the Sphinx and connect with him they begin to open to the messages from the great Star nation and the ancestors. Whereas Khnum crafts the human vessel, the Sphinx tests its structure to ensure that it can open to receive guidance and information from above.

Here you get a furthering of the grounding and tempering process—

getting the ship ready to set sail and making sure you have a compass and know where you are going. You are being given more direction here in the form of your inner map, your compass that is being guided from above rather than from the ego's limited point of view. Now that you have and are conscious of your ka, something more expansive is happening in the realm of your awareness.

There is considerable controversy regarding the origins of the Sphinx. Conventional Egyptology dates it as having been built at the same time as the pyramid complex at Giza around 4,600 years ago, however, a number of Egyptologists, geologists, and other students of the enigmatic Sphinx have suggested evidence that it is much older.

If you look at the proportions of the Sphinx, it is obvious that the current human head is much smaller than the body that supports it. A number of Egyptologists and others interested in solving the mystery of the Sphinx have posited that a different head, perhaps that of a lion, graced the body of the Sphinx ages before the pyramids were built, and before Pharaoh Khafre had it further carved to reflect his face. John Anthony West and Robert Bauval both offer compelling theories. West bases his hypothesis on geologists' studies of erosion patterns in the stone, which indicate that water rather than wind caused the erosion. This would indicate that the Sphinx was carved before the great flood, and much earlier than traditionally suggested. Bauval uses the precessions of the equinox to determine how long ago the constellation of Leo rose in the eastern sky during the equinoxes. At that time, 10,500 years ago, the constellation of Orion mirrored the layout of the pyramid complex as it still stands on the Giza Plateau.

From the realms of myth and legend come stories of the Sphinx as a guardian holding safe a library of information, likely buried deep in the earth beneath its solid structure. In actuality, that would be difficult, as the great altar is carved from the bedrock itself.

Although the origins of the Sphinx are unknown to us, we believe that it may be found in a far distant past, beyond that which we can imagine. The possibility exists that it has been reshaped several times since. The guidance that has brought in the teachings of this book tells us it was initially carved by the pathfinders who first inhabited this planet and were seeded from the Dog Star, Alpha Canis Majoris. This star, also known as Sirius and as Sothis, is located in the constellation of Canis Major. This star was well known and very important to the ancient Egyptians, who marked the first day of their agricultural calendar year by its rising.

Perhaps the original visage of the Sphinx was carved in the form of an ancient wolf, an Anubis that honored the Dog Star. Canine ancestors looked very different from the dogs and wolves of today, although in essence they held similar totemic attributes of loyalty and heart.

Regardless of its original face or age, it appears that the philosophers, teachers, healers, and way-showers of the time wanted to have on Earth a navigational tool that had encoded within it a library of information energetically infused much like the ka in our renewed bodies, within the very granite from which it was carved. As the ages turned and passed, after thousands of years, the guardian could have became a lion during the age of Leo, then been recarved with the face of the pharaoh Khafre, the son of Khufu (Cheops), who was then given erroneous credit for building the entire monument.

Each in its time showed the inhabitants of the world how closely connected we are to the heavens, and yet how heavily the Sphinx reclines upon the earth, poised to hear and relay the messages from the stellar nations above. The Sphinx whispers the mysteries of the universe into our ear when we stand and listen, whether we are there or wherever we are when we invoke the Sphinx. This is why those who would become royalty were brought to listen at sunrise. As the Sphinx stood in front of them and whispered the mysteries to them, as the sun came up and shone upon their faces, they were enlightened.

When I first visited Egypt in 1978 and 1979, I walked through the back roads of the village of Nazlet el Samaan almost every morning and visited the Sphinx at sunrise. Back then there was little security around the complex. You could walk right up to the pyramids at any time of day or night. There was a guard near the Sphinx but when I told him I wanted to pray, he let me in. I was there more than once during the equinox, when I would stand between the paws, facing outward toward the east as the sun rose directly in front of me. I would offer cornmeal with deep gratitude and prayers for good health, peace, and abundance for the land and the people of Egypt.

The imagery is thus to imagine yourself standing before the Sphinx just before sunrise, in between his great paws and leaning back against his chest/heart (the *stele*). The heart energy is there. As you are embraced by this great being, you hear those mysteries coming from his heart to yours. . . . The sun rises, and the light of understanding begins to shine upon your face. There is a sense of in-lightenment.

✍ MEDITATION WITH THE SPHINX

[Prepare sacred space. Kindle your heart flame with love and breathe the heart breath, feeling the powers of Heaven and Earth meeting within your heart. In its glow, invoke Inner Egypt, and find yourself once again flying above the land of Egypt. . . .]

You fly as the dove under the protective wings of Isis, her rainbow wings, with your olive branch in your beak. . . .

Imagine yourself flying over Cairo and onto the Giza plateau. As you soar over the buildings and the great mass of humanity that inhabits the city, you reach the desert and arrive at the Sphinx just before dawn, while the stars are still faintly visible. Make your way to the place between the massive paws, and stand as your dove self, with your olive branch. Lay the branch down between the paws as your offering to this divine messenger. You can also offer cornmeal or another appropriate nourishing gift from your homeland.

Rise now and return to your human form. Kindle your heart flame even further. See yourself sitting, leaning back against the chest/heart center of the great Sphinx of Egypt as you face east from between his paws. It is dawn and the sun has not yet risen.

Continue to breathe the heart breath, and direct your exhale through your back toward the heart of the Sphinx as you make your request to learn from the Sphinx the mysteries of the other worlds. . . .

As the sun rises and its first rays strike you and the Sphinx, listen closely (use all your senses) and perceive how this great being communicates with you. . . . [*Pause.*]

Before you in your mind's eye appears a great book that contains all of the history of the universe. It may appear as a hologram of the book of life. You can see the gold trim on the edges of the pages. When you look at the pages, you see ancient hieroglyphs and writing, and you see moving images as if you are watching a movie. Stories filled with information for your present-day journey reveal themselves as the hieroglyphs come to life. You begin to understand that your present journey began in the stars a very long time ago. Just as the cosmic library is encoded within the Sphinx, ancient future memory of who you are is in this book-of-life time capsule, which is encoded within your own DNA. The Sphinx helps you to begin to remember who you really are, and your star seed origins. You will only find these mysteries through the heart, and by connecting to the hearts of the gods of Egypt you will reconnect to the mysteries deep within. . . . [Pause.]

When the message is completely encoded in your being, rise and turn to face the mighty Sphinx. Open your inner eyes and honor this majestic being of antiquity. Give deep gratitude for his function as an Earth altar and guardian of the secrets from the stars.

Ground and center. Slowly open your eyes and return to your everyday surroundings.

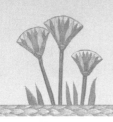

6
SOBEK AND HORUS
RECONCILIATION OF OPPOSITES
Forgiveness/Understanding

IN UPPER EGYPT, there is a beautiful temple perched on the west bank of the Nile at Kom Ombo dedicated to the gods Sobek and Horus. Sobek, the crocodile god, was worshipped as a deity of strength and fortitude, and of fertility and rebirth. He was also feared, for crocodiles were dangerous creatures. Presumably, in order to gain his protection, people needed to appease him. Sobek is the ancient, reptilian foundation of primal wisdom that has remained constant for countless millennia. His primal nature and aggressive power assured that he would survive during Earth's tumultuous youth and consequent evolution. Here we see Sobek as an aspect of the god Set, who represents the limitations of incarnate form and our egoic nature. Over time Sobek and Set have been seen as both cohorts of Horus and as his enemy.

Horus, the son of Isis and Osiris, is a complex deity with many aspects reflecting a variety of functions. Every pharaoh carries the title of Horus and many myths trace his history. They begin with his immaculate conception, tell of his youth and his battle with his uncle Set, and culminate with his ultimate victory and maturity as ruler. At this juncture in these shamanic mysteries, Horus represents the uninitiated King or Pharaoh, and is closely related to the sun and spirit. Sobek and Horus personify the polar opposites within the consciousness of every one of us. Theirs is the battle between ego and spirit, and it is not ordained that spirit should win. Each is constantly striving to fulfill his divine purpose. Consequently, they are in constant polarity, and must learn how to sustain an ongoing dance with each other.

Their battle is not about building a hierarchy, nor is it about who is going to win. Rather, it is about the eternal struggle between our humanness and spirit, as they decide whether to make love or war with each other. This battle is intrinsic to the human condition; yet there must be union between these two, for if either one wins, they both lose.

Each desires to fulfill his divine purpose. Sobek and Set are older than Horus and carry ancient wisdom. Sobek demonstrates some of the attributes of Set as he reconciles with Horus in this chapter: even though he murdered Horus's father, Osiris, Set is Horus's uncle and in many ways his mentor and teacher. He is part of the devil as well, the unconscious or dark face of God. His job is to be a shadow mirror for us in our adolescence, so that when we are given the keys to the car, or the kingdom, we don't destroy it, and ourselves. As his adversary, Set teaches Horus how to fight, which strengthens his heart and helps him develop his young power. Horus enters the battle like an impetuous adolescent infatuated with the fight and out to defeat darkness. Although he possesses the new evolvement of intelligence that we gained with our neocortex, he is still impulsive and in need of tempering. In the mythology, as their bitter struggle continued and whenever the battle seemed about to be won by one or the other, an event would occur that mitigated the situation, and they would move forward within their cycles of growth and maturity. For example, when Set gouged out Horus's eye, it was replaced with one through which he could see with a higher vision. Through this sacred wound, Horus became in-sight-full.

As he matures in his journey, Horus eventually gains understanding, compassion, and respect for Set in a different way than before. He learns to appreciate his uncle's ancient purpose. His uncle Set is there to help Horus become who he is to become. Set fulfills his purpose by being the adversarial ally.

Thus far, we humans are no longer children, yet we have not matured into the grown-up gods that we have the potential to become. This is a pivotal moment in our spiritual growth. We can now get a glimpse of our possible future and the responsibility that comes with adulthood, but we are still trying to figure out how to be grown-up gods ourselves.

In the tarot, the sixth card is usually given to the lovers. In this work, Sobek and Horus enter as opposing forces who, although they model for us the necessity of duality in our three-dimensional world, must be reconciled in order to progress. The resulting sacred marriage joins the energies, not as actual lovers, but in a divine union that restores the order and balance of Ma'at. Sobek and Horus complete each other's purpose. But they cannot do it by themselves.

Sekhmet enters the fray to reconcile these fundamentally opposite energies. Sekhmet is the lioness goddess of ancient Egypt who is the "Lady of Flame," the feminine face of the sun. Her name means "Mighty One." With great force Sekhmet pulls the two energies together. It is her power that helps create the fusion that is the sacred union. This sacred marriage is a high point in the alchemy, signaling the integration that makes way for the completion of the true empowerment. With this reconciliation, each of these opposing energies can, at least for a little while, walk in each other's shoes and have a deeper understanding and appreciation for the necessity of each other's presence.

Elementally, these two archetypes, with the help of Sekhmet, bring all the elements together. Sobek is earth and water, while Horus combines fire and air. Sekhmet brings in her fiery elemental spirit, which catalyzes their union.

Sekhmet presides over the resulting energy established in the new, more mature Horus that is an essential part of the new heart. This new seat of power now needs tempering and encouragement, the strengthening of the lion heart. It is the forces of both Horus and Sobek, presided over by Sekhmet, that accomplish the purification, strengthening, and tempering.

Another example in Egyptian symbolism is the image of the snake being lifted in the talons of the hawk. As Normandi Ellis puts it in *Awakening Osiris,* "The snake will rise to heaven in the talons of the hawk,"* or in its beak. This sky god, spirit energy, the young Horus,

---

*Normandi Ellis, *Awakening Osiris: The Egyptian Book of the Dead* (Newburyport, Mass., and San Francisco: Phanes Press, 1988).

must consume and take into itself the lessons of the snake by actually consuming Sobek. The snake, in this case Sobek, in its death or transmutation, becomes part of the hawk. And so it is with all things from the past—they are swallowed. Just as the old part of the brain (the "reptilian brain") is in some ways incorporated into the new brain.

These symbols are important to understand: Horus would not be Horus without Sobek, just as Kuan Yin would not be fully herself without the dragon, and just as the hawk would not live to see a new day if it did not eat the serpent. Life and death are interdependent, and death as we know it is not death; it is just the beginning of a new form of existence. Everything being consumed by everything else is creating the immortality of what passed before. Sobek will continue to live on in Horus at a higher evolutionary vibration.

BA

We tend to think of a soul as belonging to one person. A soul can belong to many different beings, and it is transmuted into the next incarnation.

For example, when Native Americans hunt a bear, they offer thanks to the bear for all it gives before taking its life, and they honor it by acknowledging that it will live on within them. As they eat the bear's meat and use its hide to make instruments, clothes, tools, living structures and blankets, rattles and drums, the bear takes on new incarnations, both in their bodies and in the external things they use. Evolution requires transmutation of physical form—the animal becomes part of the person, and so does its ba, its soul.

There is also a separation of the spirit of the animal. The spirit returns to the spirit world and its ba is alchemized into the human that consumed it. That's why it is important for us to think about what we put into our bodies as food. The soul of anything that we take in, including what we read or watch on TV, enters us. Therefore we want to bring more consciousness into our minds and our bodies, with whatever we are swallowing, in whatever way we consume it.

We carry forth the seeds of evolution itself and pass them on to the next generation. The ba is the evolutionary soul, which enters the ancestral lineage and ka. Because the ka includes everything that has come before, it makes the ba immortal.

Sekhmet enters the alchemical process as a powerful animated spiritual force. She blends and unifies the older energies of water and earth (Sobek) with the newer energies of fire and air (Horus) so that the fire can consume and cook the earth and water, and allow the more expanded consciousness of air to enter.

This is the threshing ground, where the wheat is separated from the chaff, where the skin is sloughed off from the old serpent, and where the old is laid to rest. In that process, the unified fields of forgiveness and understanding of the foundation and services that the old provided are integrated.

When we find ourselves in a continuous battle with a negative pattern that we cannot overcome, Sekhmet enters as a higher power and forces us to take a deeper look at our shadow, the source of the problem. In order to complete the lesson and before we can integrate the shadow, we have to look back and see what is important to carry forth.

According to Carl Jung, 80 percent or more of what's in the shadow is pure gold. By mining the shadow for its gold, you can see what the dross is, so that it can be transformed.

This alchemy honors your path, and your youthful folly. The young, immature energy desires to evolve and transform, and the old is willing but wants to make sure that what is of value is passed on so that the same limitations are not repeated. Thus the next generation moves to a higher octave.

When the gods were awakened within us at the temple of Khnum in the ka, our expanded consciousness, we were preparing the vessel to be able to receive the soul. It is the souls of the ancestors that help support these initiatory lessons, so that the new, reborn soul can evolve into greater maturation.

We are witnessing, in essence, the completion and death of everything that no longer works in us. Sobek, ruler of the ancient reptilian brain that has helped us survive, has played a vital role and served us throughout ages past. We can all identify with that in our lives and our history. However, the old, patriarchal time is over. It is time for us to become sovereign, for if we are unruly, we cannot rule. It is now time for a new ruling energy, and the following initiation brings us to a new level of consciousness and sovereignty. This is the evolutionary response to what happens after the surrender and death, and initial rebuilding of the heart.

As Horus matures and learns, he develops gratitude and compassion for his Uncle Set/Sobek. Horus is growing up.

✺ RECONCILIATION INITIATION: ACTIVATING THE HEART

[Prepare sacred space. It is best to remove your shoes for this rite. Kindle your heart flame with love. Breathe the heart breath until your heart center radiates warmth and light. In its glow, invoke Inner Egypt. Return to your dove form once again, carrying the olive branch in your beak. . . .]

You are flying above the Nile to the temple of Horus and Sobek, perched on the edge of the river at Kom Ombo. As you circle above the temple, picture opposites coming together at the point of a V. Set comes in from the left, shape-shifting from a jackal into an intimidating serpent with a cobra head. Then crawling across the sand of the desert, he shape-shifts once again into the crocodile god Sobek. Horus, the hawk or falcon god, comes in from the right, riding across the desert on the back of a being that looks like a cross between a camel and an elephant. He is dressed in full princely regalia.

Sobek stands on the left and Horus on the right. As the dove, you fly in and drop the olive branch so that it falls down between the two.

As you fly down from the top of the pyramid shape created by these three energies, acknowledge the deities and ask for permission to enter. When you descend and become the human initiate once again, you can feel your own struggle as you split into the two opposing gods. Look within and sense the natures of both Sobek and Horus within you. . . .

Take a moment to breathe deeply and feel the tug of war inside of your own being. Look for the part that criticizes your self—the critical voice. Listen to the argument that goes on, as though there were an angel on one shoulder and a devil on the other. You can feel the one that is trying to pull you forward and the one that is pulling you back. . . .

Honor and respect the fact that you have resolved this struggle often, and honor yourself for how far you've come. As you reach for a new level of maturity, you now have the opportunity to find more consistency with this resolution.

Bring up a present-day issue or reflect on a past issue, and feel deeply how it tears you apart. . . . [*Pause.*]

As you continue to reflect, off in the distance you can see swirling sand. As you focus in on it, you see that something is moving toward you from a long way off, streaking across the desert. As it nears, you see that it is Sekhmet, glinting gold, riding a chariot made of a giant triple-headed cobra. . . .

She stands tall, wearing a white veil with gold around her head. Power emanates from her entire being. Even from a distance you can see her green eyes with gold flecks in them. The cobras embody life force itself, and they are at her beck and call. Hers is the powerful energy of transformation. As staunch guardian of Ma'at, she leaves no room for confusion—these opposing forces must be reconciled.

Sekhmet's green eyes penetrate to the core of your being, and she directs her focus upon the deities within you. She admonishes Sobek for being too harsh and impatient with Horus. She says, "He's our last chance. Don't kill him, we don't have time to create another one."

She grabs Horus by the ear and says, "**LISTEN!** Pay attention, listen and learn patience! Learn how to ground your energy. Take your fiery energy and temper it with the element earth. You must learn how to stand in the fire without reacting. You must let the fire pass through your heart before you speak."

She pulls *heka* (magical power) up from the earth, up through her entire body until it shoots out her eyes and ears. It is up to you to stand in this potent sekhem (power of life force in action) energy without discharging chaos, in order to learn how to wield true power from the source.

At the same time, the intensity of the internal conflict heats the fires of transformation within you. The friction opens the cosmic or astral cervix, a vortex or birth tunnel through which the energy of Sekhmet is generated. The concentration the sekhem energy that she transmits is like the sexual life force penetrating matter. . . . [*Pause.*]

Feel as Sekhmet blows into you with her hot lion's breath, with a low purrrrr, the powerful spirit of forgiveness, self-love, and acceptance. Know that no true or lasting change can happen without simultaneously knowing that you must let go and move forward. . . .

At this time notice a softening in your divided heart. Also notice that the two opposing sides of yourself are coming into balance with each other. As a result, each side is able to feel empathy for the other, and you find you can accept yourself and forgive yourself for the places that you've been unconscious, stuck, or limited. There is an empathetic understanding that comes into your heart about the part of yourself that you've struggled and fought with. This empathy reaches deep, to where you can forgive yourself for being impulsive, irrational, irresponsible, or rash, and for lacking compassion. It reaches to where both opposing sides within you can understand the need for letting go of the past and embracing the future, with conscious awareness based on life experience.

As you feel the opposing forces uniting, you find a kind of peacefulness settling deeply within. Horus and Sobek forgive each other, inside of you and outside of you, and your past is cleansed and purified in the process. . . . [Long pause.]

The consummation of the sacred union is complete when Sekhmet, in concert with the three hissing cobras, lets loose an exuberant and celebratory victory roar that strengthens the heart and finally dispels what remains of the old energy, the old paradigm, and the old reptilian consciousness. It also tempers and strengthens the new heart that is soon to be returned to you. . . .

Place your hands upon your heart center and take a deep breath, throw your head back, and bring forth your own sacred roar, howl, or sound of celebration and gratitude. . . . As you look up into the sky, you see the dark shadow of Nekhbet-Mother-Mut flying across the bright, sunlit sky. . . . Know that she is urging you onward to your next initiation in these sacred shamanic mysteries.

Open your eyes and look around. Ground and center. Take time to be with this harmonious feeling. You are now ready to proceed to the next step in your journey, also with Sekhmet.

It's important to journal your experience to help with the integration process.

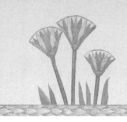

7
SEKHMET
TRANSFORMATION
Fierce Compassion/Healer

THE MOST INTENSE part of any transformation happens within the element fire. It is accomplished through fierce compassion. Sekhmet, the mighty lioness goddess whose name is synonymous with power, has the fire and the ferocity to push on through all blockages and obstacles that stand in the way of truth and higher consciousness. That's the fierce part. The compassion part comes through her great love and willingness to stand with us in the fires of transformation. She is not willing to leave us in ignorance. She is not willing to leave us in evil or stupidity. She's not willing to let us be beset with negative behaviors and attitudes, or to leave us in the suffering that comes from unconsciousness and denial. That is fierce compassion—although it may not feel like compassion when it is happening.

As you move through the alchemical process of heart surrender and renewal, your heart has been simultaneously dissolving and rebuilding. There has been a temporary conflict between the old and the new hearts: the old clinging to its wounded self, and the new reveling in its freedom. Sekhmet reconciled the two opposing energies at Kom Ombo and brought peace to the new heart.

Here Sekhmet will prepare your heart center for the return of your new heart. Up to this point, your heart has been removed, cleansed, purified, and infused with forgiveness, understanding, and grounding.

It is now time to open and offer yourself to Sekhmet, who lovingly prepare the sacred field of your heart center for the seeds she is ready to plant—seeds that will remind you of your soul's sacred purpose. With her fierce compassion and love, Sekhmet completes the disintegration of the old heart within her sacred fire. Simultaneously, the new heart becomes fully formed in the canopic jar, ready to be weighed upon the scales of Ma'at.

Sekhmet is fast becoming one of the most prominent Egyptian archetypes of our time. Her name resounds from the lips of seekers the world over, who are feeling her call and responding to the needs of the planet. When I first started going o Egypt, I had not heard of this goddess and was not taken to see her. Fortunately I was better informed by the time I started taking groups. The experience of Sekhmet at her chapel in Karnak is among the most profound for everyone who travels to Egypt. Although she has been feared throughout history as a goddess of war and destruction, it is her tremendous capacity as healer that has always showed up to help us in Egypt.

Now it is time to journey to her sanctuary at the great temple complex at Karnak. Here, Sekhmet has been standing tall in the same chapel for at least 3,500 years. Her eight-foot-tall basalt statue is unblemished and retains the ka that was initially infused into it, along with the power of all who have acknowledged her presence there since. She calls forth your newly healed and integrated heart (which has been held for safe keeping by Khnum), asking that it be brought to her so that she can infuse it with her fierce compassion. Here you are honored for the foundation that you have created, which allows this new heart to emerge.

As Sekhmet infuses your new heart with power and compassion, she also encodes it with the message of your sacred purpose. As with the acorn, the blueprint of your tree and the foliage it will bear is encoded by Sekhmet into your DNA.

Ptah is the great creator god who sees and holds the energy for the future—he husbands the seeds of the new aeon that Sekhmet implants, and that he will later bring forth and speak into being. It is Ptah who holds and protects what Sekhmet is doing. There are three rooms side by side in the temple, one dedicated to each of the three deities in triad of Memphis. When you enter the chapel, you are in the middle chamber.

Ptah's is the first statue that you will encounter. It is important to pay respect to this important deity.

The chamber on the left is the sanctuary of Nefertum, known as the lotus born, the fragrance of life. Nefertum is the son of Sekhmet and Ptah and is representative of the seed itself. Although the room dedicated to Nefertum in this chapel is empty, it still expresses the energy of what Sekhmet is planting in your heart, and you will be able to smell its fragrance, even before it has been planted.

It's a very holy moment when the human heart hears the voice of divinity and realizes what one is here to do. At that moment, attachments to the past and all illusions begin to fall away and there comes a sense of freedom and purpose.

That is so even for those who think they already know why they are here. This is a spiral process; you will come before Sekhmet many times to receive new seeds that will renew your purpose and to discover new sacred purposes. Because we are shamanic beings, each time we die and are reborn, a new facet of our sacred purpose emerges.

⚘ JOURNEY TO SEKHMET

[*Prepare sacred space. Ground and center yourself. Kindle your heart flame with love. Breathe several heart breaths to call in the powers of Earth and sky. In the subsequent glow, invoke Inner Egypt. . . .*]

In your dove form, fly with Isis to meet the powerful one, Sekhmet, the bold and beautiful lion goddess of fierce compassion. Isis brings you to Karnak and guides you into the little courtyard at what is now called the Chapel of Ptah and Sekhmet. In a singsong voice she says, "Wait here in the courtyard, little dove with your olive branch, as I go on before you. I will prepare the space for you to enter; then you will meet me in my powerful form as the great transformational goddess of Egypt, Sekhmet. Fear not, for I will do you no harm. I will take you deeper into the mysteries of your own heart and ask you to lay down that which no longer serves you."

Suddenly you notice that Isis is no longer with you. You begin to understand that she has entered the sanctuary to transform into her sacred form of Sekhmet.

As you come through the heavy door, shape-shift into your human form and transfer the olive branch to your hand. When you enter, you first stand before a statue of Ptah, to whom you pay homage. Don't offer him the olive branch; however, you can approach his statue and nod in reverence to him. . . . [*Pause.*]

Next, enter the sanctuary of Nefertum, the empty chamber. Breathe deeply to get a whiff of the essence of Nefertum, and in so doing, you get a promise, a brief savor of the fruit of the union of Sekhmet and Ptah. . . . [*Pause.*]

From there, walk back past Ptah and enter Sekhmet's sanctuary, turn left, and walk straight up to her. She appreciates your directness and lack of hesitancy in presenting yourself to her. Even though her statue before you is made of stone, her ka, her divine presence, fills the space. Feel the warmth of her inner fire emanating from the stone.

Look into her eyes and open the sanctuary of your heart center to her. Reach out and lay your olive branch at her feet. As you gaze into her eyes again, place your hand gently upon her heart and allow the energy of her magnificent heart to radiate through the palm of your hand, up your arm and directly into your heart center. Be with the tremendous force of love that is now being directed to and through you. She loves you, and you know that she, like the mother she is, wants the very best for you. Take a moment to feel the vast power of her love—and the electric charge being transmitted into your heart center. . . . [*Pause.*]

As her love pours in, feel the kundalini energy rise within you. When it reaches your solar plexus, put your attention on your third chakra. Sekhmet reaches in and pulls the energies up from your solar plexus and into your heart center, infusing it with powerful, lush green energy, so that it feels as though there is an oasis in your chest. Into this fertile ground, she places a symbol of your sacred purpose in the form of one or more seeds. Listen closely to what Sekhmet has to say while she speaks words of empowerment to you. . . . [*Long Pause.*]

If you have any question at this point about your sacred purpose, you can pose that question now. Whether it is answered immediately or not, you can trust that indeed the answer will come. Sekhmet's commitment to you is this: if you are willing to bring yourself fully to her altar, she will answer your heart's desire. . . .

Dove offers the olive branch to Nekhbet-Mother-Mut to gain entrance into
Shamanic Egypt. Isis and Nephthys stand as guardians of the Mysteries.

Khnum fashions the new human as Horus and Sobek reconcile through Sekhmet
while the Sphinx informs as the Earth altar.

Thoth and Ma'at enlighten the heart with wisdom as Khepera spins the world
through the cycles of change.

Anubis hangs from the Tree of Life, ready to meet his father Osiris in the river as Bast witnesses and urges him on.

Amun-Ra, Khonsu in his baboon form, and the goddess Sothis offering the energies
of the sun, the star, and the moon to the initiate, Anubis.

Hathor's Unconditional love helps us meet the shadow, Set, and prepare Anubis, the initiate, for Wadjet's great awakening.

Ptah issues reality as Anubis, the shaman priest enters the garden through the portal created by Nut and Geb. Thoth as the snake offers the fruit of wisdom from the Tree of Life.

The Sacred Elements: Earth/Pyramid, Water/Nile, Fire/Desert, and Air/Crested Ibis.

After the electric energy has passed through your body and you once again relax and soften, know that the energies of fierce compassion have been transmitted into your being. . . .

Express your gratitude to Sekhmet. . . . Back slowly to the door, nod your head once more in gratitude and appreciation, and turn and reverently leave the temple. . . .

As you come out and the heavy door closes behind you, go and find the sacred sycamore tree at the entrance to her temple and sit beside it, touching it for a moment, grounding the energies that are now vibrating deep within your soul. Take a deep breath and begin to feel a stirring in your heart center. It is almost time to reunite with the renewed heart that awaits you. Ground and center and prepare to fly to the temple of Horus at Edfu. Isis will meet you here when it is time to proceed on your journey to Ma'at. Ground and center, and open your eyes when you are ready. . . .

Once Sekhmet has sown the seeds of your higher purpose in the fertile ground of your heart, you will be able to sense the rose growing and blooming within. Your heart, having been cleansed of its wounds and heartaches, is being rebirthed with renewed intention and creativity.

Whether the seeds are for moving, a new career, writing a book, healing a disease, or any other creation, some of the seeds can come forth and allow you to perceive your new direction and sacred purpose. Take time to meditate on the progress of the seeds that are gestating, and you will be able to observe them sprouting and blooming into different things. Your rose is a symbol of the transformation of your awakening heart. Notice the difference in the way your heart center feels, as you should now be able to feel a sense of renewal within.

8
MA'AT
TRUTH
Radiance/Balance

AS WE CONTINUE, a review is in order, so that we might better understand the importance of this next initiation:

We wish to make it very clear that here is where the renewed heart will be returned to your heart center and awakened within you. Khnum has crafted the ka and infused its energy into the heart and body of the initiate. Every cell of the body expanded. The molecules seemed to separate, creating more space between them to allow the ka to be woven in. This happened simultaneously in the heart and in the new body, just as it happened in both the physical and energetic equivalents of the body and the ka. It is not as though the ka was placed inside the body; rather, they were woven in and out of one another. The fiery energy that filled the new vessel caused the expansion, and the ka was inserted, somewhat like mortar placed between bricks to give added strength and integrity.

The structure that was created is solid, and at the same time, infused with spirit. This spiritualized matter is the key to understanding what is meant by the mystery of how the gods become human and the humans become gods.

Ma'at has observed the entire process from the beginning. Isis made sure all the ingredients used in the alchemical process to create the new heart and body were perfectly in balance; not too much of one thing or another. The spiritualized matter that resulted had to be so full of light that the new heart is "as light as the feather of Ma'at." That is what has always been the goal of the weighing process, and all that goes with it. There are many images, primarily recorded on papyri and in tombs, depicting "the weighing of the heart." Central to most of these is the scale, which shows the heart of the deceased weighed against the feather of Ma'at. It is Anubis who reads the scale, and Thoth who pronounces the "judgment," following which the deceased whose heart is light as Ma'at's feather is led forward to become Osiris, the rejuvenating force that gives rise to new life. A heart renewed is full of light and weighs nothing.

The weighing of the heart was a clever and dramatic metaphor used to convey hidden meaning. If you were to study this process over time, you would see that it was expressed quite differently depending on who was being buried and during which dynasty or kingdom they lived.

Although the renewed heart is clearly bigger, it is also clearly lighter. Expanded consciousness weighs less; it is filled with light and space, and emptiness. This is the pregnant void, the place where everything and nothing resides.

Isis is excited that human beings are being offered the opportunity, just as her son was, to grow from adolescents into intelligent heart-minded adults. It is with great pride and joy and respect that she leads you forward into the inner sanctum, the holy of holies at the temple of Horus at Edfu to meet the hope of the world.

Isis speaks: *"My son Horus will teach you how to be a powerful, purposeful incarnated soul. He will give you the strength and the courage to carry out the sacred wisdom of the gods while in human form. Learn from his experience of having transformed from an impetuous and careless youth to a thoughtful and brave adult."*

Now that you've been through the alchemical process of reconciling Sobek and Horus and received the fierce compassion of Sekhmet, you are ready to come before the source from which flows true wisdom, and through which you find balance for your new heart.

Ma'at is the eternal divinity who has created order from chaos since the dawn of creation. Her being provides nourishment for the gods, and they thrive in and through us when we express Ma'at in our own lives. That is the ultimate reciprocity, for Ma'at is justice, balance, order, and light. She is Truth—cosmic truth, not relative truth. It is her ostrich feather that is weighed against the heart in the Underworld following death. Whether this refers to actual death or the shamanic death and dismemberment that occurs in these rites, it is Ma'at who actually balances the energies of Sobek and Horus within, in order to see that they are equalized before you can continue further on your journey.

In various tarot interpretations she is known as Justice or Strength. In these shamanic heart mysteries, the principles of Ma'at, truth and light, work closely with Khnum from the time that the old heart is being disintegrated to the time when the new heart is being born, emerging from the old like a snake shedding its skin. Inside the jar, the old skin is brittle and is cracking up around the dissolving heart, as a bigger, plumper new heart is emerging.

At last it is time to bring the heart back to life. When we are in Egypt it is at the Temple of Horus at Edfu that we do the ritual that connects the heart to the body and starts it beating again. Then through drumming and dancing and stomping, the energy rises, filling the new heart with the desire to live. All the preparation has brought us to this celebratory moment.

The temple at Edfu is dedicated to the warrior god Horus, the solar god with the energy of the hawk. It takes the full power of the intense energy of the young warrior to bring this heart to life and imbue it with courage to fulfill its sacred purpose. The full expression of Horus's energy is required, and it comes out in sound, feet stomping, voice, and drums. It takes the magic of Ma'at and the potency of Horus to start the beating of the renewed heart, and it is through sound that the gods penetrate the field of the new Horus.

You are Horus, as the initiate, the new king who is becoming divine because of what is being poured into the vessel of your restored being. All the deities have the same mission: to renew the heart and create the embodied spirit, and each is adding his or her own special touches to it, like the magi, the three wise men who come to acknowledge that Christ is born. Many of these gifts of the gods are carried into the new body on sounds.

A sign of the intelligence of this new heart is that it can receive the potent force of Horus and not revert to the primal, reptilian way of survival. This intelligent heart is imbued with the wisdom of Thoth and the encoded purpose from Sekhmet. The person with this new heart will not feel compelled to exercise power in the way of the old paradigm, nor to engage in the reckless power of youth, for this is the more mature, tempered heart of Horus. The place of peace brought about by the reconciliation of Sobek and Horus allows us to create a new use for power. In the following ceremony at Edfu Temple, Ma'at balances the energy.

The purpose of all light, all enlightenment, is to know thyself. Ma'at comes in and insists that you reflect and see who you really are at this point on your journey. You must be able to see your whole self—your light and dark. Can you do that without judgment? Can you look in the mirror of self-reflection and see your entire self, including your divinity and your humanity? Can you love yourself as you are? Can you harbor an expanded heart that is big enough to hold all of who you are? Can you bring all of who you are to the center of your heart? Can you accept yourself, and also know that this is everyone's journey? This is the journey of every soul: to meet Ma'at, to know thyself, and to love yourself unconditionally. Unless men and women can love themselves fully, they cannot love others fully either. Loving only certain aspects of themselves, they will only love certain aspects of others. This, now, is the beginning of unconditional love.

During the following initiation, Ma'at weighs your new heart to be sure that, as you are reconnecting it to the new, expanded body and ka, it has sufficient intelligence, love, and wisdom to be trusted with this new power. If we are to become the divine ones, the golden ones, the sons and daughters of Ra, Ma'at is charged with helping us find the balance of our power.

You may wish to have a drum or rattle with you to use in the following rite.

▨ INITIATION WITH MA'AT

[*Ground and center yourself. Kindle your heart flame with love and breathe deeply of Earth and sky as you prepare to return to the heart of Egypt. . . . As you continue to breathe the heart breath and meditate on your journey, you will find yourself, in the glow of your heart center, back at Karnak, by the sycamore tree outside the entrance to Sekhmet's chapel. . . .]*

Isis meets you there and whispers, *"It is time. It is time to become the hawk-headed one and to inherit my vision, my sight. This will allow you to see all things as being in divine order, no matter how tragic or how joyous. This will enlighten your heart and give you the right use of power. Come with me now to the magnificent sacred temple at Edfu."*

As Isis whispers into your ear, become the dove once again and briefly sit in a branch in the sacred sycamore tree. You have the olive branch in your beak. Isis turns into a falcon and leads the way as you begin your flight to the hawk-headed god, Horus, and to the great balancer, Ma'at. As the dove you may have a momentary experience of growing faint of heart. . . .

During your flight, however, remember Sekhmet's charge and pull up your courage so that you know you will not be eaten or destroyed. And so you as the dove and the falcon fly together to Edfu in the night. . . .

Land in front of the mighty hawk statue in the large courtyard inside the entrance of Edfu Temple. As you stand in front of the statue with anticipation and excitement, and perhaps, yes, a trace of fear, you return to your human form as Isis returns to her human goddess form. *"Fear not,"* she says, *"for tonight you meet my son."*

As you enter the hall with Isis to meet her beloved son, Horus—your next mentor—enter with your olive branch and with respect and the willingness to reclaim power from its purest source. This means you must become receptive and let go of any preconceived notions about what it means to be powerful. Pass through the central hall and into the inner sanctum of the temple. Approach the central altar and stand straight and tall in this holy of holies. With your legs slightly apart and hands down at your sides pointed toward the earth, breathe the energy up from the earth with a deep and powerful, loud breath, like pranayama (see Glossary of Terms) or kundalini breathing, and pull the life force up through the feet, the calves, the thighs, into the lower part of the body and up the spine through the belly, all the way up to your throat. . . .

The energy builds. Feel the sekhem, the kundalini serpent power as it rises up through your body energetically. As your throat opens, let sounds come out. It can be chanting or singing, noisemaking or toning, or wild sounds that come forth like warrior energy. As if in answer to your call, you can hear the sound of the hawk screeching and are joined by spirit warriors from invisible realms.

A portal opens, and Horus, the hawk-headed god, appears. His screeching hawk voice and his piercing gaze quickly penetrate your open heart space, and magically it is filled with the presence of your precious renewed heart. The youthful power of the solar god brings the heart to life and imbues it with courage so that it can fulfill its sacred mission. Your heart begins to beat like the mighty drum it is. Pick up your drum or rattle, or clap your hands and stomp your feet to feel the beating heart within. . . . Notice that your throat chakra clears and opens as this happens. . . . [Pause.]

The stomping, the sound making, the pitch of energy awakens your desire to be seen and known. You are now ready to turn your face to the world, to be known as one who fearlessly walks the path of the spiritual warrior, with integrity of heart/mind, with soulfulness, with consciousness. Feel your feet planted solidly on the earth and your hawk head in the clouds. You are prepared for illumination, and for Ma'at and Thoth.

Be with this energy until the noise and the powerful beating subsides and the space becomes calm again. . . .

Listen. . . . In the ensuing stillness, if the time is right, you can hear your spirit name being offered to you. . . . [Pause.]

Ma'at, the regal high queen, appears and walks toward you. She looks like a female pharaoh, majestic with a tall headdress, the double Ma'at crown on her head. A hawk sits on her shoulder. There is so much light around her you cannot see her face. On the top of the headdress are mirrors and around each mirror are beautiful rubies and opals. The headdress is at least two feet tall, with two large ostrich feathers coming together, long and tall and round. She wears a magnificent emerald necklace around her neck.

As you gaze upon the splendor of Ma'at, you see yourself reflected in the mirrors, and realize the true purpose of all light—to know thyself.

The harder you strive to see Ma'at, the more clearly you see yourself. . . .

This has always been the secret purpose within the mystery—the more you seek to find divinity outside of yourself, the more you are led to see it within. . . .

Although you cannot distinguish the features of her face in the radiant glow, you see yourself and the many facets of yourself reflected in the mirrors. . . . You might see a part of you as a mother or father, a wife or husband, and also as a temple priest or priestess, and again in a craft or a career, or as a visionary, and as one who feels weak and fearful, or another part that is afraid of getting old. . . . She reflects to you the many parts of yourself, and in this form, Ma'at is allowing Isis to work through her with her laser vision, so that you can see who you are in your wholeness. As you gaze at her, who is your self, you realize that it is she/you who has all the answers to all the questions that you've yearned to know—and those answers are found within. . . . [*Long pause.*]

Ma'at pulls one of the feathers from her tall cap and holds it out in her left hand. Then she places her right hand on your heart. Look at the mirrors and say, "I love and accept myself as I am in this moment."

Place both hands upon your renewed heart, stand with your eyes closed, and bask in the light of your own divine being and inner self-love. You can feel the adjustment take place as by her touch Ma'at brings your new heart into perfect balance and equilibrium. . . . [*Pause.*]

As the adjustment completes, you feel an urge rising up inside yourself to move forward, for it is not enough to feel this love for yourself alone. Prepare yourself to move ahead. The world is waiting. . . .

Open your eyes and solidly, with an air of self-confidence, true humility, and gratitude walk from the temple of Horus, back out into the night with Isis by your side. . . .

Isis says, *"Now you, too, know yourself as my beloved son/daughter, and it is time for you to go to meet your wise Uncle Thoth at my Isle."*

It is important at this juncture to realize that the renewal of your heart also awakens the healing power of your heart. To embody this initiation in a grounded way, take a few moments to reflect upon the power and meaning of your experience:

A. If you heard your name, know that you must grow into it and should keep it close to your heart until the completion of the second great round, when you reach Amun-Ra. . . . Write it down and consider why it came to you.

B. When you looked in the face of Ma'at, what did you see reflected back? And were you able to love and accept your entire being?

C. Consider what your calling in the world might be so that you can serve with the healing powers that are awakening within you.

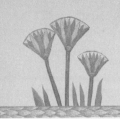

9
THOTH
ILLUMINATION
Architect of Wisdom/ Enlightened Communication

THOTH IS THE mastermind, the Magician, the overarching principle and presence that defines this work. He is the venerable god of wisdom in the Egyptian pantheon, said to have come into this world from the heart of Ra. He knows the words of power and is considered to be the tongue of Ptah because he names the dreams of Ptah's heart into being. It is Thoth, in his function as god of communications and language, who gives articulation to the essential truths of these mysteries. He is also the scribe of the gods and brought writing to humankind.

Although Thoth is most often depicted as a man with the head of an ibis, he is also seen as an ibis or a baboon. He takes the form of many birds for various functions and can speak his wisdom through all beings. Occasionally he has appeared to us as a serpent or cobra to convey Earth wisdom as depicted on the cover of this book. When viewed as a winged or feathered serpent, he combines the wisdom of Earth and sky.

Anubis is Thoth's protégé who, through his willingness to enter into the mysteries and experience them firsthand, became a master of communication and a wisdom carrier himself. Thoth and Isis are Anubis's main mentors. They are all doing this work together. The term *heart/ mind* refers to Anubis and Thoth and to the sacred marriage between them that results in the articulation of these teachings as they come through the authors.

Behind every part of this process, from when you enter the first vortex and make your offering, to the final crowning journey, Thoth is behind it all. Although his wisdom and power enable all of the other neteru to communicate with and through us, he needs to stay somewhat in the background while the initiate travels through the rites and has the direct experiences. It is Thoth who illumines the experiences to help convert the initiates' knowledge into their own inner wisdom, which is the wisdom of the neteru.

Thoth is multiplistic in his ability to speak all tongues. He is a wisdom keeper with a split tongue, like Cobra. Snakes use the two tips of their split tongue to receive independent information. To better understand the true power and nature of the maligned serpent, and consequent meaning given to the forked tongue, we must look to the mystic Gnostic texts that did not make it into the bible, before the snake became vilified:

"Scholars investigating the Nag Hamadi find discovered that some of the texts tell the origin of the human race in terms very different from the usual reading of Genesis: the *Testimony of Truth,* for example, tells the story of the garden of Eden from the viewpoint of the serpent! Here the serpent, long known to appear in Gnostic literature as the principle of divine wisdom, convinces Adam and Eve to partake of knowledge while 'the Lord' threatens them with death, trying jealously to prevent them from attaining knowledge, and expelling them from paradise when they achieve it."*

Thoth's level of communication requires the ability of one who is able to think and speak in unison with the mind and heart. That is what is truly meant by speaking with a forked tongue—one who understands duality and can speak about subjects of light and dark, life and death.

Like Raven, a totem ally who is a messenger between the worlds, Thoth sees both sides equally. Raven turns its head sideways with its ear pointing down to the earth and looks the other way as if it is listening for the worm. Thoth shows us that all things have two sides to them. There are actually many sides or facets to everything in this Earth realm,

---

*Elaine Pagels, *The Gnostic Gospels* (New York: Vintage, 1979).

although we generally think of it as dualistic. It requires the ability of one who embraces the powers of the forked tongue and can deal with the shadow and the light to fully communicate those mysteries. Forked-tongued people are gifted with the ways of the two serpents of life and death, and of all opposite things.

Enlightened communication comes from being illumined. In the tarot this attribute is usually given to the Hermit. It is called illumination here because it refers to the being that is lit from within, yet radiates as a light in the world. Like the Hermit, Thoth is the embodiment of all the tools, and he knows how to use them.

To the ancient Egyptians, Thoth represented the highest concept of Mind. His is the governing intelligence of creation and it is this high level of intelligence that he brings to your renewed heart. The ancient Egyptians called this the akh, the illumined, intelligent subtle body that is created from the marriage of the ba and the ka, the person's soul and his or her ancestral lineage. Thoth illumines a new level that brings in the ability to reason with the heart and to make decisions from the heart. When Thoth enters the heart, it completes the infusion that results in what we have been calling the heart/mind. You can then begin to experience the potential of divinity and immortality. This intelligent heart has a higher mind that does not react from victim's consciousness or ignorance and cannot be controlled by the ego mind.

Thoth is the overarching energy of all works of wisdom. He appears at the beginning and the end, and is accessible throughout, if you but ask. His place of prominence in this round, however, follows Ma'at, with whom he is always associated. She is the balance, the order, and the rule of law that Thoth serves. Although they were somewhat transparent in the beginning, it was Thoth and Ma'at who stood as the two pillars through which you first entered this initiatory path. As your material body becomes more spiritualized, you are more able to receive the illumination that Thoth represents. It is only now that higher intelligence can enter the renewed heart and the heart/mind connection becomes complete.

When in Egypt, we receive Thoth's empowerment at the beautiful island temple of Isis at Philae, just south of Aswan and Elephantine Island. Facing east you would be looking out across the lake that was created by the first Aswan dam as the first rays of the rising sun strike the temple. This meditation focuses upon your third eye: your sixth chakra center and the opening to higher consciousness.

When you reach Thoth you are nearing the end of the first great round. A great round is an entire series, a complete spiral on the initiatory path.

⚜ INITIATION/MEDITATION

[*Ground and center yourself. Kindle your heart flame with love and breathe deeply of Earth and sky as you prepare to enter the heart of Egypt. . . . As you continue to breathe the heart breath and meditate on your journey, you will find yourself, in the glow of your heart center, back in Egypt. . . .*]

Isis is with you here outside the temple of Horus, where you become the dove once again. Fly with her to the boat dock near the island temple of Isis at Philae. It is still dark, although the first glimmer of dawn can be seen on the surface of the water. You sit upon Isis's shoulder and are transported by boat to the temple entrance. Thoth meets you at the landing and you offer him the olive branch as you return to your human form. He guides you through the colonnade and to the spacious and open Ptolemaic chapel that overlooks the lake to the east. . . .

Sit at the entrance to the temple that faces the water. Isis stands to your right, and Thoth to your left, as two pillars of the temple. Remain still and quiet, focusing on your breath. Simply breathe in a calm and measured way until you are in a deep meditative state. . . . As you sit facing the water, waiting for the sun to rise, look within. Focus your attention on your heart center, using a gentle, circular breath.

Open your eyes and gaze at the dawn light reflecting on the water. While you are calmly meditating in this way, and as the first rays of the rising sun touch your third eye, you will first feel the laser touch from Isis and begin to experience a transmission from her third eye into yours. Simply be, and receive. . . .

As you breathe in the illumination of the first rays of the sun, you feel your third eye open. Your higher mind is ignited, and as your sixth chakra opens, you notice that the light is now also shining into your heart center, and you feel the warmth expanding and creating yet more space within your heart center. . . .

As the illumination pours into you and completes the heart/mind connection, Thoth, the highest intelligence of the mind, enters and permeates your heart space. While the sun shines upon your face, you are absorbing the deep blue energy of the water. Keep gazing at the dark blue water. As the sun gets higher, the water gets lighter. . . .

When the sun has fully risen and shines full upon your face, this part of the ritual is complete. Bask for a moment in the glow of the illumined heart/mind. . . . [*Pause.*]

Now when you focus on your renewed heart, you find Thoth within. Become aware that a new level of guidance is available to you. If you have a specific question, ask now, and allow your higher self to speak. . . .You can ask questions and they will be answered from this higher mind, from where your higher self speaks directly to you. . . . [*Pause.*]

As you continue to sit quietly in this warm energy, notice the soft breeze and the fragrance of jasmine. You can hear doves cooing from atop the pillars of the temple, and white birds circle above. There's a transcendent feeling of serenity and inner knowing that comes with illumination.

From this enlightened moment, you can look both backward and forward in time with a new and broadened perspective of your personal journey—where you have come from, where you are going, and how all your previous experience has served you. At this point you need to acknowledge where you came from and how you have arrived at this place of inner knowing. . . . [*Pause.*]

Walk reverently to the inner sanctum of the temple, which is an outer reflection of the holy of holies, the quiet place within where you receive the messages of the gods and embody the illumination of Thoth.

Take some further time to meditate and be still within the peace and radiance of this moment. . . . [*Pause.*]

Allow yourself to feel a song welling up from within. It is time to break the silence and offer a song of gratitude.

When you feel complete, ground and center yourself in your physical body, and notice that the expanded consciousness of your heart/mind remains as you move forward with your day, and your life.

Although you are not complete in your rites of passage, you have reached a plateau in the journey. In between your completion of this first round and the next forward movement on the spiral, the god Khepera will spin the wheel and open the portal to allow just the right amount of inner knowing to prepare you for the next great round.

10
KHEPERA
CYCLES OF CHANGE
Planetary Guardian/Spiral Dancer

KHEPERA, THE SCARAB GOD, represents the early morning sun, the first rays that reach out over the land, not yet warm, but carrying the promise of the new day. The scarab was thought to be self-created through parthenogenesis, a feat typically ascribed to females only; however, the ancient Egyptians could not distinguish the sex of these black desert beetles and believed all of them to be male.

The Egyptians observed the scarab rolling a ball of dung in which its larva was being safely nourished. In our work here, Khepera is seen pushing a spinning black ball in front of him. He is hovering over it and rolling it very, very fast while it's spinning around underneath his belly. As it spins, the black ball turns into our planet, Earth.

This image conveys the energy of transformation on a planetary level, which is in constant flux as everything goes through cycles and changes. The emergence of this archetype indicates that we are now at a place and time where we can comprehend more of the mysteries of the universe and how transformation and change actually happen.

Everything is swallowing everything else, all the time. It is a law of the space/time continuum: Once a thing is swallowed it passes through a space/time vortex and is resurrected into the next higher octave. There is a similarity in appearance each and every time.

An example in nature would be a tree going through the seasons, completing a full spiral of change each year. We don't recognize the changes from year to year unless we have the eyes to see that the branches are a little longer, the trunk a little wider, the roots deeper, and the tree taller.

This continual growth and expansion in the cycles of time speak to the meaning of Khepera as the spinning, spiraling world, the Wheel of Fortune in traditional tarot. Khepera represents equally the dark and the light, and fully understands the cycles of change. Everything passes through him in his role as guardian of the transformation process. He oversees transformations on Earth and other planes throughout the solar system.

Khepera watches over our planet and its transits, and through him we see the relationships between all the bodies (planets, asteroids, moons, etc.) within our solar system and beyond. The aspects or relationships between Earth and the other planets, such as when they are moving close to or away from us, or are direct or in retrograde, are closely monitored by Khepera, and he mitigates those relationships and alignments, and consequent influences. It is his intercession that makes it possible for us to handle the energies that are projected toward us at any given moment. As we move through the various cycles and changes, we can see and feel these planetary and cosmic forces to varying degrees. Each has different effects, all of which are important, and all of which can be somewhat regulated by Khepera, who enables us to utilize the energies appropriately. He also understands night and day, the seasons, and the other cycles of life that affect our planet and all who live upon it.

The ancients thought of the planets as deities, and gave them deities' names. They are not deities; rather they are like the familiars of deities.

Picture a deity as a wizard holding a planet in the palm of his or her hands, as though it was a magic crystal ball. It is the different aspects of the deities that govern the planets, but the planets are not deities in and of themselves. The planets function much the same for the deities as the totems do for us. Like totems, planets have intelligence and distinctive qualities, although on a huge scale, and their energies inform each human being's life according to their unique astrological aspects.

Khepera is a primary filter for these energies—he embraces Earth with his body so that they pass as light energy through him before they reach us.

The gods spin the balls of energy at different times and change their axis by degrees to the earth. The most direct hit is taken by the seraphim (see Glossary of Terms for more information); it passes through them like golden rays of the sun. Seraphim are capable of handling radiance far too bright for us to commune with directly; yet, when the light passes through their liquid air energy, it makes celestial tones. Their beautiful angelic music radiates through the universe as a cosmic celestial choir.

Beyond our solar system are an unnamed number of levels and dimensions through which various emissions from the universe travel before they reach us. After being filtered by the archangels and seraphim, these energies then pass through Khepera, and a whole plethora of spirit beings that surround our planet, and finally reach us, filtered to a level we can handle. Khepera is the protector of the cycles of change to which we human beings on Earth are all subject.

During our renewal of the heart rites, and while Khnum is creating our new being, he draws from Khepera the planetary energies in accordance with the astrological configurations of the moment. Based on one's birth chart, each person will undergo initiations at certain points in his or her life according to his or her diverse planetary aspects. This is true for all humans and all life on Earth. During the various phases, people will find themselves having shamanic experiences that are related to the planets and the neteru who govern them. These experiences include varying degrees of shamanic death and rebirth.

To one who doesn't comprehend the cycles of change and the mitigating forces involved, this could all appear as fate. When you are conscious of the influences that catalyze these experiences in your life you can begin to co-create with the very forces from which your energy derives. When you recognize that it is time to move to the next level, you can return to the rituals in this book and once again stand before Khnum on his potter's wheel to be renewed. Each time, the body, the container, will be expanded and your ka rewoven so that you can embody the next level of planetary energies and influences.

Thus it is through Khepera that Khnum draws the required planetary energies for every new body and heart. Khepera diffuses those energies to allow exactly as much enlightenment as you are ready to take, blocking that which would be too strong until the next go round of the wheel. Khepera knows how much each human can take as he spins the wheel and opens the portal that allows in just the right amount of inner knowing.

As these forces pass through Khepera, he digests and transmutes them for us, his children. They pass through us for future generations and create the stepping-stones for human evolution. What was the future becomes the present and then the past, and keeps moving through time. Whatever ancestral lineage has come before moves into the soul's journey and becomes new information, and then becomes a common piece of ancestral lineage for future generations to expand upon. We don't have to recreate the wheel over and over again. That's how the DNA has always worked, evolving itself forward to create different species. This is the way it speaks and evolves forward. The ka and the ba unite to become the akh. Through the cycles of change and the passage of time, and because we keep evolving, the akh become the future ka. A good way to understand this is to meditate upon the infinity symbol.

The Khepera ceremonies that follow are the rites of passage that complete the rebuilding of the conscious human that you have become through the renewal of these shamanic mysteries of Egypt. In your meditation with Khepera, you will perceive the energies as they come in, and create a mandala to represent and honor the images that emerge. The mandala is connected to the spiral, the cycles of change. By expressing the mandala you create translations from the illumined mind into form.

KHEPERA CEREMONY ONE— CREATING THE MANDALA

[Get comfortable in your sacred space. Take a few moments in quiet reflection on the seeds of your sacred purpose, as they were given to you by Sekhmet. . . . Start by kindling your heart flame with love. . . . Breathe deeply of Earth and sky as you prepare to enter the heart of

Egypt, where you will transform once again into the dove. Continue to breathe the heart breath while focusing your consciousness on the illumined heart/mind within. . . .]

Invoke the god Khepera. . . . See him as the great scarab beetle, his entire body and belly wrapped around the spinning ball of Earth. . . . As the dove, fly into an open courtyard or onto the rooftop of a temple in Egypt where many of your allies are gathered to support the coming transmission. Offer your olive branch to Khepera, the great god who in his winged scarab form can be seen as an almost transparent being surrounding the planet between you and the heavenly bodies above.

Return to your human form and open to receive the planetary and cosmic energies from the gods, filtered through Khepera, who knows exactly whose attention is directed upon you and how much of their radiant energy to safely allow through. . . .

As an illumined being, you are aware of what aspects of divinity are being infused into you at this pivotal moment of transformation, according to the planetary and stellar alignments that are in effect right now. For at least the next five minutes, open yourself to receive energy and become aware of the infusion of these radiant energies while this process is happening. The more you take in, the more you are able to perceive the other planetary guardian spirits that are assisting in the filtering process between you and Khepera. From this perspective, you can also perceive the greater cycles through which we are constantly spiraling. . . . [*Long pause.*]

As your perception awakens fully to this transformative process, reiterate your commitment to fulfilling your sacred purpose. . . . [*Pause.*]

When the transmission is complete, offer your gratitude to Khepera, and any other deities that you are aware of who contributed to this transmission.

Once again, ground and center yourself as you return to your sacred space. . . . Continue to reflect on your experience. . . .

Consider for a moment, or perhaps for the rest of your life, how you will honor this fusion with divinity that is your blessing. As one who has begun to recognize their god-self, how will you choose to be co-creator of your universe?

After you have completed this meditation, it is important to ground what you have learned in a physical way. Draw or paint your own mandala, using the symbols from your journey. Employ colored pencils or pens, or any tools that are available. In the mandala, it is your self, and more specifically your heart/mind, that is at the center of the circle, which is actually a turn of the great spiral of our evolutionary path. Mark it well and with beauty.

Now that you have achieved self-recognition of your divinity, what will you do with it? What kind of reality will you create? When you've expressed your mandala, the following teaching completes this chapter and round.

Create a space and time for reflection, and consider what you would like to do in service to healing our blessed planet. What would you like to contribute or create? Is there a project that is calling you, or a situation where you would like to help?

✒ KHEPERA CEREMONY TWO— RITUAL OF INTENT

[*Because this is the final ceremony in the first round, it is the last time you will enter the meditation as the dove. It is important to continue to kindle your heart flame and breathe the heart breath often, particularly when you are doing any meditative or initiatory work.*]

When you have prepared yourself and entered the heart of Egypt as the dove, honor your co-creative connection to your divine family by sending your olive branch out into the universe. Your divine family incorporates the seraphim and all the other guardian spirits that surround the earth and have joined you during this process.

Once again experience the energy of yourself in the spiral. Like a spider in a great spiral web in the stars, you don't need Khepera's protection as much, now that you have become part of the overseers of creation itself. You can begin to receive direct frequencies and vibrations from the energies that the neteru are transmitting.

You have joined with the energies of the spiral itself, and can receive and transmit higher-octave energies and become co-creators with the deities of what's happening on the Earth plane. This is creating your own reality rather than being at the mercy of fate. . . .

Envision from your higher heart/mind what you want to create—either for yourself or for the planet—and let the higher energies that are required come through you direct from source. Notice the difference between how this feels now and how it felt when you were functioning from your ego mind and still viewing yourself as separate from the gods. . . .

Take all the time you need. . . . [*Long pause.*]

Now it is time to become more independent and co-creative with these powerful tools. Within a ritual of empowerment that you create for yourself, draw up and express a statement of personal intention. Carry your statement with you into the second great round.

COMPLETION

Once you have connected to Khepera with the heart/mind, and received the transmission on the nature of change that comes through him, you will understand how shamanic death and rebirth happens on this planet in relationship with our solar system and the guiding principles, the neteru.

Now that you have completed the first great round, acknowledge your journey through the cycles of change inherent in this spiral. It is also important to remember the way through, for once you have integrated your own direct experience, you can become a way-shower for others on the path.

When you live consciously through the cycles of life, you enter the realm of the gods and become an honored member of this glorious family of the neteru of Egypt. With these deities, you become co-creators of your universe. This is the meaning of becoming divine. You are truly able to create your own reality and take responsibility for co-creating the world in a new way. No longer will you wait for rescue from any outside forces, for you have been handed the keys to the car or, as some might say, the keys to the kingdom of Heaven.

In the first round, things seemed to happen by synchronicity and fate, as though we had nothing to do with it. Yet this is not a circle; it is a spiral. Instead of circling in upon itself, the spiral extends to indicate that you are evolving consciousness forward, and to the next level. Throughout this first round you sustained a type of innocence that, once you have enjoined with Khepera, is exchanged for wisdom. Wisdom comes from experience. It doesn't mean that you will never be innocent again. Through these rites, you gained the wisdom of life experience and are ready to embrace your divinity as well as your humanity, and can take your rightful place as a co-creator of reality.

This completes one great turn in this series of rites that we are doing to renew the Shamanic Mysteries of Egypt. The next cycle, the second great round, will be similar, yet at a much higher octave than the one we have just completed. Our new heart/mind and our awakening to how transformation happens will enable us to go further than before as we enter the next round with more willingness, intention, commitment, and wisdom.

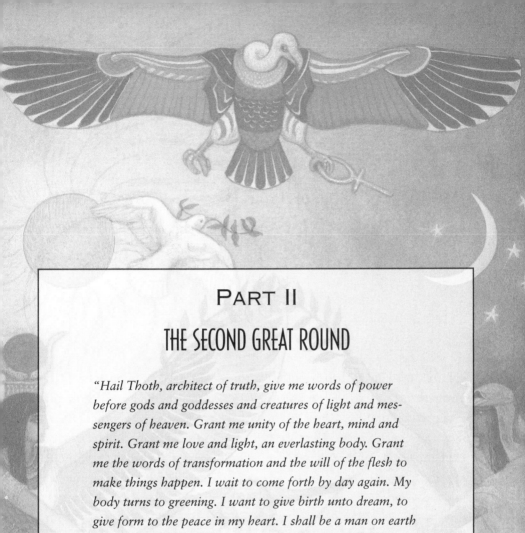

Part II

THE SECOND GREAT ROUND

"Hail Thoth, architect of truth, give me words of power before gods and goddesses and creatures of light and messengers of heaven. Grant me unity of the heart, mind and spirit. Grant me love and light, an everlasting body. Grant me the words of transformation and the will of the flesh to make things happen. I wait to come forth by day again. My body turns to greening. I want to give birth unto dream, to give form to the peace in my heart. I shall be a man on earth shaping the things of god. I am light entering unto fire, coming forth and shining through darkness. May I walk beneath blue heaven singing, my heart telling the story of light. I am a man blessed by becoming millions and millions of times."

NORMANDI ELLIS, *AWAKENING OSIRIS:*
THE EGYPTIAN BOOK OF THE DEAD

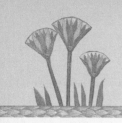

INTRODUCTION TO THE
SECOND GREAT ROUND

BEFORE WE BEGIN the second great round, we need to understand that until recently most people have had to give up their physical body in order to comprehend death and to receive the lessons of alternate realities and reincarnation. At this juncture in our evolution, human beings have the opportunity to go through many shamanic sequences without physically dying. They get to have these experiences and continue to use the same body. This was true for the initiated royalty in ancient times—who could reincarnate again and again in the same body—but not for the everyday person.

As we go through the next round, we will understand how this concept is going to weave together with these shamanic rituals. Rather than shedding our bodies and starting over, we can learn to simply speed up or slow down our energy bodies to various levels of density for lessons that our spirit wants to learn. At times we will be dense enough to have skin and bones and physical form.

Once we become skilled at using our power and our breath to stimulate the molecules of the body to open and expand, and once they move apart enough to create space for the ka body; then we can shape-shift to any form or become invisible. This is how we sustain living in the god's body, which is so vast and full of ka and akh, they are universes inside which we live. We are molecules in the body of God, and all the various aspects that are the neteru flow around and through us. As the cells and atoms living inside of them, we give them solidity. The planets live inside of them as well, and are similar to organs that govern the different energies that are part of their bigger body.

Depending upon how deeply you delved into the experiences in the first round, the higher levels of initiation encountered in the second might appear easier and smoother to you than the first-round initiations did. After you have completed all of the rites in the second great round, this map that you are learning becomes much easier to read, because you will have been down this road before. All you have to do is close your eyes, breathe into your heart, and open to what you will have learned, and you will connect to the vast heart of Anubis, and the great intelligence of Thoth, in service to the natural and cosmic law of Ma'at.

11
BAST
HOLY LONGING (DESIRE)
Instinct/Sensuality

THE GREAT CAT goddess Bast comes to celebrate with us the birth of the new human. Whether one is creating a new human form, a body of work, or a future universe, the first great round will be in place, more or less consciously in accordance with your attention. The second round prepares us for the birth of our universal creativity. The goddess Bast is invoked to inspire in us the sensual beauty that feeds our passion to create. Our renewed heart, the *ab*, is the seat of consciousness; it houses the essential desire that fuels the creative process. Later we will see that it is the polarities of Nut and Geb—represented in the tarot as the World or the Universe card, and in these mysteries as Wholeness—that create the birth canal through which our soul's purpose incarnates as it takes form on Earth.

HOLY LONGING

Bast represents the sacred side of lust and the discernment to know when to surrender to the holy longing—the desire to take form and connect to the soft, warm animal of our human bodies. The positive images she gives us of birth help us to open to that desire rather than lust. It then becomes our prerogative to utilize the desire, the hunger to burst into creativity and bring forth beautiful things in a sacred way.

We are alive to give to this earth, to experience this sacred longing.

Bast helps humans to appreciate desire and creation and to honor the instincts that call them forth. At the same time, she unites us with our higher purpose. She reminds us of the Judeo-Christian myth that humans in the original Garden of Eden were given stewardship of the garden and were meant to partake of its bounty and beauty; she reminds us of how to live consciously in that garden and keep it holy, without overindulging. It is through our interaction with Bast that we bring together the higher and lower chakras, which is the same as bringing together the above and below, or Upper and Lower Egypt. (See the Glossary of Terms for an explanation of Upper and Lower Egypt.)

It is the sensual energy conveyed by Bast that lures the gods into incarnating into human form. That's why it was called the Fall. It is the fall into incarnation. This is all about falling onto the earth, into the body. The Fall has been connected to sin and being born into sin, because it is a common belief that we should only strive to go upward. Coming onto the earth, falling, is just the other side of rising. There is nothing more sacred either way.

A baby is not born in sin. It is born in blessing. And so we begin where we ended the first great round, with Khepera, where we understand the great story of rising up through being human and becoming divine, the great story of oneness and how everything is connected in the layers we've traveled through.

Those familiar with the Isis/Osiris legend know that their birth onto this planet was held back for many ages, resulting in an urgency that is similar to what we are feeling on Earth today. With Bast, we find ourselves in the delivery room, feeling the frenetic energy of quick preparation, yet knowing calm and patience is required while the labor is completed. Remember to breathe.*

The first moments after your birth, while the memory of the oneness of being in the great heart of the universe lingers, are a time for tuning into the ab, and to the discriminating desire that awakens passion

---

*Most of the later temples in Egypt have a *mammisi,* a sacred birthing chamber dedicated to the birth of Horus. If you are in Egypt, we recommend performing the Sacred Birth Meditation in or around the mammisi at Dendera, Edfu, or Philae.

deep within your own heart. "To satisfy the *ab* is to satisfy the heart of gods, their desires and wishes. In all things great and small resides the beauty of the Divine life expression. That we exist—water and dust walking, as we are—is proof of the power of gods. For we are magical creatures. True magic is made in the heart, the magic of the desire nature to unite with the primal heart of God and, in the process of attaining that, we unfold, we become, we transform, we evolve. We are the heart of the world."*

☙ SACRED BIRTH MEDITATION

[*Create sacred space. . . . Ground and center yourself. . . . Kindle your heart flame with love and breathe the heart breath, drawing in the energies of Earth and sky. . . . Feel the powers of Heaven and Earth meeting within your heart. . . . Create a strong flame for the alchemy, and in the glow of your heart's flame, invoke Inner Egypt. . . .*]

In the light of your eternal flame, see yourself once again where you received the transmission from Khepera.

Reconnect to your experience of the Cycles of Change, and the sacred spiral within which we are all turning. Meditate on the oneness out beyond the planets, beyond the solar system. . . . Feel yourself entering into the Milky Way, and expand your consciousness all the way into galactic center. . . . [*Pause.*]

Allow yourself to experience oneness with all things, and yet feel the nothingness that surrounds you as well. This place of galactic center is the portal through the Milky Way and onto Earth. It is the grand cosmic womb from which all things are born onto this planet. . . .

Experience yourself departing from the field of plenty as you enter the void from where all things originated, and to where all things return. . . . Rest in the great void of potential. . . . [*Long pause.*]

Imagine in your mind's eye the Milky Way as the Great Mother, with her legs spread apart in preparation for giving birth. Notice the sense of longing that begins to rise up out of the great void of potential and of

---

*Normandi Ellis, *Dreams of Isis,* 221.

swirling matter and antimatter. Feel the plethora of raw powers of creation begin to affect you, pushing you, drawing you down through the vast birth canal within the center of the galaxy. . . .

Look down upon Earth, and you will be slowly, but inextricably drawn to the birthing room that awaits you. Even though you are far beyond feeling your body as form, Bast is with you, like a cat rubbing between your legs. As you are drawn closer to the planet, you see a labor room with a beautiful bed draped with silks. The Queen is in labor and the sacred midwives are wizards, or sorceresses. Nephthys and other women are around. The mother-to-be is eating grapes and imbibing nectar flavored with honey. Her naked body and feet are being massaged with precious oils. A skilled lute player creates exquisite melodies that entice you, the baby, to move down the birth canal toward the source of the music. It is a celebration, and the music draws you toward life. It lures you and triggers a longing toward embodiment.

The delivery room is open to the outdoors, where there are various animals on a spacious veranda and on the verdure leading down to a pool of water that enters a lagoon with hippos and crocodiles. You hear the croaking of a large frog and can see her sunning on a rock near the edge of the lagoon. Next to the lush garden outside the open room, a cow rests serenely among tall grasses. A hippopotamus lounges at the edge of the pool, looking up into the open spaces between the columns to the bedroom. There are many animals present and involved. This birth chamber is palatial, right down to the peacocks.

The mother is being tickled and stroked with feathers during the rougher moments of labor, and is being massaged with aromatic oils. Bells and chimes are tinkling in the wind. Bast is in charge here, and everything reflects her sensual aesthetics. All the sensations—tastes, sounds, smells, and sights—are alluring. The fragrance of flowers mingles with incense made from fine resins and sacred herbs so that the mother abides in an exquisite natural altered state.

Both men and women are present, ready to do what is needed or desired. It is beautiful! The entire space is filled with loveliness.

Under the naked woman is a red and purple silk cloth. When you emerge, you will be wrapped in silk in order to emulate what it felt like to be in the mother's womb, soft and sensual like skin. Next to the mother has been placed a soft leopard skin in which you will be cradled. At the foot of the bed is the protector, Sekhmet, a huge lioness. Graceful swans glide on the pond to complete this rich and exotic scene; this birthing chamber is surrounded with opulent sensuality. . . .

All that you see when you look up at the night sky—all of the milky, creamy substance that you see on clear nights when the sky is lit with starlight, are all of the beings in their stellar cosmic forms as they are descending through the spheres, through the cosmic universe, down through the stellar birth canal and onto the earth. All that you see pouring through that Milky Way is you and all of us. As you come closer to Earth and to your human mother and your human incarnation, feel the strong feeling of desire within yourself and honor your longing to become fully human. . . . As the sacred, holy longing increases within you, perceive yourself entering into the belly of the great sacred holy Queen Mother, who is Isis herself. . . . [*Pause.*]

Just as Isis knows how to take you apart, she also knows how to rebirth you and put you back into form. And so it is through Isis that you return to Earth.

You might feel a sense of contraction as you move through the birth canal and experience yourself being born. . . . [*Long pause.*]

Soft silk is wrapped around you like amniotic fluid, and love surrounds you. You are held and blessed and admired for the beautiful new divine human that you are. Relish these moments. . . . [*Pause.*]

Ask yourself at this time, "What is my heart's desire? What am I longing for?"

Take some time to meditate upon your questions. In the beauty of your sacred birth chamber, wrapped in silk, swaddled in fur and protected by those surrounding you, you are aware that all around you there is much to desire. The physical beauty in your sensory field of awareness is there to increase your desire and help you discern what it is that you truly long for. . . . [*Pause.*]

When the answer comes, place the longing into your heart and your mind's eye as a vision. . . .

Gradually begin to return to your outer awareness. . . .

Ground and center, and when you open your eyes, notice all the beauty around you. This is a good time to eat some juicy ripe fruit, to listen to sensual music, to smell flowers, to gaze out upon the sunset, and to partake of the beauty of this world with gratitude—deep gratitude for having the opportunity to be conscious that you are a spiritual being having a human experience.

Because of your journey through the first great round, you come back with a deeper inner knowing. . . .

12
ANUBIS
SURRENDER
Shaman/Enlightened Heart

ANUBIS, THE HEART/MIND priest who presides over these shamanic mysteries of ancient Egypt, teaches us to perceive love, life, and death from a new perspective. He is our guide, the Opener of the Way who teaches us to walk between the worlds.

In traditional tarot, the number 12 represents the Hanged Man, the initiate who perceives from a new or unique perspective. Anubis's vantage point provides you with a fresh vantage point of your own that allows you to see in a new light something that has been right before your eyes. The preceding chapters have offered a new perspective on life and death, light and shadow, matter and formlessness.

By now we have learned that life is light condensed into thick, dense form, with the molecules pulled in close and tight. Death is the vast space in between the molecules. Both are illusions, once you fully comprehend their nature and the ease with which we can move from one to the other and back. When you understand how to contract and expand molecules, then you can enter and leave form consciously, and death as we formerly knew it is over. This has always been so—life and death are about the expansion and contraction of light.

At this stage of the second great round, Anubis once again opens your heart and gives you a change in perspective, a change in view so that you can see with the illumined heart/mind. As your heart beats, you are connected to the one great source of the universe. There is contraction and expansion with the heartbeats as you move back and forth between the two dimensions. Between each pair of beats, you can perceive the condensed energy of form and the expanded energy of no form.

There is no real life and death, but rather form and formlessness. They exist within the same space. Nothing is ever really lost, and neither is more sacred than the other. They are both tremendously sacred, and we need to honor both equally. Anubis is here to help human beings grow into this wisdom.

We literally have to turn things upside down in our heart/mind's eye to have a complete change of perspective so that we can understand this. We tend to be locked into the concepts of opposites and either/or. But consider the opposites of the in and the out breath, the two beats; they are married to, rather than opposing one another. The power and beauty of this teaching is that, when you fully comprehend these mysteries, you will know with all clarity that you have never lost anything.

When the image of Anubis appears turned upside down like the image of the Hanged Man in the tarot, or like the bat hanging upside down in it's cave, or the Norse god Oden as he is pictured hanging from the World Tree, or even the image of a baby upside down as it comes through the birth canal and into the earth, you are given to perceive the message of changing your point of view.

As above, so below: At the same time you are making the ascension into realization of your divinity, divinity descends and becomes realized matter. In order to take on an entirely fresh perspective, you have to sacrifice or let die your old way of being, including your old way of seeing. Every time that a human goes upward into spirit or a god goes downward into human form, there is either an expansion or a contraction of consciousness. When gods become human they have to contract enough to forget some of their divinity in order to descend into matter. It's like having spiritual amnesia. They have to squeeze down into the density of the particles in order to incarnate in form and have a human experience in a physical body.

There is nothing evil or sinful about being born human; it is simply a limitation, to exist in a physical body encased in skin. Though there is nothing evil about it, when you move into that density, you do have to leave something behind. You don't get to have wings and fly, or remember all the mysteries that were apparent to your previously expanded consciousness. You are having a human experience, and part of that is experiencing boundaries and limitations in a physical form rather than flying above it.

In the same way, when you look from the other direction and as you ascend and move upward, you become less connected to the physicality of being human. You expand your consciousness (ka) and become more godlike. Even though you are still in form, you literally become very expanded, which is why you might feel like you are getting high or having your mind blown.

The shaman learns how to navigate the soul's journey between being human and being spirit. The resulting spiritualization of matter enables us to remember our wholeness throughout the entire journey. In helping us to see things from a different perspective, Anubis teaches us compassion for our own journeys as embodied humans.

Anubis is the shaman standing at the gate who helps us begin to travel back through our heart, and back through the earth. There does seem to be an evolutionary push right now for consciousness to remember itself more fully, whether as a god or as a human. Both/And instead of Either/Or. This is the sacred marriage. This is the beloved. The One Source, which many refer to as God, is longing for a beloved, for an Other, and that can only be found in its opposite—and that is us. Human beings are longing just as much for the One Source. We want to know if there really is a god, or something out there, that really loves us.

So God is saying, "Is there really something or someone out there longing for me, or is it all a figment of my imagination? Am I just imagining that people exist and love me?" And humans are saying, "Is it all in my imagination that there is a god who loves me?" They are unrequited lovers on separate sides of the veil, longing for one another. God says and humans say, "There must be a way that we can be united and know that the other truly exists and cares."

That way is through the holy longing and passion of Bast, and through these sacred rituals where at long last God and humans become one on a conscious level. If it weren't for the seductions of Bast, none of us would incarnate. No one would do it! We wouldn't have the desire, the courage, the catlike hunger, the drive to enter into these mysteries.

Thus Bast brings us the sacred hunger—and Anubis brings us the loyalty to the path, and they travel together, almost as consorts. Before we can embody the human experience of life that Bast has lured us into, we have to go through a sacrifice. We need to see things differently than we saw them when we were first born into human form.

Anubis now lures us into death. He lovingly presents us to his father, Osiris, and calls the energies that can take us to our ego's death. He introduces us to the promise of what will come when we die, and the knowledge that there is a renewal/resurrection.

≋ MEDITATION FOR SURRENDER

[Prepare sacred space. Ground and center yourself. . . . Kindle your heart flame with love and breathe the heart breath, feeling the powers of Heaven and Earth meeting within your heart. In its glow, invoke Inner Egypt and the birthing chamber of Bast. . . .]

After completing the birthing ritual with Bast and opening up to your sensual nature, you are ready to encounter the great shamanic priest of Egypt. As you rise from the birthing space, walk out onto the white and gold marble veranda. Receive acknowledgement and blessings from Bast, and from Taueret, the hippopotamus goddess who is one of the midwives in the Egyptian pantheon. . . .

Walk past the lagoon and through a cluster of trees and vines until you eventually emerge at the edge of the Nile. On the shore there is a large tree with twisting branches that remind you of the ram-headed god Khnum's horns. One branch is leaning out over the Nile, and from it, Anubis is hanging upside down with his head only a foot above the water, in deep meditation with his ears flattened straight out, horizontal to the river. He looks like a mummy with a golden rope around both his feet. His arms are crossed over his chest. As you come to this place you are struck by this image; it's as if he is in the womb, or incubating some- how, or as if he is a great yogi in deep meditation awaiting the answer to some important mystery.

As if in response to his receptivity, the Nile says, *"I am the reflection of the Milky Way. I am the mirror of galactic center. Just as all the cosmic material is swirling in the Milky Way and you reside there as your star self. Here, beneath my surface, are all of the primal elements that are needed to become human. This is where human beings were born, in my waters. I am the reflection. I am the Duat. Some know me as the Underworld, but the truth is, I am the inner world, for you were born within my arms, within my body. You become part of me as you walk to the shoreline now, as the transformed human ready to offer Anubis your intention to learn what he has to teach you about surrender. . . ."*

Sit facing the river and ponder Anubis, and the concept of surrender he is so eloquently expressing to you. Take as long as you need to fathom what it might be like to face letting go in this way. . . . [*Long pause.*]

Suddenly the golden chord turns into a golden snake. It uncurls itself from around Anubis's holy feet. He is Jesus. He is Kuan Yin. He is you, we. He is every god/goddess that has become human. When the snake has loosened its hold, Anubis drops sleekly into the water. He doesn't even make a splash as he disappears from view. . . .

At this moment you must trust in that which you cannot see. Go to your mind's eye and ask yourself the question, "Can I trust in that which I know but do not see?" Sit with this koan* by the river's edge and meditate upon it to see what comes. . . . [*Pause.*]

After sitting in this reflective place of the heart/mind, take a deep breath. Put your feet in the water. Know that you, too, are entering more deeply into the sacredness of becoming fully human. . . . [*Long pause while you ponder this new perspective and prepare to meet Osiris.*]

Ground and center, and return. . . .

Next we go to Osiris, Anubis's father, whom we find in the Underworld where Anubis has gone to learn the mysteries of beauty—the mysteries known in our world of humans as Death.

Because of our past karma and childhood wounds the ego is formed as an adaptation. When we "make the turn," we become ready to change perspective. Christ nailed to the cross, and Oden in the Norse tradition,

---

*As per *Webster's Collegiate Dictionary,* eleventh edition, the word *koan* means, "a paradox to be meditated upon that is used to train Zen Buddhist monks to abandon ultimate dependence on reason and to force them into gaining sudden intuitive enlightenment."

pictured hanging from the tree, are other symbols of the willingness to surrender the ego's agenda to a higher perspective. (See the Glossary of Terms for more information on Oden.) It is through surrender, and when you embrace death, that you realize that death is nothing to be afraid of at all. Everything will grow from that death and become more beautiful than the old belief systems and the ego's fears that you've been holding on to.

13
OSIRIS
REGENERATION
Transmutation/Beauty

THE OSIRIS MYSTERIES are at the forefront of the search for comprehension of the questions that compel us to grow and evolve. His is everyone's story, and in Egypt it was the goal of every person to become and awaken as Osiris. It is by our inevitable journey through the dark mysteries of the time of the missing sun, the dark hours of the night of the unknown, that we are re-membered and are conjoined once again with the neter-world of consciousness and divinity.

Osiris, the first-born son of Geb and Nut, was given the fertile lands of the north of Egypt to rule with his sister/wife, Isis. Their rule was one of peace, expansion, and great learning for the people of Earth. Osiris was murdered by his brother, Set, an act that caused great grief and mourning throughout the land; yet his death and dismemberment were essential to make possible our capacity to regenerate and renew life. Isis, under the tutelage of Thoth, and with the help of Nephthys and Anubis, sought and learned the magic required to raise her Underworld husband into the future Horus, the next incarnation of rule for our planet.

Osiris brings us a message of hope. He assures us that it is not too late to envision seeds for the future and the new world. *It is not too late!*

Isis and Osiris are true consorts, just as are life and death. Isis is about the beauty of life and its wondrous manifestations as the embodiment of spirit in flesh. She dances with death, her beloved counterpart Osiris, lord of the Underworld. Their dance transmutes matter and energy into new forms of beauty.

Osiris's body is much like the seed beneath the earth, or the butterfly wrapped up in the chrysalis. He holds the energy of death, which is transmutation itself and that results in the renewal of life. Isis awakens Osiris from his Underworld sleep and he rises up to meet his beloved, issuing forth his energy, up through the earth, to create new life. His message is a promise of hope and renewal not only for the gods, but for the human beings who reside on the world above him. The great mystery that is revealed here is that human beings, while they are embodied on this planet and taking on the most difficult lessons of the universe, are as sacred as the highest gods in any dimension. Ours is a sacred mission, and it is a blasphemous misunderstanding of dogmatic teachings that views humans as despicable underlings, separate from the gods who created them.

That is not to say that some of the actions and behaviors of human beings are not despicable. They are. Yet sometimes from our narrow or clouded vantage point we don't see the whole story. It is when we enter back into the spirit realm, and have some distance from our earthly incarnation, that we see the perfection of all things. For then we see the big picture with the single all-knowing eye of the gods.

In the myths and legends and stories told about the gods, their behavior sometimes seems deplorable as well. For example, we hear about the wrath of Yahweh or the destructive sides of the Greek and Hindu gods or the dark aspects of Egyptian deities such as Sekhmet and Set—yet whenever we delve deeper into these mysteries, rather than relying on the pop culture interpretations of them or the fundamentalist point of view, we find that the gods deeply embrace the dark and the light of their own nature and comprehend the consequences of their actions.

The main difference is that, regardless of the inaccuracies of the myths as they come to us through time and misinterpretation, the gods take responsibility for their actions, because they have a greater understanding of the necessity for the choices they make, whether it be light or dark. They are the alchemists of the universe. Without their greater understanding of the right combinations of the elements of light and dark, there would be no existence for humans and all other creatures of Earth. This is not only true for Earthlings, but for all forms of existence in the realm of matter.

When you realize that Osiris must die in order to give birth to the light and the hope of the new world, which is the new Horus, then you can understand that Osiris is pushing up from the Underworld all of the new seeds of consciousness, the birth of springtime, and the continual growth cycles we each pass through in our own dark night of the soul. Osiris speaks in whispers to his progeny about the beauty of death and rebirth.

The dove represents the first stage of initiation when you are learning life's lessons. During this second round, now that you are making the conscious choice to die and to be resurrected in a new way—ready to listen to the new spirit rising up inside of you, to your own inner divinity and authority, to your inner shaman—you embody the energies of Anubis. You will complete the rest of these rites in his form.

You know that you hold the seeds for the future world. It is in your death, in your willingness to surrender your old form, that you give birth to future generations.

Although it is Anubis who leads you into the water, the catalyst for the transmutation that awakens you into the shaman is Osiris. It is then up to you to create beauty, for you become a true co-creator with spirit. It is out of your own demise—your death and your disappointments— that you get the choice to either awaken or stay asleep. When you speak of being conscious for seven generations forward, you are calling upon the power of Osiris.

Death is simply that which decays and becomes formless. It is from the formless that all forms develop. When matter breaks down, it goes back into that place of formlessness through time. The more formless it becomes, the more birth springs from it—from death, from that other world. The void, the other world, gets filled up with emptiness, and from that emptiness form is born. From that emptiness of expansion it bursts into a condensed physical form. The molecules of form are tightly woven together, born out of that which has expanded, decayed, disintegrated.

There is no need to think that when anything dies it is gone. Death, so fearsome to so many, is simply a going from here instead of a coming to here. It is a temporary immersion into a divine, blissful energy state, not a boring, blissful place of eternal harps. The heaven or nirvana one seeks is not a sacred place; rather it is a sacred intelligence, in which we are form, or formless. This is the Osiris mystery.

🪷 JOURNEY WITH OSIRIS

[*Prepare sacred space. Kindle your heart flame with love and breathe the heart breath, feeling the powers of Heaven and Earth meeting within your heart. . . . In its glow, invoke Inner Egypt. . . .*]

You will find yourself sitting by the river with your feet in the water where you saw Anubis sink into the depths below. Imagine yourself now as Anubis, hanging from the tamarisk tree over the waters of the Nile.

Hear these words as they travel from another time to come to you:

Yea, though I walk through the valley of the shadow of death,
I will fear no evil: for thou art with me; thy rod and thy staff
they comfort me.

PSALM 23

As Anubis, you take the plunge into the Underworld to meet Osiris and your death. Surrender yourself completely. . . . Let yourself fall into the deep waters. . . . Let yourself die to all that has been. . . . [*Long pause.*]

Within the absolute peace of your experience, eventually you will become reoriented and will notice that there is a cave beneath the waters under the earth. Its entrance is the portal through which you pass in order to join Osiris in the depths of the Duat (the tomb/womb). When you enter the cave beneath the waters, you see him, looking at you with his bright blue compassionate eyes as he embraces you briefly and you let go into his watery arms. . . . [*Pause.*]

Magically, you feel yourself being lifted back to the surface and gently returned to your position upon the welcoming earth beside the water.

Lie down beside the river and put your ear against the earth with your eyes closed.

> *Goin' home, goin' home*
> *By the waterside I will rest my bones*
> *Listen to the river sing sweet songs*
> *To rock my soul*
>
> FROM "BROKEDOWN PALACE,"
> ROBERT HUNTER, GRATEFUL DEAD

You may feel a strong sense of longing as you listen for Osiris. Listen. . . . His message is stirring beneath the earth. Allow it to come into your being as it stirs you and stirs your heart. . . . [*Pause.*]

Feel the transmutation as the seeds that Sekhmet planted inside your heart now begin to sprout. . . .

Perceive the seedlings as they send down their tiny roots. . . . The roots spread down through your heart, down through your body and through your legs and feet. . . . They spread out through your arms and your hands. . . . They come out of your fingertips and your toes and reach deep down into the earth so that they continue to be nurtured from this rich Underworld energy. . . .

Simultaneously feel the tiny sprouts emerging from your heart as if they were a bouquet of flowers planted upon the earth of your being, like the lotus that grows from the mud and the waters, or a rose bush climbing. . . . You can see all of the wildflowers in the mountains growing and generating out from your heart, and from all across the top of your body, and spreading onto the land. . . . There are water lilies and lotuses blooming over the water, and all the plants that grow around the marshlands and the wetlands. . . . Forests spring up from the mountains, and flowers fill the valleys. . . . Fruit trees bloom. . . . Butterflies and hummingbirds, the bees, and all the birds emerge. . . . The great cornucopia of life in its myriad of forms springs forth as the insatiable urge toward life responds. . . . Nothing can hold it back.

Continue to contemplate these images of renewal and awakening. . . . [*Long pause.*]

When you are ready and the feeling of completion is upon you, slowly open your eyes and see the beauty that surrounds you. Ground and center. Express your gratitude to Osiris and Anubis for these teachings. With a deep inner knowing, continue to contemplate the mysteries of transmutation from death to life and rebirth. . . . Take some time to journal before you return to your daily activities.

Through these rites we are attempting to become adult gods so that we can comprehend this mystery of conscious death. The following visualization offers an additional possibility for experiencing death. Take some time to integrate your first plunge before you enter into this next journey, which came to me (Nicki) in a dream that burst forth on a morning when I was going to visit the tombs in the West Bank in Egypt. It can be read as poetry, or better, experienced as a visualization:

꧁ HAIL OSIRIS!

[Prepare sacred space. Kindle your heart flame with love and breathe the heart breath, feeling the powers of Heaven and Earth meeting within your heart. In its glow, invoke Inner Egypt and find yourself somewhere along the river Nile, near where you found Anubis earlier. . . .]

I dreamed death this morning and it was final. No platitudes could soothe the sting nor turn back the tide of time. The honeyed cake of laughter caught in my throat. Stop the wheel—I want to get off. But I can't—there is nowhere to go. Oh great merciful grief, wash away this pain, for I shall not see another day from this frail shell.

Anubis stands in the doorway, piercing yellow eyes gleaming from velvet black darkness
Holding you
Knowing you
Calling you . . .
His features are hidden, but his demeanor is clear. He stands poised to hear the faintest whisper of the western wind.
Surrender.

There is no choice.
You are held in the vice of destiny. Relinquish the last vestiges
of resistance. . . .

Your body is placed in a stone coffin. Its walls are marked with
eyes through which your spirit can see.
You hear the sound of stone scraping against stone as the heavy
lid is set in place.
You wait in the house of eternity. . . .

Like a snake that's outgrown its skin you shed your life in the
darkness, layer by layer—scene by scene—as the tapestry of
your life unravels.
Each knot untied lightens the weight of your heart as it rests
on the scales of Ma'at striving for balance. . . .

When the last fantasy is stripped of pretense and the last thread
is but a wisp, then gone—
You enter truth. . . .
In the company of Gods, you awaken to the god you are. . . .

Hail Osiris, risen in light.

NICKI SCULLY,
EGYPT 1998

When you awaken as Osiris, you step forth by day to meet the next
archetype: Hathor.

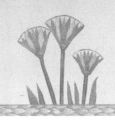

14
HATHOR
MAGIC
Medicine Woman/Integration

HATHOR'S MOST DEFINING symbol is the sacred cow, the cosmic cow of the night sky whose nourishing milk is the substance of the river of the night, the Milky Way. By some she is considered the oldest goddess and she is intimately related with Nut, the sky deity, for it is her loving nourishment that is radiated from the cosmos. She is also considered part of the triad that includes Sekhmet and Bast, and by some accounts is interchangeable with Sekhmet (see the Glossary of the Gods at the end of this book). It was veneration of her—as the golden calf—that instigated the furor at Mt. Sinai, resulting in upheaval and the consequent split that divided pantheism from monotheism. Hathor is vast and complex, and her functions in this work are not at all at odds with her more conventional representations as the goddess of love, sensuality, celebration, and intoxication, but here she conveys her magic in very specific ways in order to prepare us for what follows.

To enter relationship with Hathor, return to the lagoon beside the birthing chamber of Bast. The water is clear, and there are palm trees around the edge. A beautiful swan glides on the water. Notice the serene energy of the swan as she swims to the shore and steps onto the bank. She transforms herself into a gorgeous, sensual woman with long golden hair. She emanates love and grace, although her function in this chapter is the further union of opposites in order to create the magic of higher love and wisdom. Hathor brings us to the next level of the sacred marriage that we experienced with Sobek and Horus in the first round.

Wherever Hathor walks, conflict resolves. As she walks forth from the lagoon to her garden, notice how things change. You can imagine nations warring, and in her wake the people lay down their arms and come together in a warm embrace. As conflict resolves, there is no need for tension in the way that we have experienced it up until now.

Hathor has a cow's tail, and as she turns and laughs, you realize that she is the most beautiful of all the goddesses we have seen. She carries herself with an eminence that, when combined with her inner peace, conveys an unhurried grace that is the result of having brought opposites together. When you understand that nothing is lost and all things that happen are comings and goings in the natural cycles of the universe, there is no worry, and no hurry. There is simply alchemy, which is the same thing as love.

Alchemy is the art that turns whatever is considered to be ugly, such as a lump of coal, into its highest potential, such as the diamond. Whatever is lowly in form, when blended with love turns divine. In the dimension of form, the greater the darkness the greater the light. In the past, we've needed intense experiences such as war and other suffering to birth higher levels of consciousness.

Much of human suffering is unnecessary. Perhaps we only need a small bit, like the tiniest pinch of a strong spice in the soup, to create transformation in the world. In physical form, suffering creates the friction that heats up the fires of transformation. A great deal of the suffering may become unnecessary as we learn to create from beauty and consciousness rather than from the intensity of suffering. As we evolve consciously, we are able to create our spiritual lessons without so much drama, and with beauty—perhaps even in another dimension—and peace and harmony will naturally occur. There is a certain amount of disintegration that is necessary in order for beauty to burst forth.

Hathor, the medicine woman who works her magic as an alchemist, digests the dark and light energies of opposites into a third thing. With Hathor, the energy is not only of reconciliation, but an actual merging where the two become the divine third. As we learn from her, we are preparing for the coming age when we will be able to transform whatever is happening around us with her love.

Whereas Sekhmet's energy is fierce compassion, Hathor's is fierce grace.

❧ HATHOR'S JOURNEY

[*Prepare sacred space. Kindle your heart flame with love and breathe the heart breath, feeling the powers of Heaven and Earth meeting within your heart. In its glow, invoke Inner Egypt. You will find your-self back where you encountered Osiris. Rise up from beside the river as Anubis, the shaman priest who has awakened within you. . . .*]

Now walk to the edge of a circle of trees in which there is a large clear-ing filled with animals. Hathor is in the center of the clearing, cooking. She is stirring her giant cauldron with a big wooden spoon. Like all good chefs, every so often she tastes to see if the full flavors of your life, the experiences, lessons, and spiritual awakenings, are coming together into a beautiful and delicious delight. She continues smiling as she checks again and her brew gets further along. . . .

Enter the circle of the animals that are gathered in around her. There are rabbits, wolves, coyotes, and deer. Birds of all kinds are gathered in the trees. Lion, fox, beaver, bear, all of the creatures, the totems, are standing in the circle. They come from all parts of Earth—Egyptian hippo, Indian elephant, crocodile and alligator, blue heron, all the insects—all are here, because they are the familiars and totems of the initiate that you are. Ant and beetle, snake and lizard, turtle and fish. In the brook nearby, fish leap out of the water so they can see too. The fairies are here, like beads of lights, glittering like Tinkerbelle, or fireflies. Wispy clouds with angelic beings float above. All are here as you approach the circle. You join and stand in the circle with all these brothers and sisters. . . .

They are here in response to Hathor's love. You can't see the deities, although you can feel their energies coming through the other beings and creatures.

We're all there watching Hathor mix the ingredients, and as we watch her we feel love growing in our bodies for all our relations. We feel love generating through all our chakras. . . .

Let yourself bathe in the love of all these beings. Feel it enter your solar plexus and flow into your heart. This is the empowerment, for when you are filled with Hathor's love, you know you are not alone. You have all of these beings walking with you, connecting with you. . . . [*Long pause.*]

Now the primary beings that want to show themselves to you step forth from the circle toward you. Greet them. . . . These are the ones who want you to know that they are with you. They have been sent to be with you whenever you go through shamanic death and rebirth. These are your allies. . . . Remember them, and call upon them when you are dying and being reborn, and they will take you to Hathor, Lady of the Beasts. . . .

Acknowledge that these beings are now present with you. Invite them into your life, and they will show you how they can assist you. . . . [*Long pause.*]

Hathor now hands you an obsidian blade so that you can cut a lock of your hair and offer a strand in gratitude to each of your guides for making themselves available to you. . . .

Take a deep heart breath and open your eyes. Ground and center. . . . Come back slowly, knowing that you never travel alone through any dark night you may encounter, or any joyous day. Your allies will always be with you. *Mitakuye Oyasin.* *

As you walk forth from this initiation with Hathor, you have embodied the heart/mind shaman in the form of Anubis, and are ready to encounter that which you most fear. It is important for you to feel how much you are loved in both your dark and light forms, and in your struggle to integrate them. Once you've called forth and acknowledged your helpers and allies from the animal kingdom and the angelic realms, you can call upon the deep magic of these shamanic relationships, to assist you in your capacity to co-create and to make significant changes in your life.

---

* "For all my relations," in the Lakota Sioux language. When the Lakota use this expression they are referring to all of creation, not only to their human relations. It reflects their belief that all beings are related to one another. It is used here because in this ritual, Hathor can be seen as related to the Lakota icon, White Buffalo Calf Woman.

Hathor's love and higher wisdom are particularly important in relieving stress. When you bring the heart/mind energy into your life, you are able to relax into whatever unfolds, no matter how chaotic or stressful the situation. Hathor's alchemy helps you bring yourself calmly and purposefully to each moment, being fully present with each breath and action, and letting it go in the next moment. (This is not about attachment or detachment.)

Hathor's magic is art in its highest form. She shows us how to honor negative energy rather than repress it. As it moves through us, we can infuse it with love and higher wisdom, thus inviting the magic that blends the energies together and creates something entirely different; something that is greater than any of the original ingredients. As the consummate medicine woman, Hathor has mastered the art of tempering and its resulting integration.

This is the next level of the reconciliation of opposites that we experienced in chapter 6 with Horus and Sobek. Blending the negative, dark, or shadowy energies with higher love and wisdom solidifies the sacred marriage. The result of combining the lower energies with unconditional love is spiritualized energy in matter.

People who judge themselves and others and feel shame and self-loathing are prone to despair, and are incapable of higher, intelligent love. Hathor's magic is essential for anyone preparing to fearlessly face their shadow self and the chaos that surrounds life's most difficult situations; it helps you to realize true and lasting change in your character. Only when you have unconditional love and acceptance for yourself and others can you see without judgment, through the eyes of Hathor.

In this path of the shamanic mysteries of Egypt, you encounter Hathor and let her create the sacred marriage within your soul, so that you can meet Set, who is symbolic of the shadow. As long as you limit yourself to loving the light, you are only half a person, and you are not in your fullness, wholeness, or godself. Through Hathor's magical art, you can release your own and others' confusion and shadow difficulties into the hands of the goddess, and be supported as well by the totems and allies and their additional skills and perspective.

15
SET
SHADOW
Adversarial Ally/Trickster

HATHOR HAS LED us to integration and unconditional love for our whole selves. With the understanding of alchemy and the power of love, we can have the courage now to meet Set, the powerful archetype that reflects to us our shadow and helps us embrace it with love. As the trickster, Set performs his divine purpose by opening people to their dark side, their shadow nature. His is a sacred function, because he continues to show people what it is that they need to transform in themselves and in the world.

As the god of storms and the desert, Set's is a harsh power, personifying chaos and confusion. The animal that is used to represent Set is a very mysterious creature of unknown lineage. Traditional views tend to conjure a conglomeration of depictions—jackal, crocodile, donkey, goat, and even an aardvark. There are other even more obscure suggestions in the available literature, as well. Set personifies the limitations imposed by physical reality and our constant struggle to overcome them.

Healing and transformation are not intellectual pursuits, especially when dealing with the shadow. There are many emotional components, which often bring up irrational, reactionary, and confrontational or aggressive behavior. The embodiment of qualities that some would refer to as devilish or lower, even evil, brings in aspects of creation that are essential to the alchemical process, even if we cannot perceive or fully comprehend their necessity from our limited perspective. For example, many of the most potent healing plants are poisonous; it is the dosage that determines whether they heal or kill.

Although Set represents the shadow, he also possesses trickster magic, and will use most any means to show us what we need to learn about ourselves and our behavior. A force to be reckoned with, the conjecture has been that he is evil; but he is not. The term *evil* comes from the energies behind the devil, yet it is more about people trying to find a way to make a space for the energies of Set in their lives.

Without him, nothing can be born. In the most common story of his birth, Set spears his mother's side in order to escape a long-drawn-out gestation. Whether it's cutting open his mother's side or forcing open the cervix of consciousness through suffering and pain, he moves us forward into awareness. In this work, he also functions as a scapegoat in order to carry whichever of our burdens feel wrong, immoral, and unholy. He gives our perceived sins a voice and presence in the world, and we are forced to become more conscious as a result.

Set acts out for us the unholy energies, thoughts, and actions that have terrorized our world throughout history, and which are most often projected unconsciously into the world. The key to transforming these issues is to be able to express them, embrace them, and feel the negative emotions associated with them—anger, grief, jealousy, or whatever comes up—in a safe and holy container of self-love, forgiveness, and acceptance. This transformation can be accomplished in a sacred ceremony such as a sweat lodge, through shamanic breathwork or alchemical healing, or in the kind of process we are offering in these shamanic mysteries.

Following the last chapter's work with Hathor, Set's role is to bring up the negative thought forms and experiences that are most repugnant to us so that we can feel the repulsion toward our unconscious behaviors and also feel the consequent feelings of sadness, or of shame and remorse—whatever we don't wish to see or face—in order to bring them into the light of day. If you are willing to face them and feel them, you can heal them. Hathor and your family of neteru, along with your allies from the preceding chapter, are here to assist. When we delve into and face with love what is locked in our unconscious minds and karmic patterns, the possibility of forgiveness is born and we learn to embody the true spirit of humility.

Forgiveness is a high aspect of love. As the personification of your enemy, Set helps you come to a place of forgiveness. When you can experience forgiveness for a person regardless of how they behave—whether it is a loved one or someone you truly dislike who is being a shadow dancer or shadow partner for you—you will feel a tremendous sense of freedom and lightness of being.

By doing this work in a safe, preferably ceremonial space, you can proactively deal with the individual and collective unconscious shadow and do not have to act out inappropriately in the world. As a result, we are able to call in our divine nature and behave as more mature gods, conscious co-creators in the world around us. We can no longer deny that we, too, are Set, and therefore are no longer controlled or unconsciously influenced by that archetype.

If Set didn't keep the balance, all of life would perish. That is part of what he was doing when he broke out of his mother's womb—he was creating an exit for survival. Additionally, in some stories it is Set who creates the ladder upon which the dead are said to ascend.

◎ JOURNEY WITH SET

[*Ground and center yourself. Kindle your heart flame with love. . . . Breathe deeply of Earth and sky as you prepare to enter the heart of Egypt. Continue to breathe the heart breath and meditate on your journey. . . . In the glow of your heart center, when your heart flame has grown bright and strong, you will find yourself once again as Anubis, walking forth from Hathor's sacred grove. Traveling with you are Hathor and your animal spirit guides and allies, who will assist you as you encounter your shadow in the personification as Set . . . .*]

As Anubis, you walk toward that which you fear, and when you come to Set, you see that you are looking at an aspect of yourself. . . . Set/Anubis.

Notice how contrary Set appears to what you feel you are, as the great heart/mind shamanic warrior you have become. . . .

Look into your father/uncle's eyes and see your own reflection. . . .

Go within and imagine a recent conflict or situation that troubles you, or perhaps an old issue or pattern that pops up again and again. . . .

Look into the eyes of the so-called enemy. . . . Focus on the places that you feel triggered, that you hold a charge around this situation as you carry with you the frequency of Hathor.

Now ask Set to speak to you directly and show you what you need to know about yourself that you cannot fully comprehend without this lesson. . . . Listen with humility and with an open heart and mind. Continue to look into his eyes. As you focus on those places where you have issues, be willing to know and accept the truth without judgment or blame for yourself or the other(s) involved. . . . While you receive this lesson in whatever way it comes to you, feel the unconditional love of Hathor and your allies upholding and supporting you, and flowing through you. . . . [Long pause.]

Set will give you a message or symbol from the dark side. It will help you to bring your shadow into the light of higher consciousness. . . . [Pause.]

When the teaching feels complete, offer your gratitude to Set for having been willing to hold and carry this energy for you until you were ready to face your shadow. . . . Give thanks to Hathor and the other beings who came to support you in this process for teaching you about love. . . .

Slowly bring your consciousness back to your surroundings. Ground and center. Spend some time in reflection and perhaps journal your experience.

We call to ourselves our enemies, our shadow figures, our adversarial allies. They show us who we must become in order to walk in wholeness and balance. They live within us. Other important characteristics of the trickster shadow are impatience, rash impulsive behavior, unpredictability, instability, and false pride. These lead to the next energy in this process, which in the tarot is called the Tower.

16
WADJET
LIFE-FORCE ENERGY
Purification/Divine Awakener

WADJET IS AN ancient, predynastic goddess known by many names and forms. In her primary image, the cobra, she has often been depicted as the protector and guardian of Lower Egypt. She was also considered to be a fierce protector of children, and later of pharaohs. Closely related to both Sekhmet and Nekhbet, her image is seen at the entrance to many temples and sanctuaries. It is her form as Wadjet that is sculpted on the diadem of Sekhmet. The joining together of the Two Lands of Upper and Lower Egypt is symbolized by the images of both Wadjet and Nekhbet side by side on the double crown worn by the pharaohs.

In one Egyptian creation legend, Atum was the first god of the Universe. Wadjet was his daughter, whom he created to be his eye and sent in search of his lost twins, Tefnut and Shu. When she found them, Atum cried tears of joy, and human beings were created from those tears. From that moment forth, she has held her position on his forehead. From her place as the living *uraeus crown* (the circlet adorned with the cobra) at his forehead, Wadjet was said to have spit fire at the enemies of every pharaoh who wore the uraeus crown.

Wadjet is known as the Divine Awakener. She is the kundalini energy, the powerful life force that manifests in sekhem. She is also synonymous with and representative of the silver serpent of the Nile.

Only after learning the lessons of love and alchemy from Hathor, and meeting and embracing the shadow side of your nature with Set, are you ready to meet and embody the Great Awakener. This powerful archetype must be approached with a sense of humility and awe and embraced in a powerful and creative manner. If you choose to remain in your shadow, rather than transform it, Wadjet will tear down all that you have constructed around your ego personality.

As she awakens in you, there are circumstances that, because of your Set characteristics, you will unconsciously "set up" to help destroy the old egoic structures that no longer serve your conscious evolution. The more attached you are to these, the more they can become addictive in nature, and the more likely you will become paralyzed and stuck.

Like Sekhmet, with whom she is closely associated, Wadjet's tremendous compassion compliments her power. She is determined to assist you in your spiritual growth and will stop at nothing. She is magnificent, with green piercing eyes. Her chest is broad and golden. You can see through her eyes for a moment as she shape-shifts back to Nekhbet-Mother-Mut, who reminds us that she is working the alchemy through all these characters. Nekhbet is particularly fond of Wadjet, one of her strongest aspects and closest allies, because when Wadjet comes and curls herself up through the spine, when she winds herself through the DNA and the cerebral spinal fluid, there is no hiding from the truth. She opens up compartments in the brain where things are hidden and brings forth within human beings, at a cellular level of experience, what we refer to as *processes*. These sometimes manifest as hot and cold energies coursing through the body, and occasionally as symptoms such as shaking, nausea, double vision, and ear problems. All the senses are affected tremendously as Wadjet changes the chemicals in the brain so that we can function at a higher level of awareness. She has a huge job.

Wadjet is another of the underappreciated archetypal principles that appear here as the neteru. In comparing these archetypes with traditional tarot we have represented Anubis as the Hanged Man, Set as the Devil, Osiris as Death, and Wadjet as the Tower. Wadjet, as have serpents in many traditions, has been subject to powerful negative projections, yet within these misunderstood deities are some of the most loving energies of all. It is they who are willing to mine the dark primal realms in search of the base materials that we ultimately recognize and alchemize so that we can shift consciousness and become co-creators in conscious evolution.

When you have been able to incorporate the conscious awareness of dark and light within yourself, when you find that healthy balance of what is known and unknown about yourself, you have a deeper level of understanding and compassion. There is no blame; you can forgive the people around you. You are then ready to be a space holder for others because you are able to move past judgment. You understand that we are all part of the great change of awakening throughout the universe, and in the fullness of time we have all been everywhere on the wheel of awakening. Therefore we have all been murderers, polluters, rapists—we have all been unconscious in various ways.

Set arranges the circumstances that require divine intervention, and Wadjet then creates the bottom that people hit. This can be navigated with conscious awareness or it can happen through what looks like fate, which is unconscious awareness. Ultimately, all of us have a destiny to awaken, whether we do so through wisdom or woe.

As noted, in traditional tarot Wadjet would represent the card called the Tower, an often unsettling card that usually depicts fire, sometimes in the form of lighting, tearing asunder the false tower of pride and our arrogant assumptions. The tower can also stand as a symbol for the institutions erected to connect us to the gods (or perhaps to keep us separate from the corruptions of Earth). Regardless of the interpretation, it portends a humbling revelation, usually accompanied by a startling and sudden change in fortune. Here, Wadjet is engaged in bringing down the twin towers of ignorance and greed. Ignorance can mean more than lack of knowledge. It can also mean to ignore, to not see. It can refer to the unwillingness to see the truth in any reality or situation that presents itself. Greed is about hunger. It is about a feeling of insatiable emptiness and the inability to deal with the powerful sensation of the void.

If we human beings can learn not to ignore but rather to experience and embrace emptiness, and to dance in the void while holding space for the energies of the heart/mind, we can create and eat of the divine fruits of our labors and creations. Unless and until we can do that, we will mis-create, while continuing to believe that this will bring us more.

Our creations that come from a lower level of consciousness will *always* turn upon us.

Although it often looks as if people are getting away with something, spirit is incarnated in many different forms through what we call time and space. Somewhere, someday, there is karmic retribution—not to be confused with punishment. Punishment does not exist in creation. Karmic retribution is simply the balancing of opposite energies into a harmonious state. Harmony does not consist of the positive only; it is the presence of love and truth in the midst of chaos and confusion, and it exists within the darkness.

Another important aspect of Wadjet is her unique digestive system. Whether as Cobra or as Vulture, in the form of the goddess Nekhbet, who picks away at the dead and eats what is generally poison to us, she can transform within herself all that she consumes. Consequently, she is one of the greatest healing allies.*

If a person is not willing to see what's before him or her, or is unwilling to embrace the void and consequently is eating too much and too often, then the experience of being torn apart, of having your world destroyed and your realities busted, becomes the natural course of events. Yesterday's soul's purpose is today's ego's agenda. We will continue to grow past that which we have come to know. If we do not release yesterday's soul lesson consciously when it is finished, we become fixated on an ego ideal—and Wadjet will strike. She will strike because she is merciful and has our highest good as her purpose. All souls have a contract with her to help them evolve while they are here. This might be contradictory to the ego's idea is of how things should be.

Wadjet will most certainly strike if we are walking in denial, ignorance, or greed. She *may* strike even when we are not. How we choose to relate to her visit is what makes the difference: we either welcome her and her powerful energies and change, or we perish.

Even as she awakens us by tearing us down, Wadjet is merciful. It is an illusion to think otherwise.

---

*For more on the healing aspect of these goddesses, see Nicki Scully, *Power Animal Meditations* (Rochester, Vt.: Bear & Company, 2001) and *Alchemical Healing* (Rochester, Vt.: Bear & Company, 2003).

Although the following journey with Wadjet may appear to be short, please allow yourself sufficient time to fully receive the experience, and then explore it through journaling when you are done.

You might wish to read this journey first, and then simply take it on your own. Rhythmic, energetic music can enhance your experience. It is important that you enter this journey with reverence and humility, and in the form of Anubis. It is also imperative that you come before Wadjet with Hathor's unconditional love and acceptance for who you are, as well as some recognition of your Set shadow self. . . .

✒ JOURNEY FOR AWAKENING WITH WADJET

[*Prepare sacred space. Kindle your heart flame with love and breathe the heart breath, feeling the powers of Heaven and Earth meeting within your heart. Give yourself plenty of time to build a strong fire for the alchemy. In its glow, invoke Inner Egypt and find yourself once again fully present and whole and having become Anubis once again.*]

Set and Hathor, as well as your animal and other allies, accompany you as you walk forward. You are now ready to offer what you have learned about your shadow to the Great Awakener, Wadjet. Gather your intention. It takes all of the loving openness and willing acceptance that you have been gathering through this second round to be able to come before her. . . . Stand humbly in the presence of Wadjet with bowed head. You are aware that this giant cobra is raised fully upright and towers above and between the twin towers of ignorance and greed. . . .

Offer Wadjet the aspects of your character that no longer serve you. . . . Ask Wadjet to awaken you from the sleep of denial in any further places where you have been ignoring that which you need to know, accept, and change in yourself. Ask her to show you where you have grasped or grabbed with greed out of fear of being empty, abandoned, or alone. . . . [*Pause.*]

As you stand before her consciously seeking her responses, her tender mercies will flow through you and perhaps instead of terror, you will experience relief. She enters you like a bolt of lightning and fills you with the spirit of truth. . . . Take the time you need to allow yourself to be fully infused with her potent energy and wisdom. . . . [*Long pause.*]

When you feel complete with the insight you have gained, be sure to give thanks to Wadjet for her mercy and for the powerful initiation that you have received. You may need to take some additional time to ground and center before you return to your everyday surroundings.

After you have returned and reflected, it is important to look at what you've learned. In your journal, prepare two spaces—either columns or pages—in which you can record your insights about ignorance and greed. Make notes on what you have been ignoring and also what you have been indulging in.

The gods work closely together and are interrelated, and although we must deal with them here in a linear way in order to understand their functions, in actuality this path spirals like the snake—it is a spiral that turns back upon itself. As you move through these energies, especially the energies of Set and Wadjet, they spiral back to and around Hathor in order to deal with the powerful and raw energies, transmuting them to create the alchemy that takes us to the next whorl of the spiral.

Having swooped through the loop and gathered more energy, and with Set and Wadjet working hand in hand with us, we have created the space in which each person's individual star can rise—and this is the next journey in these shamanic mystery teachings that awaken the healing power of the heart.

17
SOTHIS
STAR CONSCIOUSNESS
Generosity/Bodhisattva

WHEN YOUR STAR rises, you begin to take your place in the garden of the gods. You become a part of the great star nation and of the great awakening for humanity. It is from this place that Sothis—Isis in her star form—rises up in the sky. Each one of us must become that star.

The star Sothis is more commonly known as the Dog Star, or Sirius. The Blue Star, as it is also known, is the brightest star in the night sky. In the sky as seen above Egypt, Sothis follows the neighboring constellation of Orion as it sets in the west and disappears from view for seventy days beginning each May. When it appears on the eastern horizon in July, it heralds the flooding of the Nile, and it marks the birthday of Thoth, god of wisdom, and the first day of the Egyptian agricultural calendar year. The embalming rites for the pharaoh were given seventy days, as that is how long it took for Sothis to proceed through the Underworld. (Anubis was in charge of the embalming, just as he is in charge of the shamanic heart mysteries.) Living on the horizon encircled by the Duat, Sothis was thought to guide the pharaoh in the afterlife by assisting him to fly into the sky to join the gods and become one of the imperishable stars.*

---

*The Dogon tribe of the southwestern Sahara Desert in Africa accurately described the three stars associated with Sirius long before they became visible through our current technology. They are considered stewards of a complex system of knowledge sourced from amphibious beings who were their teachers from Sirius.

The constellation of Orion was associated with Osiris, and Sothis with Isis, who vowed to follow her husband and raise him from the Underworld. In the heavens as well as on Earth, the love and wisdom of Isis sparked the inundation and the fertilization of the Nile Valley, and the conception of Horus, to whom this star was also linked.

Depictions of Sothis from as far back as the First Dynasty show her as a woman wearing a tall crown surmounted by a star with five points.

Sothis creates the cosmic pouring out onto the world, and as the cosmos pours out its energies onto the world, conscious awareness pours out of a vessel into the waters upon the earth. The waters are related to consciousness as well as the inundation and subsequent fertility.

The star that is rising, Sothis, is the individualized star of each person's soul that rises when the person has been through death and rebirth. With each sequence, she rises anew, much like Inanna, the Sumerian goddess who goes into the Underworld and then rises again. Inanna is the mirror reflection of Sothis, and like her, also Queen of Heaven and Earth.

Sothis shines as the star of wisdom gained through her Underworld experience. She pours that wisdom out through her own being, through her body, back to the earth. She is what you might call emotional intelligence, and she is the true beginning of Sacred Purpose. She looks to the cosmos and to the grand story of the universe to inform her, and then she pours that wisdom out through her compassionate heart to the suffering masses to give them meaning, purpose, and understanding for their journeys.

Sothis represents the ascension of matter, a type of resurrection. She is matter spiritualized and expanded with sufficient ka so that she is able to walk on water. She is lifted, filled with the elements of air and breath. Sothis is Sacred Purpose, for she gives purpose and meaning to our spiral path of shamanic death and rebirth. Her delight is to pour this cornucopia of joyful celebration back into the hearts and minds of men and women and all beings. Each of us is like a blade of grass (as the Talmud says) and Sothis is the one who sends encouragement back to Earth and whispers to us, "Grow, grow, grow."

Each of us is waiting for our blue angel, Sothis, to remind us that we, too, after our dark night of the soul, can rise again and ascend to great heights—providing that we have been willing to descend to great depths. Sothis is the light that we receive when we remember that our true home is in the stars.

A bodhisattva is an enlightened one with a generous spirit who pours his or her higher love and wisdom back onto the Earth to all suffering beings. As a bodhisattva, Sothis has a commitment to share all that she has attained and learned during Earthly incarnations with her sisters and brothers until all beings on Earth ascend to higher levels of consciousness. In the true sense of the word, a bodhisattva is a shaman, a walker between the worlds with a compassionate heart.

Upon awakening to the deeper truth of our light and shadow, we in our Anubis form are ready to take our initiatory experiences and convert them into wisdom teachings to share with humanity. Out of compassion for our own suffering and sorrows, a deep desire rises up within our own hearts and minds to intelligently share with others so that consciousness can evolve forward to a higher octave upon our planet. It is in this spirit that we offer the following Bodhisattva Initiation.

◎ BODHISATTVA INITIATION

[*Prepare sacred space. Kindle your heart flame with love and breathe the heart breath, feeling the powers of Heaven and Earth meeting within your heart. In its glow, invoke Inner Egypt and once again step forward from the fertile valley to the edge of the Nile. . . .*]

It is night. As you approach the water's edge, you are Anubis. . . . Take a moment to reflect upon your journey through these mysteries thus far. . . . [*Pause.*]

Look up at the starry night and the twinkling stars above. Take some time to feel the love of Isis surrounding you and upholding you. . . . [*Pause.*]

Step with faith onto the water. . . . Ma'at appears and nods as you walk out upon the starlit Nile. You are uplifted by her wisdom and begin to rise as though you have wings, as though some divine presence such as an angel or some great being is lifting you. It is Isis, who comes up behind your Anubis form and wraps her wings around you and lifts you up. There is starlight upon the shimmering water. You are lifted from the water up toward that starlight. As you continue ascending, you gain the larger perspective of what your life path has been about. . . . [*Pause.*]

Any remaining bitterness vanishes as your burdens are lifted. . . . As you become lighter and lighter, you begin to feel gratitude for the very human experience of your life. You have a radiant inner knowing of your purpose in relationship to the wisdom gained from your experiences. . . . [*Pause.*]

Feel yourself begin to shape-shift once more, this time into a star. . . . You are becoming a being with five points, like the five-pointed star with a person in the middle that Da Vinci drew. . . .

Each ray emanates back to the world as a ray of hope imbued with the results of your powerful lessons, not only for your own conscious evolution, but also as illumination showering the world. . . . [*Long pause.*]

When the journey feels complete, gently find yourself back on the earth. . . . Beam your gratitude up to the stars. . . .

Ground and center, and return to your everyday surroundings with star consciousness activated in your DNA. Notice how easily you can navigate back and forth between the heart of ancient Egypt and the place from which you embark on these journeys. Remember to practice seeing the bigger picture as you embrace the lessons you've learned along the way in your daily life.

Now that you are ready to shine and pour your gifts back upon the world, it is a good time to reflect upon your journey and to write down or discuss what those gifts might be, and what lessons you can share with others. You might wish to consider teaching, writing a book, creating a work of art, or simply walking your talk and reaching out to others, one soul at a time.

18
KHONSU
LUNAR ENERGIES
Divine Timing/Blood Mysteries

KHONSU IS AN ancient lunar deity whose name means "king's placenta," a name reflecting some of his various functions throughout history. During the Old Kingdom, he was said to have slain and consumed lesser gods, prompting the people to call him bloodthirsty.* In intermediate times he was associated with childbirth and fertility. In later times he was known as a great healer and exorcist. He was said to celebrate the demons of disease and prepare feasts in their honor, so that when they had been fed and honored, the demons would go away happy.

Like the many phases of the moon, Khonsu is depicted in a number of forms and with many faces, including those related to Ptah, Osiris, and Horus, and also to Thoth, with whom he is closely associated. It was with Khonsu that Thoth played draughts and senet, games similar to checkers, chess, or cards, with a deep connection to strategy and oracular magic. They may have actually been using a form of ancient tarot as a divination tool to foresee the future of creation. They worked in conjunction to manipulate the game pieces, such as the weather patterns, in order to

---

*The hieroglyphs or sacred symbols associated with Khonsu may have literally translated to "bloodthirsty," or one who eats the hearts of gods. This is true, as he did consume the lesser gods. Human beings also eat the gods and are bloodthirsty, for we must have the blood that is formulated from what we eat. When we eat of the body and blood of gods, we create the new blood within us and we become what we eat: the gods themselves. This is the meaning of communion.

create the conditions on Earth for the inundation to be sufficient to allow birth to happen. Through this pursuit, they earned enough wisdom (light) to create the five epagomenal days, the days outside of time added to the 360-day agricultural calendar year of ancient Egypt, during which the goddess Nut delivered her divine children. These became the feast days between year's end and the New Year that started with the birthday of Thoth and the flooding of the Nile. Giving birth is always a gamble, and the gods worked collaboratively to help co-create what we have come to think of as fate.

In the beginning of this work, we saw the great alchemists as Nekhbet-Mother-Mut, Isis, and Nephthys. Here we see that there is a triad consisting of Thoth, Ptah, and Khonsu, with each god holding a similar place. It is they who play the game, knowing when and where to move the pieces—the gods—to bring them to life and activate their consciousness so that what needs to happen will happen.

Because of his identification with the moon and its cycles as it travels through the night, Khonsu was known as the wanderer, a god of travelers and also a measurer of time. In that capacity, he could both influence gestation and determine the life span of the humans and other creatures of Earth. It was thought that Khonsu stimulated fertility and conception through his association with the shining crescent moon that is often seen resting upon his head, encircling the red disc of the sun.

Without the various phases of the moon and its cycles of change, all life would perish. The moon's cycles remind us of death as well as life. The fourteen days of the waning moon represent the fourteen lost pieces of Osiris, and the waxing moon includes the fourteen days it takes to put him back together again in his fullness. The phases of the moon also control the tides and influence the weather.

Whereas Thoth is bold and bright in his function as the god of wisdom and moon magic, Khonsu reflects the hidden side or the dark mysteries of the moon. Many of the feminine mysteries, especially the blood mysteries, have been misunderstood, misrepresented, dishonored, and even defiled throughout history. The wisdom of both Thoth and Khonsu are essential and the interplay between them is constant; yet we are most often aware of Thoth as the great sage who is also the architect of wisdom teachings throughout the ages.

The Star as Sothis and the Moon as Khonsu work together. Some Old Kingdom references may have been referring to his role as the guardian of the blood mysteries. With Sothis, he governs all things having to do with water and the tides on Earth, to which those mysteries are closely related.

The Apis bull (see the Glossary of Terms for more information) was worshipped as the embodiment of Ptah, and later Osiris. It is his horns that hold the moon, and he stands for great strength and virility. According to these mysteries, if the inundation did not follow the rise of Sothis, and a drought occurred, the Egyptians would bring a great bull to the place where the water's edge should normally be. His throat was slit in a sacred, ceremonial way. Even though it was Khonsu who was conducting this ceremony, it was Ptah that would ride the bull's back to the water's edge to meet Khonsu. As Earth drank the blood, the Silver Snake would rise. The waters would begin to flow again as the rains finally came in the south. During the feast that followed the Sed festival rite of renewal for the Pharaoh, he, too, was nourished and revitalized through ritual offerings of massive amounts of various meats and other ritually prepared foods through which he, too, consumed the gods.

Khonsu is also in charge of the ritual of communion, to which all of the above named functions are in some way related. Although we know it more as a Christian tradition, Khonsu reflects it back to the pre-Egyptian communion conveyed in Inanna's story of the rituals of the bread and the waters of life. Inanna became known as the magnificent Queen of Heaven only after her willingness to make the descent to the Underworld, to meet her other half, her shadow self, her dark sister Ereshkigal. Ereshkigal was perceived as a despicable, pathetic, monstrous creature. The split between the two was vast, one being the archetypal light and the other the archetypal darkness. When Inanna went into the Underworld, Ereshkigal killed her by stabbing her in the back and hung her for three days on a meat hook. The Sumerian moon god, Enki, also god of the floods and tides (a counterpart of Khonsu) sent tiny invisible beings that flew down into the Underworld and took with them the bread and the waters of life, the communion, to restore Inanna's soul so that she could be resurrected and emerge from the Underworld. Until they could meet, connect, and die to their old forms, neither could reach the full expression of their potential. Ereshkigal became more compassionate and released Inanna so that she could ascend and become known as the Queen of Heaven and Earth.

Inanna's is one of the oldest, if not the oldest story that we know of a goddess from pre-Egyptian times. The later stories of death and rebirth, including the Isis and Osiris myth, the myth of Demeter and Persephone, and thousands of years later, the Christ mythos, came from her.

Inanna's story is Osiris's and Christ's stories, and they are relevant to Khonsu because he is the universal principal of the life-giving waters and the bread of life. Without the waters, there is no bread; there would be no wheat in the field of plenty. The ancients believed that the moon governed the weather and the rise and fall of the Nile, which in turned governed what would grow in the fields and when the waters would flow so that a person could be born.

The part of the ritual known as the Holy Communion later became associated with the Last Supper, but long before that, it had always been a means of calling on Khonsu through an act of drinking the blood or the wine and eating the bread, to honor and continue that flow of life-giving water and crops.

According to Normandi Ellis, the hieroglyphic symbol of an altar cloth, a loaf of bread, and a bowl of wine shown together is *emhotep,* meaning "peace."* The symbol represents the traditional Egyptian offerings for the dead of bread and wine for sustained life and peace. As in the Eucharist or Holy Communion given today, the bread and the wine remind us that we are taking in the body of the divine god—the divine body lives in the wheat from which the bread is baked. The divine blood is represented by the wine in the chalice. When we partake of emhotep, or the Eucharist, we partake of the consciousness that came before us; we become part of the god, and the god becomes part of us.

The elements themselves are manifestations of the neteru, and when we drink the water, when we eat of the things that come from the earth, we are literally eating and drinking the gods. The elements live inside of us and give us life. Whatever we take in becomes our body; it creates what we are and affects our brain and blood chemistry.

Accordingly, we are food for the gods, for as we eat and become part of them, they are also part of us. In essence, we are swallowed by the gods. We expand or contract our consciousness in accordance with what

---

*Normandi Ellis, personal communication.

we take in or eat. Whether it is actual food or another person's emotional life, we absorb that which is around us. We need to be thoughtful
about everything that we take into ourselves, and make it sacred. It is
important to define our boundaries around people, places, things, and
situations.

One reason that Khonsu, rather than a female, is the guardian of the
feminine mysteries and our receptivity and fertility is that his energy is
related to what we take in—in other words, that which penetrates us.

As Sothis the star rises, our expanded consciousness moves to a
higher perspective, and we are prepared to encounter the divine feminine. We can then open to the goddess, and to her life-giving waters, her
fruits and grains, her fertile valleys. We can open ourselves like a woman
opens her womb, to receive the seeds of a new consciousness. You are
now ready to be impregnated. However, first the divine womb must be
prepared as a sacred container for the fertilization of the world egg.
When you eat of the divine mysteries, you bring into being the divine egg
within your womb, preparing it for conception.

In preparation for the following meditation, prepare an altar that includes
some food made from grain and some grape juice or wine. You can add a
candle, incense, and whatever you feel would add to the sacredness of the
ritual space. If you are in Egypt, I recommend as a good place to practice
this ritual any of the temples in Luxor that have chapels with statues or
images of Khonsu, such as Karnak or Medinet Habu. Luxor Temple has
the benefit of being open at night.

❧ RITUAL OF HOLY COMMUNION

[*Prepare sacred space. Kindle your heart flame with love and breathe
the heart breath, feeling the powers of Heaven and Earth meeting within
your heart. In its glow, invoke Inner Egypt, where you will find yourself
in one of the sacred temples along the Nile.*]

Your star is shining brightly within you as you step forth once again
as the shaman Anubis. Whether you are male or female, practice being
as receptive as you possibly can. Take the time you need to meditate in

stillness and quiet, regardless of what might be happening around you. You are being invited to open to receive the seeds of a new consciousness. Open your heart/womb and take in the Holy Communion. As you receive the sacred waters and bread of life from Khonsu, you receive the infusion of the holy elements of water and earth. . . .

Khonsu appears. He may show up for you in any of his many forms or phases, perhaps as the baboon or the ibis-headed man/god with the great crescent moon upon his head. His form might shift from one to another as he stands before you. Greet this great god with respect. . . .

Take a moment to fully relax and open your heart/womb in preparation to take in the Holy Communion. . . . [*Pause.*]

Opening fully in this way connects you to the void and the Great Mystery as a place of renewed innocence and trust as well as raw potential. This is not about controlling the outcome. Rather, you are open to the will of the god/goddess, the universal mind's intention for you.

Perceive with all your senses as the spirit of these elements permeates your entire being. . . . [*Long pause.*]

When you feel you have become as receptive as possible, stay fully conscious as you consume some of the holy sacraments, the food and drink you have placed upon your altar. Take in the energies in order to receive the blessings of water and earth, the Holy Communion. . . . [*Pause.*]

Sit in meditation for a few moments and allow that which you have taken in to work its miracle of fertility and inner nourishment. The seeds of love that Sekhmet planted into your heart during the first great round are now ready to enter the world egg, deep within your belly, in preparation for fertilization. . . .

When you are nourished and the communion feels complete, slowly open your eyes. Ground and center . . .

You are now in a waiting mode. Allow some time to go by before you enter into the work of the next chapter, Amun-Ra.

19
AMUN-RA
SOLAR ENERGIES
Transfiguration/Alchemical Gold

AMUN AND RA (sometimes spelled Re) are flip sides of one another. It cannot be said that either one comes first, because they are the two sides of light, the seen and the unseen.

Our radiant sun feels as though it is the most powerful source of light and fire with which we come in contact. It is so potent that we can only take it in a very limited amount. Many kinds of energies exist between us and the sun that filter and dilute its rays so that they can penetrate us without harm.

Even as we acknowledge the potency and power, the glory and royalty of our sun, it is important to remember that the sources of sacred light in the entirety of our universe are exponentially vaster and stronger. The sun is a reminder of the possibilities of the light.

The essence of Ra, the royal, potent life-force energy, reminds us that gold is one of the highest alchemical elements—gold, glistening in the sun, golden statues, pyramids of gold, streets of gold, radiant spiraling gold energy of Ra. Conversely, the essence of Amun is the hidden power of the sun and the great mystery of our sun's journey through the night, when its light is invisible to us.

In the alchemy that happens when we eat and are eaten by the gods, we pass through the *negredo*, the obscured mystery that includes the prime matter as it traverses the impenetrable darkness, before moving

148

into the sun's light. The gold energy is about royalty and reaching the highest state of transformation. The energy of this light is almost beyond comprehension. When a person reaches this state of consciousness, he or she becomes the kind of pharaoh that was acknowledged as a divine being.

If we are taking in the right substances and energies, and if we are in the right relationship with that which we consume, our godlike nature will shine as we are transformed into gold, into the radiant light bodies of Ra, in his Eagle energy form. When we step into this place we become our own inner authority, and in the intimate connection with our divine higher power, much of what we need to know and do comes to us directly. There is no need for intercessors when we achieve and sustain this level of consciousness.

The danger of too much light is spiritual arrogance, and the rigidity and inability to learn anything new. A truly wise person will understand that the great tides governed by Khonsu will turn again, just as the Nile rises and falls, and that this place of highness will move into another state over a period of time.

We can remember, however—at those times in our lives when we are traveling back through the rounds again—this state of illumined consciousness. Each time we travel this road the path becomes more deeply worn. We learn it so well we could almost walk it blindfolded, and the more we follow this map, the more joyful and less burdensome the journey becomes. At times it can even be fun as we come through the energies of Wadjet, because we understand it's just a part of the path.

When you have emptied yourself with Khonsu and are open to the sacred feminine, the universal womb of the void; when you are willing to open to the not-knowing, which is the way of the soul and the path of the heart, you start the process of healing ignorance and greed. From the place of being fully open that you achieved through your work with Khonsu, you rise and move into the energy of the sun. You will be penetrated and filled up by the forces of fire and air.

In that fullness some initiates feel the consummation as an orgasmic experience. This full-filled feeling of satisfaction is an antidote to greed and to the grabbing for those things that can never satisfy you and never fill you. Opening to your true powers and divinity, the true powers of the divine masculine to direct and guide you in the right use of your creativity in the world brings forth your royalty and your highest self.

When you enter willingly into a shamanic ritual of death, which is formlessness, and then willingly step back into form and embodiment, your death and rebirth become conscious and you learn what you need to transform into the Golden One, Ra. You become the grown-up son or daughter of the god/goddess who knows and embodies the mystery of life eternal, which is not dependent on form or lack of form.

The person thus initiated is filled through his or her higher chakras with the radiant light and energies of the sun and shows up in the world as Ra. His or her emanation is Ra; but underneath and behind, unseen, is Amun, the hidden power of the sun. We cannot look directly at the sun. What is being shown can't be seen. This is the mystery of alchemy.

The heart/mind engenders a union of thoughts and feelings and creates a higher energy than either would have in its separate form. The higher love and wisdom that are the offspring of the marriage of thoughts and emotions, mind and heart, are greater than either one alone. The yin/yang symbol illustrates how both are contained within the greater whole. The eyes in the light and the dark sides are the portals through which each transforms into its opposite. At times we are mainly focusing on one side or the other and can travel through that portal in order to change sides. The two are dancing and spinning with one another in the dance of Ra and Amun, their movement of energy creating synthesis, which is implied rather than visible, as with the dance of Shakti and Shiva.

This is the dance of Ra and Amun. This dance, this alchemy that happens between the energies of Ra and Amun is the unseen, and what is created—the book or child or work of art that comes forth—is the third thing, the resulting aspect of Ra that is known as Ra Horakhty (see the Glossary of Terms for more information). Horus becomes the spiritualized matter that is also known, among other things, as alchemical gold and the philosopher's stone. In terms of the Egyptian subtle bodies, it manifests as the akh, and the simultaneous germination of the seed that becomes the *sahu* (see Glossary of Terms). This fresh embodiment of spiritual power is always the beginning of a new paradigm. It is that which in the physical world is reflective of the Great Mystery of the unseen—Amun, the hidden face of the sun. As above, so below—as without, so within. The best articulation I have found of this process is clearly written and illustrated in the chapter entitled "The End of the Underworld Journey" in Jeremy Naydler's book *Temple of the Cosmos*:

> The human being as reborn Horus realizes an inner identity with Ra. . . . The child Horus is equally Ra rising in the east as Ra-Horakhti ("Ra-Horus-in-the-Horizon"). . . . In terms of human consciousness, what has now been achieved is the radiance of spirit characteristic of the *akh*. The human being has become a shining one. The *ba* has been divinized through having been brought into union with the source of its existence—the self-creating, self-renewing spirit. The realm of Osiris has been effectively transcended, and now the primary experience is that of being merged with the cosmic light that emanates from Ra.*

Although you will be placed in a sarcophagus to undergo this initiation, this is not about physical death; rather you will be asked to surrender to your DNA, to the god/goddess's will, your highest potential, your essential self. Prior to this, you may have been operating from your human will only. It is time to move to a higher octave, for you now have the spiritual maturity to open to the Great Mystery in depth as never before.

❧ TRANSFIGURATION RITUAL

[Prepare sacred space. . . . Ground and center yourself. . . . Kindle your eternal heart flame with love. Breathe several heart breaths to call in the powers of Earth and sky. Feel the warmth as your heart fire intensifies and begins to radiate throughout your being. . . . In the subsequent glow, invoke Inner Egypt. . . .]

Now you are ready to enter the Great Pyramid and climb the grand gallery to the King's Chamber. . . . You find yourself standing in front of the Great Pyramid as Anubis, the shaman priest, in preparation for his own rite. Take some further deep heart breaths to prepare yourself. . . .

---

*Naydler, *Temple of the Cosmos*, 280.

The entrance to the pyramid is on the north face. Although you know that your allies and the neteru are with you, you are alone as you enter through a rough-hewn entry like a cave that opens onto some stairs. The stairs lead up to an ascending shaft that is like a square tube. You crawl up the shaft for about forty yards before coming out into the Grand Gallery, a huge vaulted space that continues upward for another fifty yards or so. At the top, you have to crouch down to pass through a short tunnel that leads into what Egyptologists refer to as the King's Chamber. It is a plain, stone room with a high ceiling and a stone sarcophagus off toward the west end of the chamber. There is no lid.

You have already received the nourishment of communion in preparation for the consummation to follow.

Lay yourself down in the sarcophagus as you open to the death of your old being, your old ideas and belief systems. . . . Allow yourself to feel the unfathomable emptiness of the void as you prepare to be divinely impregnated. . . . [*Pause.*]

As Anubis, open to your feminine form; call forth and embody the sensual fertility goddess Bast. . . . As you lie in the sarcophagus and open wide, you feel no fear of the void. You feel no fear of the feminine mysteries. You feel no fear of that which disintegrates into nothingness. As you open to that which you are prepared and ready to receive, Amun-Ra enters the chamber. You are penetrated with a shaft of light. . . . It fills you up with the fires of transformation, the heat of the sun, the wind, the breath, the air. . . . In the sanctuary of the sarcophagus, you are flooded with energy and light as Amun-Ra calls you forth as your divine self in this consummation, this Hieros Gamos, this sacred marriage between human and spirit. . . . [*Long pause.*]

Bask in the glow of these energies until you have been completely filled with the energies and light of Amun-Ra. Now you have reached the moment when Ra rests in Osiris and Osiris rests in Ra. . . .

As the fully initiated shamanic priest Anubis, step forth from the sarcophagus transfigured as the new Horus, Ra Horakhty—a light in the world. You now realize that in this new iteration of these ancient mysteries, Anubis rests in Horus and Horus rests in Anubis. Prepare to enter into the company of gods. . . .

From now forward, when you stand before the people on Earth and walk your path with this kind of initiation in your heart, you are transfigured, and others can feel the depth of your being. Your presence alone, even in silence, has so much dignity and clarity that others will be inspired, healed, motivated, and awakened. This is what occurs when the avatars and healers work with people and connect with others around them.

Enjoy this place of honor while you prepare for the next phase of this journey. In the next chapter, with Ptah, you will find that you are able to go in and out of this exalted state while you proceed with your life. Savor the moments. . . .

20
PTAH
THE NEW AEON
Imagination/Visionary Prophet

PTAH IS THE great creator god of the North of Egypt who is said to have issued forth all of creation with the utterance of words. He creates the world by "thinking of it with his heart and producing it with his speech."* His feet are bound like those of Osiris or a mummy, and on his chin he wears a pharaonic beard. A blue skullcap adorns his head. It is as if his feet are embedded deep in the Underworld and his head reaches into the sky. Ptah has dominion over the Underworld, Earth, and the cosmos, and all the space between. As the one who manifests creation with his thoughts and his voice, he is also the deity of craftsmen and builders. His consort is Sekhmet, the Power, and together they bring forth their son Nefertum, the lotus born, who represents the fragrance of life.

With the blessing of Ptah, you can create a whole new era that is royal and beautiful, for he has been holding the image of the promised new aeon in all potential future realities in his vast mind. Ptah is working to remain very clear in the energies and messages he is sending to the people of Earth about what the world can look like and where we can be going at this time. He loves beauty, and he is a leader in creating this new

---

*Erik Hornung and Betsy M. Bryan, eds., *The Quest for Immortality: Treasures of Ancient Egypt* (Washington, D.C.: National Gallery of Art, 2002).

world. His desire is for a world rich in beauty, crafted from the elements that are produced from the bodies of the neteru. As with the elegance we experienced in the birthing chamber of Bast, there is nothing overdone or greedy about his vision.

Take a moment to imagine one individual's view of what this world might look like—whether this be a real city, or a metaphor for an inner landscape:

This world of pure waters and clean, fresh air is for all beings. It is a manifestation of our vision of what heaven or nirvana would be like, except it would be here on Earth, in this dimension and realm. Streaks of gold, rich blues, and deep red energy are the most prominent colors. Everywhere you look, this magical city reminds you of our imaginings of Shangri-La or of Egypt in its splendor.

No one is hungry in this Golden Age city, for the tables are piled high with the fruits of bountiful harvests, and there is enough nourishment for all. Money is obsolete here, because all goods and services are based on equal exchanges. There is a balanced ecology between the people and the environment that everyone understands. The people all serve each other. In this age, every person loves doing whatever it is that he or she is doing, whether preparing a meal, giving a massage, planting a garden, or cleaning a bathroom. The consistent energy here is of enjoyment, for when we are fulfilling our purpose, we are content.

The little toe in our body is no less happy than the brain. No one part subjugates another; all simply are what they are. Different energies choose to incarnate in certain roles and that is their function and purpose, and their great joy.

Knowing that all form is transitory, in this new aeon people can come and go easily. Because of the ease in moving back and forth between form and formlessness, there is no major attachment to any one form. There are always enough people to perform a particular function on the planet, according to the basic concept that nature abhors a vacuum; thus, there are people to fill every role. In this higher ecology, things work with harmony and grace.

Life and death as we know it are transformed to coming and going, and there is a natural flow, in and out, like the breath pervading this earthly paradise.

If it is Ptah who creates the aeons, it is we who must be able to imagine in our own minds what is possible. The seeds for this new world exist in the universe in the minds of gods, and as human beings, we are entrusted with those visions. It is we who hold those potential futures in order to embody, enact, and create them.

Although the idea may at first seem improbable, this bold and beautiful new aeon is alive and well in the mirror world of this dimension, waiting to be brought into the Golden Age that we have heard promised. Even if human beings wreck the car and destroy themselves, this world continues to exist. The gods have a genuine interest in creating this long-held dream in physical reality. As our divine parents, they want to see us, their children, become co-creators and continue to create new worlds and new dimensions. If we allow ourselves to fulfill our sacred purpose, if we can bring this new aeon into physical existence, we will have surpassed our teachers—which is what all teachers of merit wish for their students, and all conscious parents wish for their children.

If humans waver in their response-ability, they start using creative energy in a way that is of lesser intent. That is what may have happened eventually in Egypt—and before and since, in many other civilizations that have disappeared in the process. The forward motion of evolution comes grinding to a halt when human consciousness sleeps and corruption takes over. In the past there have been great floods that Khonsu helped bring to Earth in order to purify the land of negative solar energies, rendering Earth barren of many, many of her previously abundant life forms. Atlantis and Lemuria were two of the civilizations that rose and fell along the way.

We need not be dismayed about the cycles of change, nor be upset that we have to make this journey over and over again between the rise and fall, the in-breath and out-breath of thousands of years, because the path is getting clearer. Even though in the new aeon we will still go through the twenty-six initiations, it will happen with fluidity and grace. None of the victimization and tragic misunderstanding will be part of that journey, yet it will still require effort and courage, strength, perseverance, and a drop of suffering.

While Ptah is meditating—dreaming the world like Brahma—he

speaks the words and they are made into flesh as they are spoken. At all times, and especially following these rites, we have to be careful about what we speak, because it is instantly created. It is through sound coming through the opened mouth that creation happens in the physical world.

As Ptah dreams this new world, he comes to us in our thoughts and our daydreams, in our visions and our nighttime dreams. When we receive sudden downloads of information and don't know where they are coming from, it is Ptah whispering his love for us, his creations. His nature is of love, and he loves this world, this existence, and all things manifest. When he opens the mouths of those who can see and speak creation into being—whether it is his mouth, or your mouth, or the mouth of a pharaoh or a god—stars and moons pour out of it; all creation flows from out of the mouth, including the Milky Way, the Nile, and all the vegetation, the golden cities and the paradise on Earth, as well as the next neteru, Nut and Geb. He issues forth the Garden of Eden, replete with royal temples and palaces.

When we know how to use form wisely and become divine co-creators, we are given the keys to the car—or, better yet, the keys to the kingdom. By now we have enough illumination in our awakened heart/minds to be trusted. We've survived with our battle wounds and our ups and downs, and maintained fidelity to our heart path. The neteru believe in us; they believe that we have enough self-discipline, courage, and faith in this process to remain committed to the shamanic mysteries that awaken the healing power of the heart.

Just as many traditions, including some Native American, Mayan, Tibetan, Aztec, and other worldwide mysteries are being brought to the fore, so it is with these Egyptian Mysteries. Although in times past, these sacred teachings were held secret by the highest clergy and most insulated priest/priesshood and pharaonic lines, where they and their scribes were the only ones allowed to see them, now it is different. It is time for the sacred rituals to come out of the inner sanctum and into the heart/minds of all who are ready to receive and carry them forward. There are many whose DNA are being activated through the various spiritual arts of our time, and who are contributing to the activation of the ka energies to make ready for these most ancient shamanic rituals to return so that we can restore the healing power of the heart in preparation for a greater role in co-creation.

It is time, as part of the awakening process and because you have taken in the power of Amun-Ra, for you to begin to help create the new aeon, the Golden Age. When you have successfully melded the heart and the mind, the soul and the intellect, the ba and the ka, you become the akh, the illumined being. The profound illumination that results is so great that others are drawn to you, especially those who are on the path but not yet fully awakened in this way.

THE RITUAL OF THE OPENING OF THE MOUTH

The Opening of the Mouth is an ancient ceremony performed on the pharaoh during his shamanic initiation experience, and on his mummy during the embalming process. Through Ptah, it is Isis whose voice is awakened, for Isis is the mother of Horus, as she is of us all. It is through her recognition of her divine child that this hawk-headed god is ready, like his mother, to serve all creation and all humanity by ushering in the new era of the golden rule. His greatest gift is to serve with the awe-inspiring power of embodied love and wisdom in its potent masculine form. It is with this new level of inner authority that you are able to give birth to the new world. Through Ptah you are able to create the new aeon.

In preparation for the following ritual, you need to formulate your statement of intention for the world. It can be in the form of an incantation, an invocation, a mantra, or a statement. Think of it like a political platform: this is who I am and this is what I've come to do.

As you prepare to open your mouth in the ritual, remember that you are opening the mouth of your cosmic womb so the world egg, the potential of the world's creation and of your sacred purpose, can be born. When Ptah opens your mouth, it is Isis's mouth, and you speak this sacred purpose forth into the world from your lips with her voice. From your human lips, the word is made into flesh. When it is complete, you can say, "Sa Sekhem Sahu," the Egyptian mantra that conveys the magic words of power (heka) that complete your intention. A rough translation would be

"May the breath of life mightily liberate the highest possible outcome for the transfigured, divine human."*

As you observe yourself after having risen from the sarcophagus, become aware that you now embody both Anubis and Horus, and will find yourself shape-shifting back and forth between the two. This new Horus has integrated the refined, new masculine power of Horus with the renewed heart of his shamanic brother Anubis. The ancient wisdom of the neteru is woven into your cells and bones.

With Khonsu you opened, with Amun-Ra you felt the energy come in and were brought forth out of the darkness into the radiant light. The enlightened power that has risen up inside of you is not attached to the result, leaving it free to co-create without needing to control the outcome or abuse or misuse the power.

In the following rite you will be given your sacred *ren,* the power name that expresses the essence of the new power that you will carry out into the world as the warrior of light that you have become. If you were given your name at the temple of Horus during the Ma'at initiation, it may well be a reiteration. Either way, now may be a time you wish to express your sacred name as you integrate its power and meaning into your life.

Names were extremely important to the Egyptians. According to ancient Egyptian thought, everything is created by the utterance of its name by the god Ptah. Consequently, a name given in a shamanic birth carries the power of the neteru who call it forth. Some gods and pharaohs used different names in different places, and for different purposes and functions. Names were considered to be invested with magical powers, and certain names were held secret in order to keep that power concentrated.

Ptah will confir upon you the *was* (or *uas*) staff, the scepter (wand) that acknowledges your dominion over the forces of darkness, and was earned through your passage through the rites of these mysteries. You will also receive a crown that conveys that you are a sovereign, a fully

---

*Literally, "Breath of Life, the Sacred Might, Realized Human." See Robert Masters, *The Goddess Sekhmet* (Ashland, Ore.: White Cloud Press, 2002), 73–74. See also the Glossary of Terms in this book for further explanation.

realized divine human, consciously infused with the neteru of Egypt. You are open and connected at your crown chakra, and able to co-create, and to receive and transmit accordingly.

✍ THE CORONATION CEREMONY

[*Prepare sacred space. Kindle your heart flame with love and breathe the heart breath. . . . Feel the powers of Heaven and Earth meeting within your heart. In its glow, invoke Inner Egypt. . . .*]

You will find yourself where you left off, standing in the King's Chamber of the Great Pyramid as the divine human. Ptah and Sekhmet are there with you. Ptah stands before you in full regalia. He presents to you the *was* and *ankh* scepter that is your wand of power. He then places a crown upon your head. This crown has been fashioned from all of the olive branches that you have offered to the neteru throughout your journeys of initiation. . . . [*Pause.*]

Ptah looks deeply within you, then closes his eyes and focuses on that which is within his heart, longing to be born. . . . He opens his own mouth and issues forth your true name. . . .

As the sound of your name rings through the universe you experience a flash of recognition, a quickening that elicits your response and causes you to open your mouth and allow the energy of your sacred purpose to rise. . . .

Sekhmet adds the power of her divine roar to your voice as you make your declaration. Go ahead and speak out loud the intentional statement that you have prepared. . . . [*Pause.*]

Take a deep breath and begin to let a sound or tone, a roar or growl, a screech or howl, well up inside of you and burst through your throat. . . .

As you let forth this sound, you realize that your new voice is that of Isis. You may experience a powerful, unparalleled feeling of resonance, at-onement and wholeness. This sense of wholeness of human, soul, and spirit can be orgasmic bliss. . . . [*Pause.*]

To complete this part of the rite, pronounce the words Sa Sekhem Sahu. . . . [*Pause.*]

Ptah now steps forward with his hands up and across his chest and his heart. He closes his eyes and breathes into your heart/mind and into your third eye the feelings and images that are the vision for a new world. Open and let your imagination be filled with the visions of your awakened being. Notice how this great opportunity to fulfill your sacred purpose becomes the ground that anchors your light body to the earth as the light of Amun-Ra is grounded into every cell and molecule of your being. . . . [*Long pause.*]

When you've fully received Ptah's vision, he leads you out of the pyramid and back into the world, where you can create that which you have envisioned.

As you move back into the everyday world of your life, you will find that you can remain cognizant of more than one dimension simultaneously. You can move with ease in your worldly dimension and at the same time, you can clearly perceive the pantheon of Egypt inside and around you—it is simply a matter of your focused attention.

AFTER THE CORONATION

Once your mouth has been opened it is especially important for you to be aware that spoken words create reality. The gods live in the sounds of words, and it is their desire to be manifest into form. Ptah brings the energies sent from the neteru to the open mouth, and we speak as the sound rises up in us. Our words are infused with the energies of the gods in the combinations of sounds that make up the words.

You can use language, and through it the gods, to bless or curse. Therefore it is essential to always feel the energy and listen to the sound coming through words, as well as the words themselves. And be mindful of how you say things.

In order to sustain the consciousness that we have raised with these rites, you might wish to incorporate a simple ritual into your morning meditation or practice: Ground and center yourself and connect with your awakened consciousness through breathing the heart breath. Bring into focus your intention for the day—and remember to be grateful and to include your desire to bring love into your thoughts, your feelings, your actions, and your speech.

21
NUT AND GEB
WHOLENESS
Creation of Sacred Purpose/
Divine Parents

NUT AND GEB are the conduits through which Osiris, Isis, Nephthys, Set, Horus, and Anubis make the journey from Sky to Earth. The way one version of the story goes, it was the job of Tefnut and Shu, Ra's children and the parents of Nut and Geb, to keep Earth and Sky apart by literally holding them separate. Tefnut and Shu are the dry air and the mist that form our atmosphere. If there was only one reality, or if Nut and Geb were locked together in constant unity, nothing could be born and our three-dimensional reality would not exist. Shu and Tefnut are there to support duality by creating the divine tension between these lovers so that consciousness can be seeded into the fertile earth. We need "other" in order to love and to create.

The holy longing between the two ultimately resulted in a pregnancy that defied the edict of the Sun god, Ra, who did not want any other gods to be born during his rule, or so the modern version of the myth says.

In actuality, divine timing is everything, and Ra's all-seeing eye knew that the time was not right to birth the new level of consciousness on Earth at the time it was conceived. The way was not yet properly prepared. Therefore he sent Thoth and Khonsu to the drafting table to strategize by playing draughts* (an ancient game of chess which was degraded in modern times to checkers), and through their skill learn when the right time would be, for it was beyond known time—outside of time as they knew it in order for the impossible to happen. They were the divine architects who were attempting to bring consciousness to Earth by infusing matter with spirit (by making the spirit flesh) yet the matter at that time wasn't strong enough to contain the alchemical process required. It was Khnum who was the craftsman who took the plans that they drafted and created the new human on his potter's wheel.

Nut and Geb are pictured opposite one another, her hands are touching his feet, and his hands are touching her toes. Together they form an archway in both directions, a vortex or birth canal for creations to pass through as they are born into this universe and onto Earth. This is also the conduit through which Ptah's dreams are born.

When a person initiated in these sacred heart rituals encounters the divine couple Nut and Geb, they have completed a major cycle of transformation and are inspired to bring into form the visions that they have received. They are ready to step out as a divinely incarnated human being with sacred purpose in the world and connected to the cosmic energy of the universe. In the past, we have known these beings as avatars, gurus, savior, pharaohs, or other enlightened beings. It is for us, now, to become fully awakened and step out into our sacred purpose and into the new Aeon.

When we complete this part of the journey, it is now, in this moment, not in some obscure or future age. Those who have walked this path and come to this point have an opportunity to realize the creator-like and magical feeling of being empowered and on-purpose. This is a familiar place for many of us who have been courageous enough to make this journey. Yet until we've walked this spiral road numerous times, we forget that we've been here before.

Each time we take the journey, we have the opportunity to function at a higher octave of the spiral. The great hope is that if we continue, and enough of us go through it again and again, that we will be able to

*It was through that ancient game of draughts that Thoth determined the five epagomenal days in which they could eventually be born, and which extended the agricultural calendar of Egypt from 360 days to 365.

embody this big picture, this vision that we have been shown in the last chapter, for longer and longer periods of time, and for all beings.

Nut and Geb and the energies they represent express the perfect yin/yang, the perfect sacred marriage for all human beings. They govern the amount of feminine and masculine energies that each person embodies, and they display a balance of those energies. By touching each other's toes and hands and forming a circle, they show the connection between these energies, and the space in the middle allows for creativity, balance, and wholeness. If they were on top of each other, there would be compressed energy with no room to grow, no space for something to manifest. Both connection and space is required between all things, not just between people and lovers.

This image of Nut and Geb describes a perfect sacred union, which is wholeness. In order to be an empowered person with sacred purpose, you need to balance both masculine and feminine within yourself. In our reality we cannot be fully empowered until we are and feel whole within ourselves, with our receptive and directive energies in resonance with the energies of Nut and Geb.

Geb presents another aspect of Osiris, and Nut of Isis. Whether mother and father, Sky and Earth, or Underworld and outer world, this is a picture of unity and wholeness—it is representative of the maxim, as above, so below. What we know as the Underworld is really the inner world, and it is reflected in the sky.

Another way to view this image is that Nut has the whole world, which is Geb, in her hands. The overarching sky mother is watching over us all. Geb is her beloved, and she is watching over the earth with tenderness and love, and the earth is reaching back to her with its longing for her fertility, and for her gifts that come from the star nations that live in and around her. She bestows upon the earth and all the creatures of the earth the great love that emanates from the stars. With this knowledge comes the realization that the ones who brought us here, those who reside in the cosmos, still love us and are with us.

Allow yourself plenty of time to enjoy the following journey in its fullness. It is best to do this journey under the stars, ideally out in nature; however, a rooftop or your imagination will also work.

🪶 JOURNEY OF COMPLETION WITH NUT AND GEB

[*Create sacred space. . . . Open your heart and breathe the earth breath by pulling the breath up from the heart of the earth. . . . Allow yourself to become Anubis once again. . . . You are an Anubis priest or priestess, fully initiated in these Shamanic Mysteries of Egypt. . . .*]

Take a moment to honor Anubis, and this wonderful process that brought you to this place on your journey. . . . Then, wherever you are, gaze up into galactic center, into the Milky Way and feel the love emanating from your Star Mother. . . .

As you gaze up into the night sky and see the blanket of stars, allow yourself to transform from Anubis into both the Earth Father, Geb, and the Sky Mother, Nut. . . . As you open you begin to remember your larger self, and your DNA. A memory stirs within and you know that you are a spiritual star being having a glorious earthly experience. . . .

As your memory awakens, you know that you come from the stars as well as Earth. With this knowledge you are given the gift of feeling whole—human and spirit unified by the children who are the soul qualities that the various gods that were born from these two exemplify. The star children who were born from Nut and Geb were all created to embody the human heart/mind, the intelligent heart. They were created to be the elementals, the neteru, that create the alchemical birth of the heart/mind through their trials and tribulations, and their victories and celebrations.

As you gaze heavenward, feel Nut's love and energy pouring down upon you. Let yourself feel the sacred longing for the stars, and allow yourself to be pulled upward, drawn by the stars into the sky mother's milky womb. As you begin to rise into her starry firmament, you enter and discover that you are not alone. It may take a moment to adjust your perception. . . .

When you focus your attention on the cave of the womb, there before you stand Isis and Osiris, Nephthys and Set, and Horus, the five children of Nut and Geb. They are standing in the configuration of a five-pointed star.

The five of them represent the Star of Humanity at this time. They invite you to join them in your rightful place in the pantheon of the neteru as the counterpart of Horus, Anubis. It is the bringing together of Horus and Anubis that completes the unification of spirit and matter. If you accept, the star will transfigure into a six-pointed star. In that configuration, Heaven will truly come into Earth.

In order for the transfiguration into divine humanity to unfold, first you must recognize and make peace with all five of these aspects of yourself: with Isis, the mother who gives you a physical body and life; with Osiris, the father who sees you and brings you to death and transformation; to Set, who shows you the parts of yourself that you must love, accept, and integrate; to Nephthys, the mother who teaches you to believe in what cannot be seen, and to trust your inner spirit and intuition; and to Horus, the part of you that is the new seed that has sprouted, and is ready to be fully incarnated as the new consciousness on Earth as soon as you accept that you are both human and spirit—as soon as you are ready to accept your divine heritage and lineage as a fully embodied spiritual human.

Take time to encounter each one of these energies, and make peace in whatever way is necessary with all of these parts of yourself. . . . [*Long pause.*]

When you are complete and ready, when the time is right, step fully forward out of the womb of Nut, the Galactic Mother, and into the space between Heaven and Earth. Imagine Nut overarching and protecting you from above and Geb underneath, circling from the opposite direction and grounding and supporting you from below. . . .

All five of your kindred siblings step forward with you and you join together and become the six-pointed star, with the tip of the top pyramid touching the heavens and the tip of the downward pointing pyramid touching Earth. . . .

Welcome home, Star Brother, Welcome home Star Sister. Welcome home, Anubis.

PART III

THE ELEMENTS—TOOLS FOR MANIFESTATION

"*Across the sky gods and goddesses pass. Fire and air, spirit and light. What we imagine comes to pass. Thought finds its form. All forgotten things return. This moment marks a time. I endure the ages. My heart contains all I am, all flood of love, all thoughts invisible and vital as air.*

"*I leave the fields and enter the house. The journey ends there. I am a man returning home. Welcomed by family, embraced by ancestors, I am again that which I was, a soul, a fire clothed in heaven, a sparrow. Born of stars, I am a god naming the life that was always mine.*

"*Long tables are stacked with cakes. The scent of sandalwood rises. The house fills with birds and the smell of beer and ale. I enter the circle of sun. I speak with priests and hermits. I know words that draw light into the darkness. I know the vulture and the carcass. I know the eggs in the nest. I am a silver star hanging above the world, courage in the blackest night. I am swift water running, a lowing cow, the thought of myself in my father's forehead.*

"*I stand in peace before the world. I nourish and am nourished by love. Like a lotus, quiet upon the water, I listen and repeat the silence. I am Osiris: man and god, black obsidian reflecting light.*"

NORMANDI ELLIS, *AWAKENING OSIRIS:*
THE EGYPTIAN BOOK OF THE DEAD

INTRODUCTION TO THE ELEMENTS

THE TWENTY-TWO archetypes offered in the previous chapters are the neteru that are prominent during this round of our spiritual evolution. They represent the supernatural element of akasha, spiritual energy. When we are filled with this energy, we are able to become skilled alchemists who can utilize the natural elements of earth, water, fire, and air. Our journey through the mysteries allows us to master the elements and become conscious members of the family of the neteru.

It is especially important that we become conscious, now that humans are technologically advanced enough to affect the weather and climate, for to become gods with that power, but without awareness, is dangerous. We have to accept responsibility for our godlike nature. We cannot afford to be asleep at the wheel, for the ignorance of our divinity is destroying the planet. When we ignore that our spiritual lineage makes us kindred offspring of the gods, we feel separation and isolation, and the emptiness leads us toward greed and insatiable hunger. We try to fill ourselves with the elements of the material plane. When we are informed with akasha, with the spirit of these twenty-two archetypal energies alive within us, then we can spiritualize the other elements in every thought, action, and creation, and we become divinity in form.

The neteru repeat themselves over and over in various combinations, just like the DNA, and the components in our very blood, mix and match to create all the various functions of being alive. When you use the name of Isis, you are talking about Nekhbet and Hathor and Nephthys. When you speak of Ptah, you are also referencing Khonsu and Thoth and Osiris. It is the various combinations of the neteru that create all of life.

The neteru appreciate our struggle with our training in linear thinking as we attempt to concretize our understanding and ability to articulate. We are now being pushed beyond our limited, contracted awareness to see the ways our divine family works in unison and in various configurations.

In the Christian mystery, when they say "the mystery of the trinity," the mystery is that three are in one; and in the older pagan mystery of maiden/mother/crone, all are contained within the one. Nekhbet-Mother-Mut contains all the neteru, and in Egypt, she is everywhere— all live within her. The wise old woman, the grand dame of Egypt, holds within her all of the lovers, all of the divine couples, all of the children, and all of the grandchildren.

The next emanation from Nekhbet-Mother-Mut would be to see things in their four elemental forms, because all of the neteru work within those four forms. In the tarot, the elements are expressed as Cups, Discs, Wands, and Swords. To express them here in *Shamanic Mysteries of Egypt,* we have a symbol for each of the four elements, and embedded within each is the whole story of water, earth, fire, and air. Based on the four perspectives and within each are the story lines of all human beings' lives—all their daily dramas and melodramas. It is the twenty-two akasha, or spiritual archetypes, however, that give true substance, meaning, and purpose to the natural elemental human experience.

Because most of the people of the world at this time are living primarily in a separated or divorced state from the spiritual archetypes, they have dispirited the elements, and therefore dishonored them and their own humanity. They no longer see that the elements are connected with akasha, which is the element of spirit. When they relate to the elements, including their physical bodies, without reverence for spirit, the result is power without the spiritual integrity necessary to make responsible decisions. Most often, those who claim they are living a spiritual life through their religions are doing so through attachment to rigid and dogmatic traditions that are actually cut off from their original source.

The elements are the physical representation of the neteru in the material world. They influence and are connected to all of the other archetypes, and they are informed and animated by the archetypes that are the facets of akasha. Each time we have journeyed with an archetype in this alchemical process, we have experienced the overarching essence of the deity as it brings us the necessary element for wherever we are in the bigger picture of our journey. For example, Sekhmet, in the first round, gave us a deep understanding of the essence of the element fire as the agent of transformation, as did Wadjet in the second round.

In addition to learning the primary element of each archetype, we experience all the elements within each journey. As the dove, you start out feeling a calling. You are being inspired, and you feel it from the element water. You connect with the element earth, knowing that you need to be grounded in your journey. When you take action and make the leap, you are moving into the fire. When you are flying through the air, moving to a new place, a bigger understanding, you are with the element air.

Each archetype is like the alchemist mixing the four ingredients within you. As you become the dove and fly over the Nile to meet Nekhbet-Mother-Mut, you are like the baby in the womb who has been called to the birthing process. The preparation for the journey, the grounding and connecting with earth, is the foundation that requires the element earth. Fire is associated with the energies that move as you begin to take action. The understanding and completion, which is air, helps you to breathe and let go into the next archetype: Nephthys. And so it goes throughout the entire journey. These twenty-two emanations are like facets of a diamond within your own consciousness that you merge with for a period of time as you learn spiritual lessons from them and complete the great rounds of consciousness. When you reach the end where once again Isis and Osiris, Geb and Nut, Set and Nephthys, and Horus and Anubis—the sacred twins and pairs—are reunited, then it is not long before you will be called to return to the dove and move up to the next whorl on the spiral.

On Earth, the four elements are powerful symbols of the invisible energies from other dimensions. The qualities of the elements convey the basic attributes upon which our individual characters, and the whole of nature, are created. To know and understand the elements gives us the tools with which we co-create with divinity the entirety of reality. What we see and appreciate in our physical world is the result of the elemental combinations. As you learn the attributes of the elements and begin to perceive the world around you, including people, animals, and other forms of nature, you will be better equipped to step up to the cauldron as the alchemist that you are, and mix and stir and create with the elements, with the magic of Isis and Hathor.

Always use these powerful tools of manifestation with great care and respect.

22
THE NILE
SACRED ARCHETYPAL ELEMENT OF WATER

WATER BLESSES US. It blesses all of life. Everything in nature thirsts for water: trees, animals, mountains, and human beings. In our human bodies, water is synonymous with our blood. It is Earth's lifeblood, the lifeblood of the Earth Father, Geb. As we live upon his body we feed upon his waters.

The Nile is the bountiful river that is the reflection of the river of the night, the Milky Way. It is our Star Mother's counterpart on Earth—"On Earth as it is in Heaven." Nowhere on Earth is there such contrast between fertility and barrenness, between life and death, and between abundance and desolation as in the Nile Valley, especially where the river's influence halts at the desert's edge. In Egypt, all of life is dependent on the Nile, and the Nile in her generous and gracious flow feeds all life.

As the Nile flows through Egypt, water flows through our lives, teaching us about both ascension and descension. It teaches us about ebb and flow, and about the cycles of coming and going, and of manifestation and disappearance. It shows us its many forms: liquid and solid, vapor and mist. Water teaches us about eternity by showing us how to have faith as we move from the different states of being and consciousness as well as of form.

We learn about feeling and emotions through water, and about unconsciousness. It asks us to go deep, to return to the primal waters of unknowing, to trust that we will be fed and nurtured by that which we do not know, the Great Mystery.

The water reminds us that from time to time we are called back to the womb, back to a place of deep introspection and reflection, where we are invited to let ourselves float for a period of time, to become embryonic and to be formed anew. Occasionally we have to return to the beginner's mind in order to reclaim our innocence. When that happens, we have to let go of the language—all of our words of description that give many of us our outer security—in order to be renewed once again.

Through the element of water we learn to trust that we are upheld by the waters of life.

☙ WATER ACTIVATION

Carefully submerge yourself in a hot tub or bathtub, or a lake or other body of water. The temperature of the water should be comfortable and the attitude should be one of walking into the water gradually and allowing yourself to float on the water. Receive the water's blessing and allow all your senses to be connected to it: feel it, smell it, allow it to go into your ears so that you can hear it. . . . Offer a prayer to the water of gratitude and thanksgiving for all the ways that water sustains us. . . .

Offer your blessing to the water. Bless the water in whatever way feels right to you. This can be shedding your tears into the water, laughing into it, tasting it, offering words out loud, or a chant or a song. Or you can simply touch the water and say, "Peace." Or "Peace be with you." Let your spirit guide you on how best to bless the water. . . .

23
THE PYRAMID
SACRED ARCHETYPAL
ELEMENT OF EARTH

PYRAMIDS ARE NOT just about the pyramids in Egypt; they represent the archetype of the Pyramid itself. This archetype is related to the Sphinx and functions similarly as a connection between Heaven and Earth. There is a gold cap on the top that reflects the sun's powerful solar energy.

Consider what the pyramids could have been made of: electrum and gold inlaid with lapis and carnelian, malachite and turquoise. It is speculated that at one time these and various jewels such as diamonds were embedded into the pyramids and have since been removed and stolen. Gemstones are minerals of the earth world.

Pyramids give us the understanding of how to build consciousness from layer upon layer of foundation and work. This is how consciousness evolves. The teaching around this is that foundations are essential for building. Strong foundations, like roots, are a key requirement for constructing anything. A solid foundation is the basis for the correct configuration of building blocks in consciousness as well, all the way to the pinnacle at the top.

If you don't put the time and energy into the foundation of whatever you are building, then it will collapse or won't have the right angles to come together in wholeness and symmetry at the top. This is all about the earth element at work. If you think of the different levels and layers as consciousness itself, and you apply care and "Thothfulness" at the base, then you will have the same level of consciousness continuously all the way to the top.

There's less margin for error at the top, but also less opportunity for making mistakes. There is less effort as you come closer to the top, because you are actually narrowing the options. You get to move in a more direct, straightforward fashion. This is where right thinking, right speaking, and right actions come in. It is where you get the concept of the straight and narrow; yet it is not narrow-mindedness.

Because they hold lessons about discipline and structure, pyramids are a perfect formation for teaching human beings about Earth's wisdom. When you have your feet firmly planted on the earth, then you can have the pillars that stand tall and carry the weight. In ancient times, many attempts were made to reach into the heavens by means of towering structures such as Jacob's ladder. Most of those structures have fallen or disintegrated because the builders didn't understand the principles of building. Although they were trying to get into the other world, they didn't have the right foundations in their thoughts, feelings, speech, and actions. We have similar situations happening today as humans attempt to reach other worlds, or heaven, or paradise. They think they will leave the earth behind. Most don't understand their reason for being, their divine purpose, so the foundations are crumbling beneath them.

The top of the pyramid acts like a satellite or radar, or a parabola or antenna—all devices that pull in signals, and thus they inform. We are each capable of functioning like a pyramid in that way: we can reach up with the crown of our heads, our crown chakras, and inform our bodies with the messages that are coming from beyond and from within. In order for us to interpret those messages correctly, they must pass through the heart. The heart is the connecting bridge between higher mind and physicality.

◱ EARTH ACTIVATION

This activation is best accomplished outdoors, preferably in a natural setting. Go to a quiet spot and stand like a pyramid, with your legs apart and your head in alignment with the center of your body, your spine erect. Arch and stretch upward from your spine and the crown of your head, while simultaneously sending the energies heavenward through your crown chakra and downward through your feet into the earth. As you stretch in both directions, begin to breathe deeply into the heart and use circular breathing so that the flow is both downward and upward as the breath goes around.

When you feel the gravity as unshakable and solid, take ten very deep circular breaths, allowing the energy to move through and out beyond the body, until you have a sense of expanded awareness throughout your entire body. . . .

On the next breath, aware of the expansion, open the heart and chest area and just as you stretched up and down, now stretch forward and back, so that you are expanded in all four directions. . . .

Allow yourself to feel the centeredness of a grounded physical heart in your earthly body. . . . Feel it beating. . . . Sense the power of your heart to keep you alive. . . . Notice how your heart connects you to the hearts of other human beings, and all beings on Earth. . . .

While you open to receive a message from Earth, bless this planet on which you live.

Listen to what the element of earth has to say to you about being grounded and connected. Ask it to show you your honest limitations and boundaries. . . . Also ask it to reveal the false rationalizations about why you cannot become more, or why you cannot do what your heart tells you to do. . . .

As you receive your message, offer blessings and gratitude to the earth. . . . You might bow down or lie flat on your belly and touch your head to, or kiss the earth. In some way connect your heart to the earth. Whatever you are called to offer, feel your gratitude as you bless the earth.

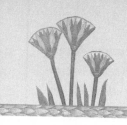

24

THE DESERT
SACRED ARCHETYPAL ELEMENT
OF FIRE

IN THE DESERT, there is nothing but sand and a fiery red sky, with sun pouring down on the sand creating wavy energy in the air. This is not a mirage, but rather another dimension—the domain of fire. Many mystics have quested for answers to life's deepest questions in that place of aridity, fire, and heat, for it is a place of true transformation. Just as we saw Sekhmet riding the chariot of cobras, barreling across the desert at full speed, the energy of fire is quick; it can consume everything in its path in the blink of an eye.

When you think of the cauldron, you think about heating something up. We humans have the ability to create a contained fire rather than a fire that burns wildly out of control, although that containment is not meant to stifle the power of the fire. The desert itself contains a certain amount of geographical fire; it is like a fiery cauldron that holds the heat. Everywhere you look in a desert you see the results of the relentless heat, where everything has been cooked and turned into sand. We are also cauldrons that must be able to contain enough heat for the transformations that we need to make within ourselves.

Fire compels and repels us more than any other element. We are mesmerized as we gaze at the flame of a candle, a fire in the fireplace, or a campfire.

When you are in a desert, unless you pay attention to where the sun is in the sky, you cannot tell where east, west, north, or south is. It can be a pall of confusion.

The energies of fire push us toward the death of the old and the struggle for birth, for when you go out into the desert you realize how tenuous your hold is on life, and how easily and quickly you might perish. Yet it is in our willingness to die to the old and leap into the fires of transformation that we surrender the outcome and the future to something that knows, beyond our ego minds and ego designs, what is really true, and where we need to be headed. Trial by fire speaks of the tempering quality of fire. It burns away the dross, which includes everything except the essence of what needs to be carried forth.

You enter a vision quest in the desert pure of heart and with trust and the willingness to allow that which no longer serves your future self to be burned away. In that alchemical crucible before birth, you leave behind the old world and fight for your life in a struggle to be born.

Yet it is out of the flaming heat, the scorching fires of transformation, that true wisdom is born, rising up out of the desert pyre like a phoenix with brilliant multicolored feathers glinting off the relentless sun.

🪶 FIRE RITUAL

In order to willfully encounter birth and death, rebirth and transformation, you must withstand thirst and hunger. The peak shamanic encounter occurs when the flames are turned up in our inner and outer realities; it requires an experience of some discomfort. No matter how easy a birth might be, there is always some pain and sacrifice in order to make it sacred. You need to feel the heat physically. Of course, entering a desert would be optimum; however, building a fire in a field or on a beach, or even in a fireplace, fire pit, or brazier will suffice. You must allow yourself to be physically close to the heat, not dangerously so, but to the point of feeling discomfort.

Let yourself become thirsty and dry. . . . Allow yourself to open to your inner thirst and hunger. Stay with this sensation and the realization that you are cooking. As the fire moves through your body, let it speak to you and give you its message. . . .

Feel the kundalini rise within, as the birth energy moves up from your base chakra, up through all the chakras. . . . As the birth energy stirs within you, feel the passion as it moves through you. . . . Birth and Death, the fires of transformation are simmering within. . . .

Ask Fire what it has to teach you. Receive its message and gift, which includes the death of the old self, of that which no longer serves you.

Call on your power animals and guides, the allies that support you. . . . Feel yourself shedding your old skin into the fire. It helps to raise a sweat if possible. As you shed your old skin, bless the fire in whatever way you are called. Perhaps you could respectfully place some sacred herbs into the fire, or a message written on a piece of paper, or a clipping of hair, with a request to the fire that it might accept you in its embrace and guide you safely through your transformation. Tobacco is a sacred offering in many traditions. You can offer whatever is sacred to you.

Fire teaches you to trust your own alchemical process when the heat is on. . . .

25
THE CRESTED IBIS
SACRED ARCHETYPAL
ELEMENT OF AIR

THE SACRED CRESTED Ibis, known to ancient Egyptians as the akh bird, is associated with the element of air, and with Thoth as he relates to the cosmic mysteries. The root of the word *akh* in hieroglyphic writing means to shine with the transcendent light of transfiguration, and it refers more specifically to spirit and the pineal body. It is the illumined subtle body that is created when the ka and the ba merge. Without having gone through the trial by fire, one cannot be crowned as pharaoh and rise like the resplendent crested ibis.

The crested ibis is a symbol of rebirth of the akh, and the clear thinking that gives you the understanding of your journey. The symbolism refers to the ability to conceive of the resulting creation in advance of its actualization. It refers to both the preconceived idea and the goal.

The dominion of the element air includes both communication and the word. It is through air that we speak words of power, and it is by making sound and music—toning, chanting, singing, speaking, and breathing—that we express the element air. Through our connection with air we find sound within ourselves and communicate directly from the throat.

When the baby is born and the cord is cut, the baby breathes in and out and generates the sounds that make its voice heard. Air is the last alchemical ingredient, for it is when air is added that the baby is fully incarnated. Water, earth, fire, and air are individual elements; breath is related to spirit and is separate from air. Breath is akasha. It is the breath that breathes in air and activates the fire, the earth, and the water inside the human being. As we breathe, we are being breathed by the unifying spiritual principle that connects all the elements. The wooden spoon that stirs all the ingredients together is the breath, in the hand of the one source stirring, blending, and unifying all the elementals.

In ancient times, pharaohs were crowned during sunrise. Simultaneously, the words of power that are connected with the Sacred Crested Ibis were spoken on the breath through the element air, like a magic spell or incantation. Sekhem, the power, is carried on the word and rises upon the air itself. As conveyed in the biblical sense, the word is made flesh in the full incarnation of divinity. In the last of the elements, air, the bird rises with the word *sekhem*.

The Sacred Crested Ibis is Thoth, our beloved god of wisdom and communication, the highest concept of mind. He is associated with mercurial thinking and the free association and rapid succession of thoughts that result in expanded consciousness. Expansion of consciousness is achieved by opening the mind to thought patterns that reach outside the normal way of thinking. Thoth is every new idea. With the goddess Neith, Thoth weaves together thoughts that create patterns and structures for language, communication, and outward expression. He puts the symbols in our mind's eye and then urges us to find physical sound and utterances to express and convey the energy of the symbols.

For example, the word *bird:* in truth, the word is not a bird. But the hieroglyphic symbols that represent the spelling of that word have the vibrations of the gods, the neteru themselves, in various languages. Thoth is responsible for weaving together the gods with their glyphs and sounds into language, and into outer expression.

The mind was never meant to be divorced from the heart. Thoughts were never meant to be separate from love. It saddens Thoth to think of people using their minds in thoughtless ways to create reality. He and Anubis are equally determined to reunite the heart with the mind.

Once you have figuratively stepped into the fires of transformation and allowed your outworn selves to die, innocence is reborn, and in the newness and rebirth, the dove is created again. In some traditions, the white bird and the symbols of white feathers have been associated with rebirth and higher consciousness.

ॐ AIR ACTIVATION

Go to a high place. It doesn't matter whether it is a mountain or a roof-top, or even whether you imagine a high place in your consciousness—some place where you can see birds flying. From that place, ground and center, kindle your heart flame . . . open your mind with the breath. . . .

Breathe into your thoughts and allow the thoughts to come and go with no attachment. . . . [*Pause.*]

A great white bird, possibly an ibis, will come to you, bringing to you a sense of flying. . . . Envision the bird lifting you above the earth to where you can have a larger view, a bird's eye view of how far you have come on your journey. . . . [*Pause.*]

Perhaps there is a situation that you have been struggling with, a past life review or any other need you have to look back over your life from this bird's-eye point of view. Allow the air to speak to you and give you a message from the perspective of the highest viewpoint possible. . . . [*Pause.*]

From this expanded vision, bless the air for its gift of freedom, which is that of remembering who you really are beyond life's trials and travails. Bless the air and thank it. One of the ways you can bless the air is through sound. Let sound spontaneously rise up from within your chest. . . . Sing a song. Make a tone. Screech like the hawk or eagle. . . . Howl like the wolf. . . . [*Pause.*]

Once you are shown the larger perspective, you are also shown the cosmic joke. Then you can give back to the universe, and to Thoth and Anubis, gratitude, laughter, joy, and celebration.

Come down from the hill when you're ready. Slowly ground and center—this is a time of optimism and joyful celebration.

A VISION FOR THE FUTURE
AWAKENING THE HEALING
POWER OF THE HEART

> *"All you need is love,*
> *All you need is love,*
> *All you need is love, love,*
> *Love is all you need."*
>
> THE BEATLES
> (LENNON/MCCARTNEY)

AS YOU COMPLETE the work of this book and move forward, striving to maintain the impeccability necessary to sustain and enliven your experience, you might find yourself slipping backward. In our personal journey through this work during the writing, we noticed that we would regress from time to time, and that certain things seemed to influence the level of consistency with which we could maintain ourselves. When we were tired or stressed we noticed that we became irritable, which is the first sign of regression.

When you notice irritability for any reason, this is a good time to revisit the chapters that will remind you and bring you back to awareness. Your vigilance is your own best support. If you pay attention, and stay in relationship with your allies and the archetypes who are your close family on the other side, you can easily maintain the awakening you have received, and continue to move forward. It is important to recognize the people around you who are allies as well. Ask for and listen to feedback from those closest to you. If you can find others with whom to share this path, it might make your continuing journey easier and more enjoyable.

When you do the meditation that follows, it will become apparent where you are constricted, and your body may have a visceral response to the action of combining love and breath as you direct it to the places that are blocked. The result will be an immediate adjustment—a spiritual chiropractic adjustment—that rebalances the heart and enhances your ability to stay open to love, and to perceive the love that surrounds you.

THE POWER OF LOVE

Love is strong. Love tells the truth. Love is neither passive, nor weak, nor codependent. A truly loving person does not view others as less than, or as victims who need to be taken care of. We give loving support even in difficulty or disagreement by sharing our loving concerns and acknowledging that which we may not see or fully understand. We are simply expressing ourselves and inviting others to share their perspectives.

Love is not about being silent or holding back. Anytime we hold back, we are not allowing the energies of love to flow through us. Love does not try to control, fix, or determine the outcome of anything; it trusts, and allows, and makes space for things to unfold in accordance with spiritual and cosmic principles. Love does require the courage to stand in the fire and trust the healing power of the awakened heart.

Anubis has peace in his heart as he stands on a ledge over the great canyon where we first started our journey. He is enjoying the breeze with a serene look on his face as he gazes at the setting sun. He stands in his integrity.

There is a sense that if we could all stand in this place, watching the sunset time upon the world as we know it, we would begin to wake up and use the power that has been given to us appropriately. If we don't, the human experiment is over. It's over!

When mass consciousness makes the simple shift from ego's agenda to soul's purpose, human beings will live from the heart and peace will prevail. The entire world will shift its focus, and the resulting celebrations will usher in the new aeon.

Gods are not codependent with humans. The neteru allow us to experience the consequences of our actions. They send messengers and signs to support human beings. They cannot interfere, nor would it be appropriate, if a person needs to learn the hard way. They don't judge us, and they do love us. They radiate love energies to us, but they don't control us. Each individual has responsibility to evolve his own consciousness, to feed her own soul. Just as we all have the responsibility to care for our physical self, it is also true for our emotional and spiritual well-being. Because we are all connected, we have a responsibility to share what we know with the world; we then leave the responsibility to others to make their own shifts, no matter how attached we may be to them. One of the highest forms of love is to trust someone else's spirit to do what it needs to do.

When one speaks of the heart and the heart/mind, one is actually addressing the energy and healing power of love. People generally have a misunderstanding about what love is, often confusing love with chaotic and sentimental notions. Love is the most powerful and potent force in the universe. When harnessed, it is more powerful than anything we can construct—more powerful than nuclear energy. Although people refer to many different feelings when they speak of love, those feelings are often mere shadow images mixed up with longings and unmet needs from childhood trauma and family-of-origin issues.

To understand the true meaning of love, we must separate it out from the immature sentimentality commonly found in books and movies. Love is not sex, although sex can be a powerful component of love. Our most common definitions of love do not reflect its true power, nor the various gradations and expressions that comprise the energy of love as it is associated with the heart/mind.

Love guides the way. Love is a felt sense of knowing that you are in the right place at the right time, doing the right thing, regardless of what anyone or anything around you might be saying differently. Fidelity to your own heart and path is the truest form of love—it enables you to let love flow abundantly and bless all those around you. That kind of love has the ability to wear down the toughest resistance and judgments, your own and others'.

AWAKENING LOVE THROUGH
THE CHAKRAS

Love emanates from our heart center and from our other chakras as well. When you do the final journey, you shall see how love elicits the response associated with each chakra center.

Because of the nature of the first chakra center and its relationship to the element earth, you will notice certain issues being fed there. If love is emanating from the first chakra, there is often a sense of loving your home, where you live, and your surroundings. Because survival issues and security are based in the root chakra, self care and how you take care of and nurture your physical body comes into focus. Breathing love to the first chakra helps you to develop trust.

A lack of love in the emanations from the first chakra results in hunger. You might find yourself eating impulsively. You might find yourself seeing only lack, and fiercely or violently defending what you have for fear that there is not enough. Or you might default to not caring for yourself or your home, or whatever it is that would give you strong roots.

When you are emanating love from the second chakra, whatever you are creating, whether it is baking a pie or writing a book or building a home, you will be unifying with it in a creative mode. If love emanates from the second chakra, then indeed the connection to a sexual partner may feel very loving. If love is not guiding the life-force energy that flows from your second chakra, you might not have discernment about your urge to merge. You might lack the discrimination you need to choose appropriate partners for your relationships or projects. Your boundaries might be weak and you might have difficulty making choices from your authentic being.

When love comes into the third chakra in your solar plexus, your power—the power that you walk with in the world—is shared with others, and actually supports others in being powerful as well. You feel happiness when you see others coming into their true power. There is no competition when you have love emanating through the third chakra. If there is not enough love coming through the power of the third, tyranny and self-righteousness occur, and there is the potential for abuse of power. Fear of power and victim's consciousness also come with the feeling of lack of power in your life.

If you radiate love through the center of your being, the fourth chakra, your heart chakra, you radiate compassion, wisdom, acceptance, understanding, and peace, and people feel safe in your presence. The heart center is one of the strongest places you can come from, even more so than the higher chakras, because the heart is the melting pot for all the other chakras, and blends the energies from them all. The heart is the Holy Grail in which you pour all the energies of love, from all directions, and then emanate them back out into the world, as in the heart breath. When the energy is in your heart, yet you are not able to radiate it, people feel that you are holding back your love energy and that your heart is withdrawn, judgmental, and disconnected, and it is not safe for them to be vulnerable around you.

When you bring love energy into your throat at the fifth chakra, you speak truth. Although you speak your personal truth, you also speak a higher truth beyond and inclusive of your personal truth. You don't use words to control, manipulate, or hurt another, nor do you hold back words that are spoken from a place of integrity out of fear of hurting others. If your motives and intentions are coming with love through this chakra, what you are saying is not hurtful, even though sometimes others may interpret it so. When you don't have love coming through this chakra, you can be critical and judgmental, or you will withhold your truth.

When you bring your loving energy into your sixth chakra you see things as they truly are, from the highest, most expanded state of awareness. You have true understanding and your actions are aligned with a higher vision that sees into the heart of the matter, and from this vantage point it is impossible to be reactive. If you do not bring love into this chakra, you will not be able to see with the single eye, which reconciles the opposites.

Love in the crown chakra connects you to the one source. When you bring love into this center, you feel the loving connection to all things and all beings. It's like a fountain of love springing up out of your crown chakra and pouring radiant light and energy like a fountain all around you. There is a sense of oneness with everything, which makes it impossible to do harm to yourself or others. You realize that all things deserve to be loved and blessed by this energy. There is no separation between you and anything else. Without love coming from this chakra, there is either a sense of profound aloneness in the universe, and disillusionment, or simply a floating in the imagination. There may be visions and insights, but love isn't connected to it, leaving you with a kind of a cool, aloof connection to the archetypal world.

We know all too well the consequences of our actions and words when they do not come from love. There is no articulation for what happens when all chakras are fully open and running the energy of love. This can only be sensed and experienced in a profound way.

We recommend starting your day (or at any time you feel the need or desire) with the following meditation as an offering of gratitude for your life and the beauty that surrounds you. Incense or a spray of flower water can be useful to help clear the air. Feel free to add any unique ingredients that you find helpful to create a supportive and nurturing environment, to assist you in opening to the spirit of love.

During the meditation, you will move from chakra to chakra, starting with the root chakra at the base of the spine, and experience the impact of love on each center. The first time you take this journey, it is important to honor and connect with each one of the neteru that engages with you. Over time, as you integrate this process, it will be sufficient to use the meditation as an exercise to simply call on the power of love. You will know when it is time during your various alchemical processes and journeys to repeat the meditation in its entirety.

❧ EXERCISE TO AWAKEN THE HEALING POWER OF THE HEART

[*Kindle your heart flame and pour love upon it. When you have created a strong heart flame for the alchemy, breathe the heart breath, drawing the breath from Earth and sky simultaneously, breathing into and out of the heart center. . . .*]

Begin to focus your attention on the first chakra center. . . . Imagine drawing the energy up from the heart of the earth and pulling it up through your body. Imagine the cobra goddess, Wadjet, coming up into your body and clearing the central channel that is your spinal column. . . .

Consciously invoke the energy of love as you focus upon your first, or root, chakra center. Open yourself to the energy as it moves through that chakra, and move the attention of the heart breath so that your first chakra is receiving the energies of both Earth and the cosmos, as you allow Sothis to pour her healing energies of love into your being. Stay with this for several breaths, until you feel the energy of love fully permeate the first chakra center and pour out around you from the opened center in every direction. . . . [*Pause.*]

Move your attention to the second chakra and repeat the heart breath through this chakra. . . . Open once more to the powerful loving energies of Wadjet and Sothis as love moves into your second center. In this chakra, Hathor joins Sothis and Wadjet to bring forth any needed sexual and emotional healing. As the alchemy resolves those issues, love pours out around you. . . . [*Pause.*]

When you bring your attention up to the third center, the creative power rising up from the first two chakras begins to activate your power center. . . . Continue to breathe the heart breath to this center. . . . You may see a round, golden disc as the solar power enters your solar plexus and Ra helps infuse this part with the strong, radiant golden energies of love and protection. . . . Feel your personal will coming into alignment with divine love. . . . [*Pause.*]

With this newfound sense of personal power, return to the heart breath and direct it to your heart center. . . . As you continue to breathe the heart breath, open to the unconditional love that Anubis contributes to the energies that are building, and feel the love as it radiates out from your heart in every direction. . . . [*Pause.*]

The energies of love continue to rise up through you with growing urgency and force. . . . When you put your attention on your fifth center, your throat chakra, continue to breathe the heart breath fully. . . . It is Sekhmet that enters to help you find your unique musical note in the universe, your own magical words of power that can be expressed in every vocalization. . . . [*Pause.*] Give voice to this sound now. . . .

As your attention moves into your third eye, the energy of love rises into the sixth chakra. . . . Isis appears as a white bird flying around in a spiral pattern in your mind's eye. She opens your inner sight to create the single, all-knowing eye and perfect vision of Ptah. . . . Together they call in the powers of divine creativity and imagination imbued with the powers of love, so that what you envision can be brought forth with the vibration of the highest wisdom and embodiment of love. . . . [*Pause.*]

When you rise to the crown of your consciousness and rekindle the heart breath, Osiris can be seen lying in the sarcophagus. . . . Keep breathing the heart breath and infusing it with love. . . . Osiris rises up as the divine integration of his two sacred sons, Anubis and Horus.* As you become completely upright, the neteru, the seraphim, the angels and fairies, the star beings—all the spirit beings of the universe surround you as you are resurrected. Golden energy encircles your entire being. Osiris has risen in his full glory and every part of your/his being is united with love for all things and all beings. You are one with the entire creation, and there is no separation—only beauty. Let the love energy pour up and out through your crown as a great fountain of love and light. Let it continue to flow until you feel it spread out around you into the world. . . . [*Long pause.*]

You will know when you are ready to move forward with your day, and your life, open and connected to your entire ka and the love that holds it all together. . . .

When we remember this oneness in ourselves we pour it out into the world as though from a great fountain and know that we are all one, and the beauty of love is all there is. . . .

Hail Horus and Anubis, reunited. . . . Hail Osiris, risen in Light. . . .

---

*This gives new meaning to the raising of the *djed*, the backbone of Osiris.

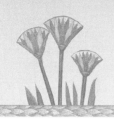

GLOSSARY OF THE GODS
A GUIDE TO THE SACRED
NETERU OF ANCIENT EGYPT

THE NETERU (nature spirits/deities) featured in *Shamanic Mysteries of Egypt* are archetypal guides and principles from the Egyptian pantheon. With ancient wisdom and abiding love, they lead us on our shamanic journey of transformation—a journey designed to awaken the healing power of our hearts.

You can find many wonderful interpretations of these deities—both scholarly and anecdotal—in the Egyptian literature. Our work approaches the neteru from a more personal point of view. It is concerned with a deep, rich inner experience of the neteru based on our own spiritual communion with these ancient gods. The first archetype listed here—the Dove—is not initially one of the neteru. Instead, the Dove represents you, the initiate, as you enter into these mysteries and approach these venerable spirits for guidance. Just as they did in ancient times, the neteru are coming forth to assist us in meeting the challenges of today's world.

In this glossary we present the neteru in the order that they appear in *Shamanic Mysteries of Egypt*. (Other deities mentioned in the book can be found in the Glossary of Terms.) The first part of each description is based on our direct phenomenological experience of these powerful deities. We follow our own understanding with a few brief comments on generally accepted history and interpretations for each deity.

0. THE DOVE
INITIATE/INNOCENCE/TRUST

The Dove represents the reader as the archetypal principle of the innocent initiate who responds to the call to enter these mysteries. The Dove
trusts his or her own inner knowing in the face of the powerful transformational forces encountered on this path. The initiate carries an olive
branch as an offering of peace and to honor each of the neteru that
are our guides throughout the journey. The white Dove is the bridge
between the present world of humanity and the ancient past. For most
people the Dove will automatically evoke some kind of spiritual connection, as the olive branch does for peace and reverence.

The Dove transcends history and culture as a universal symbol of
peace and innocence. It is seen as the soul and the Holy Spirit in Christianity and is sacred to the goddess Athena, the Greek goddess of wisdom.
The dove appears on the Fool card in some tarot decks. Although doves
are plentiful and live in the temples throughout Egypt, they are rarely
mentioned in recent historical mythology.

1. NEKHBET-MOTHER-MUT
ALCHEMIST/WISDOM KEEPER/
GRAND MOTHER

Nekhbet-Mother-Mut is the most revered and ancient grand dame of
Egypt. She is the wise old crone and honored elder of the pantheon of
neteru and comes to us in this work as a blend of the two vulture goddesses Mut and Nekhbet. As with all gods, she must be approached
with respect if one wishes to gain permission to enter into these sacred
mysteries. One does not trifle with this goddess, for she is a disciplined
taskmaster who assists the initiate in making the decision to engage fully
with this process of transformation. Once the decision has been made
to move forward, her loving watchful eye is always upon the initiate to
ensure safe passage through the portals of shamanic initiation.

Nekhbet-Mother-Mut is one of the oldest gods in the Egyptian pantheon. As Nekhbet, she was a protector goddess of Upper Egypt in the
south, closely related to Wadjet, the cobra goddess who was the protector of Lower Egypt in the north. Both were also guardians of the king
and of women and children, especially in childbirth. In her Mut aspect,
she was generally an anthropomorphic goddess, often depicted holding

her son, the moon god Khonsu, on her lap, yet she also has a leonine visage. Her name means "mother" and it is represented hieroglyphically as a vulture. As the feminine counterpart of Amun (a creator god), she was the stately queen mother who wore royal crowns and maintained a regal presence. Mut and Amun were considered parents to all the pharaohs from the reign of Hatshepsut forward. Mut's great temple in the vast complex at Karnak held most of the statues of the lion goddess Sekhmet, many of which are now scattered in museums around the world.

2. NEPHTHYS
HIGH PRIESTESS/INTUITION/MYSTERY

Nephthys is the hidden or veiled one who serves as a medium between worlds. She comes to us in dreams, flashes of intuition, and visions. Along with Isis and Nekhbet-Mother-Mut, Nephthys is an aspect of the Triple Goddess. She relies upon spirit to direct her in all things and she holds the mystery teachings of life, death, and rebirth deep within her essence. In our shamanic visionary experience, Nephthys inspires the initiate as she whispers her secrets into the wind and dances exotically under the starry sky, with magnificent serpents winding around her beautiful bronze arms.

Nephthys is the twin sister of Isis, the night to Isis's day. They are almost inseparable, although Isis is much more renowned. It is intrinsic to Nephthys's nature to be secret and hidden. She was primarily considered a funerary goddess, guarding the canopic jars and other aspects of the mortuary rites. When Isis's husband Osiris was murdered and dismembered, Nepthys helped her sister find the lost parts of his body and reassemble them.

Nephthys was paired with the shadow god Set, yet it was with Osiris that she conceived and gave birth to the shaman priest Anubis. The sisters Isis and Nephthys are often seen standing behind Osiris, giving him energy through their hands. They are found at either end of every sarcophagus from the later Egyptian dynasties, presumably guarding the dead.

3. ISIS
HOLY QUEEN MOTHER OF US ALL/
EMBODIED MANIFESTATION OF LOVE

Isis is the pure clear essence of spirit embodied in matter. She is always with us on this journey as a loving supportive force through every transformation we undergo. Isis re-members us when we die the sha-man's death; she makes us whole again as she urges us forth into a new incarnation—a new way of being at a higher octave of consciousness. She is the Queen of both Heaven and Earth and unfolds her brilliant rainbow wings to build a rainbow bridge of love between the worlds of form and formlessness.

Isis is the Great Mother who is also a magician and student of Thoth (god of wisdom). According to the most prevalent myth, Isis and Osiris fell in love while in the womb of their mother, the sky goddess Nut. During their earthly reign over Egypt, peace and harmony prevailed. Agriculture developed and Isis taught weaving and traveled the land as a midwife.

When Osiris was murdered by his brother Set, Isis grieved and searched until she found her husband embedded in a sacred tree in Byb-los. By the depth of her love and magic, and the wisdom teachings of Thoth, she was able to conceive their son Horus after her husband's death. In their search for the murdered Osiris, both Isis and Nephthys were associated with the kite, a small hawk that flew about seeking car-rion and screeching. Their hawklike cries are similar to the keening of mourners throughout Egypt.* It was in the form of the kite that Isis was able to enter the dimensions beyond life to conceive Horus with Osiris. As the Mother of Horus, Isis's popularity grew and she was venerated for her powers of nurturing, protection, and healing.†

Over time, Isis has become one of the most popular goddesses ever known. She has absorbed many goddesses who preceded her and has influenced or suffused many who have followed. The myth of Inanna and of Demeter and Persephone, as well as the legend of the Virgin Mary and Christ, bear remarkable resemblance to her story. Her veneration spread from Egypt throughout the region. Ancient sanctuaries dedicated to Isis can be found in Byblos, Rome and Greece, and more modern sanctuaries exist throughout most of the world.

---

*Richard H. Wilkinson, *The Complete Gods and Goddesses of Ancient Egypt* (Cairo: American University Press, 2003), 147.

†The full story of the Isis/Osiris myth is quite complex and lengthy. For a wonderful account of the myth, see Normandi Ellis, *Feasts of Light* (Wheaton, Ill.: Quest Books, 1999). See also, Jean Houston, *The Passion of Isis and Osiris* (New York: Ballantine, 1995).

4. KHNUM
MASTER CRAFTSMAN/
CREATOR OF FORM/ORGANIZING PRINCIPLE

Khnum is the highly skilled Master Craftsman who creates the eternally evolving varieties of material form upon his potter's wheel. He holds the universal secrets of the organizing principles of DNA and of life itself. Khnum lovingly and carefully re-creates the new body, or form, that will house our renewed heart after its transformation in these sacred heart rituals.

The word *khnum* means "to unite," as in uniting the ka (the ancestral lineage) with the physical body and the ba (the soul). Khnum was variously known as the ba of Ra, the ba of Geb, and the ba of Osiris.* He was closely associated with the Nile and was said to have controlled the inundation from his domain at Elephantine Island. Elephantine is located near the first cataracts, which were considered the source of the Nile by the ancient Egyptians. Khnum is distinguished from the other ram-headed gods by his horns, which grow horizontally outward in swirls. Khnum was also quite closely associated with Sobek (the crocodile god) at both Elephantine and Essna, and with Amun, another ram-headed creator god.

5. SPHINX
DIVINE MESSENGER/
COSMIC LIBRARY/EARTH ALTAR

The Sphinx is a Divine Messenger and repository of cosmic akashic (spiritually informed) wisdom. As an Earth Altar and Cosmic Library this mysterious one holds the stellar messages from our ancient ancestors— messages that have been waiting for centuries for our readiness to receive their sacred transmissions.

For thousands of years the enigmatic Sphinx has inspired deep thought and questioning. Its source remains a mystery and its very existence is a riddle that challenges our knowledge of history. Conventional Egyptology claims that the Sphinx was created by the Pharaoh Khafre about 2500 BC. There is a resemblance between its current visage and that of Khafre, however the disproportion between the Sphinx's large body and small head might indicate that its current face was carved from a previous one, perhaps that of a lion.

---

*Wilkinson, *The Complete Gods and Goddesses of Ancient Egypt,* 194.

There is a stele, a large upright slab of granite, between the paws of the Sphinx. It tells the story of how Thuthmose IV, a general around 1400 BC, sheltered himself from the afternoon sun beneath the head of the Sphinx, whose body was buried to the neck in sand. He fell asleep and received a message from the Sphinx in a dream. The Sphinx told Thuthmose that he was suffocating under the weight of all that sand. If Thutmose cleared the sand and freed the Sphinx, he would become pharaoh. Thutmose had the sand removed and soon afterward was crowned as king.

6. SOBEK AND HORUS RECONCILIATION/FORGIVENESS/ UNDERSTANDING

Sobek and Horus represent two powerful opposing psychic forces found in all human beings—the old and the new parts of each of us. The crocodile god, Sobek, is associated with the reptilian brain, the primitive nonverbal part of the brain that ensures our physical survival at the level of stimulus and response. The reptilian brain holds the most ancient evolutionary patterns from which we have evolved. It has kept us protected, alive, and growing forward. In opposition to Sobek, Horus is associated with the neocortex, which serves as the center of higher mental functions for humans. The neocortex is also associated with our higher chakras and, among other things, relates to our connection with spirit. To create balance in our lives, Sobek and Horus have come into this work as adversarial allies. It is their task to create a harmonious union within our psyches.

Sobek is an ancient creator god who is linked with both Ra and Horus and who shares a temple with Horus at Kom Ombo. Throughout the long history of Egypt, his representation has changed. During the Old Kingdom Sobek was revered as a god of the Nile and the floods, bringing fertility, while at the same time feared as a god of destruction. From the Middle Kingdom onward he was closely associated with Ra (the sun god) and during Greco-Roman times Hathor (goddess of reconciliation) was considered to be his consort and Khonsu (the moon god) their child.

It is probable that some form of the falcon god Horus was venerated as far back as predynastic times when rulers were called Followers of Horus. It would be impossible to cover but a fraction of his attributes here. Horus is considered twice born, once of Nut and Geb, and again as the son of Isis and Osiris, conceived after Osiris's death through the love and magic of Isis. As a young prince he was groomed and trained to inherit the royal leadership of his father. His primary image is as falcon or hawk and his primary identification is with the sky and the sun. Yet there are leonine images, as well, and by the New Kingdom he was associated with the Great Sphinx and with many other gods who through time assimilated his power. His child form was usually anthropomorphic and thousands of amulets were created depicting the image of Isis suckling the young Horus on her lap. The story of his conception, birth, development, struggles for sovereignty, and eventual and continuing reign as the ruler of the gods makes Horus one of the most prominent gods of Egypt. Much of his mythic battle with Set is described on the walls of his temple at Edfu.

7. SEKHMET
TRANSFORMATION/
FIERCE COMPASSION/HEALER

Sekhmet is a compelling fiery neter who comes to us when we are in the midst of the fires of alchemical transformation. She shows us her fierce compassion as she assists us in healing the dual nature within. She also helps us to shape-shift into our future selves—the selves we are struggling to become. As we evolve to the next level of consciousness, Sekhmet opens and purifies our heart space, creating fertile ground that can receive the visionary seeds of who we will become.

Sekhmet's name means "the power," or "the mighty one." She is the feminine fire, feared by many, yet known as the quintessential healer in Egypt. She is a fierce guardian of Ma'at (goddess of truth), with whom she became associated in later dynasties. She is also interchangeable in certain stories with Hathor. She is a daughter of the sun god Ra and consort of the creator god Ptah.

In one of the prevailing myths, Ra calls his daughter Sekhmet to Earth to deal with some humans who have become disrespectful of his reign. Enraged by what she encounters, Sekhmet begins a slaughter that, once she has a taste of human blood, threatens to annihilate all of humanity. Ra knows that he can't control his daughter, so he calls upon Thoth to come up with a solution. Thoth advises Ra to have his priests brew huge vats of barley beer, dyed red to resemble blood and spiked with herbs to make her calm. This they pour out upon the land surrounding Sekhmet while she sleeps. When she wakes up, she drinks the beer and becomes intoxicated, returning to her more docile nature. This myth is also attributed to Hathor, with whom Sekhmet is very closely linked.

Sekhmet's color is red and her breath is the hot wind of the desert. In a manner similar to Wadjet, the cobra goddess who is seen at her brow in front of the solar disc that she wears as a crown, Sekhmet is thought to have breathed fire at her enemies. Sekhmet's powers are associated with healing and protection, as well as destruction and war. She was considered the one who brought plagues, yet she was also the one called upon to cure them. There is a current resurgence of veneration for Sekhmet today, particularly in her aspect as the healer who is in touch with the magical aspects of medicine and transformation.

8. MA'AT
TRUTH/RADIANCE/BALANCE

Ma'at is the powerful balancer and adjuster who helps us to accept and love the truth about ourselves. "The light the dark no difference." Her brilliant radiance reflects our own back to us so that we may truly see who we are and know where our "work" lies as we move toward greater wholeness. She is the Regal Mistress who reigns over the Hall of Mirrors. She sees beyond right and wrong and creates divine justice in our affairs.

Ma'at represents cosmic law, divine order, and justice; she is also the balance for which we strive. She is closely associated with Thoth, for wisdom and truth go hand in hand. She can be recognized by the tall feather that she usually wears, probably that of an ostrich, and is most often represented as an anthropomorphic deity. In dynastic Egypt, her image was offered as sustenance for the other gods who "live on Ma'at." In her association with judgment, the scales of Ma'at weigh the heart of the deceased against her feather, which is sometimes substituted for her image. An enlightened heart is full of light and weighs nothing. It was the purpose of all Egyptian kings to uphold the truth, balance, and order that Ma'at personifies.

9. THOTH
ILLUMINATION/ARCHITECT OF WISDOM/
ENLIGHTENED COMMUNICATION

This sacred holy scribe and wisdom keeper urges us ever upward toward higher learning so that we are able to understand the deeper meaning of our lives. When we have embodied the truth of our lives we are able to articulate and share that wisdom authentically from an enlightened place. This form of communication has its basis in the soul's fountain of wisdom.

Thoth is usually represented as either a sacred ibis or a baboon, or a man with an ibis head. In ancient times he was called Djehuti and he was associated with Hermes by the Greeks. The Hermetic tradition, the Western magical tradition, and the tarot are all sourced from Thoth. To the ancient Egyptians, he represented the highest concept of mind. He is closely associated with the moon, and therefore knows the secrets of time and measurement. As the god of writing, communications, language, medicine and healing, architecture, mathematics and accounting, astronomy, science, and magic, Thoth has long been known as the "teachers' teacher." He is also considered to be the author of all great Egyptian books of wisdom. The Romans called him Mercury, the messenger of the gods, yet he is much more—he is the mediator, the one who sees the big picture and finds a solution for every problem. Whereas Ptah was said to have created the world with his thoughts, Thoth was said to have named those thoughts into being and is sometimes called "the tongue of Ptah" or "the intellect of Ptah." Another creation myth suggests that Thoth rose up from the primordial mound and created, out of the primeval chaos, the Ogdoad, the original eight principles of nature from which all life emerged.

10. KHEPERA
CYCLES OF CHANGE/
PLANETARY GUARDIAN/SPIRAL DANCER

The mighty scarab, Khepera, serves planet Earth as a loyal guardian and spinner of cycles, bringing forth necessary changes that allow creation to keep moving forward. S(he) is a Spiral Dancer who faithfully filters and transmits the powerful stellar and cosmic energies that radiate to all Earth's creatures. Khepera knows how to spin the energies and hold the balance of time and the Turning of the Ages in his/her mighty feet.

Khepera is the Becoming One, the ancient scarab beetle who pushes the solar orb above the horizon at dawn. The scarab represents the morning sun and is closely associated with creation and resurrection. Although there was no specific cult following for Khepera, his image is found all over Egypt. Scarabs started appearing as amulets in the Fifth Dynasty. Their popularity continued to grow throughout the lengthy civilization of ancient Egypt and continues up to current times. Scarab beetles are considered protectors. In some instances scarabs were placed in mummy wrappings and over the heart of the deceased.

11. BAST
HOLY LONGING (DESIRE)/
INSTINCT AND SENSUALITY

The sensual cat goddess Bast creates the compelling desire to be born into form from the disembodied ba in the realm of formlessness. Her instinctual holy longing is irresistible in its urgency to create new life. She shows us that birth is sacred and being born into form is a blessing not a curse. She is our guardian through the birthing chambers each time we are ready to renew our form. Without her alluring promise of new delights, we would never have the impetus or courage to reenter the cosmic birth canal and be born over and over again. With each birth we celebrate the joy and magic of our precious incarnation here on Earth.

Originally seen as a leonine goddess, and as such a Daughter of Ra with the aggressive, protective tendencies of a lion, Bast became the Cat of Ra in later times, perhaps because she mellowed and became tamer. She is closely associated with both Hathor and Sekhmet and is often seen as a cat-headed woman carrying a sistrum (rattle) and/or menat (amulet). There is suggestion that she was a northern, or Lower Egypt form of Hathor (as was Sekhmet), as she was most popular in Bubastis in the eastern Delta. Her festivals were unequaled for the exuberance and intoxication of her adherents.

Cats were loved and revered in ancient Egypt, where they guarded the granaries from snakes and vermin. Bast was worshipped as a goddess of motherhood and protector of pregnant women. She was also worshipped as a goddess of fertility, abundance, and pleasure.

12. ANUBIS
SURRENDER/SHAMAN/
ENLIGHTENED HEART

Anubis is the enlightened heart shaman who is the Opener of the Way, meaning he has gone before us, as one of us, to pave the way so that we might follow in his footsteps. Anubis knows how to surrender his heart and his truth to ever-expanding cycles of death and rebirth, in order to step more fully into his divine humanity here on Earth. "On Earth as it is in Heaven." He is the original Wolf Spirit from the Dog Star, Sirius, who is our ever-faithful companion, assisting us in our ego deaths and renewal of our soul's true purpose. He is a walker between worlds and knows how to sniff out the path that comes and goes from form to formlessness. Anubis cares deeply about us and will guide us if we call upon him during our own shamanic journeys between the worlds.

In ancient Egypt, Anubis was known as the Divine Embalmer, and was said to have worked with his mother, Nephthys, and his adoptive mother, Isis, to help find the scattered pieces of Osiris's body. He helped prepare the body and wrapped it in the mummy cloth. He was considered an Underworld god, the son of Osiris, who became a guardian and guide, leading the deceased along all the pathways from the darkness back into the light. Anubis is often depicted reading the scales during the weighing of the heart against the feather of Ma'at.

13. OSIRIS
REGENERATION/
TRANSMUTATION/BEAUTY

Although Osiris has long been associated with death and called the Lord of the Underworld, truthfully it is more appropriate to acknowledge him as the archetypal regenerative principle that transmutes outworn, deteriorating form into its renewed, shining manifestation of beauty. Osiris invites us to let go and rest deeply upon his earthy green chest as he wraps his supportive arms around our bodies and turns us into that which we are in the process of becoming.

Osiris was said to have been a beloved and benign ruler of Egypt, whose reign featured harmony and great expansion. He brought civilization and prosperity to the people and taught them agriculture and trade. According to the myth, his brother Set became jealous, possibly because of Osiris's prosperity and popularity, and possibly because Osiris fathered Anubis with Set's wife, Nephthys. Set murdered Osiris, after which Isis set out—with the help of Thoth, Nephthys, and Anubis—to find her dead husband and restore him to life. His ensuing resurrection made Osiris the god of regeneration and growth.

14. HATHOR
MAGIC/MEDICINE WOMAN/INTEGRATION

Beauty permeates this Medicine Woman who has integrated the light and dark into a magical blend of higher love and wisdom in her gold-and-silver cauldron of healing. Hathor's resolution of inner conflict results in a sacred marriage within that brings forth the possibility of unconditional love for yourself and others. When you are healed by Hathor's magic, you experience a peaceful empowerment and the ability to co-create your outer world. All Earth's creatures feel blessed and safe in her presence and long to be close to her heart.

Hathor is a complex goddess with many attributes. Although her origins are hidden in prehistory, throughout her mythic presence she has integrated the polarities of love and hate, creation and destruction. Her name means "house of Horus." She is linked to Shekinah in the Jewish tradition, meaning the dwelling place of God. Hathor has long been worshipped as the golden calf, sacred cow goddess of the night sky who nourishes both gods and humans with her milk—the Milky Way. She is honored as goddess of love, sensuality, sexuality, celebration, intoxication, and joy, and she is also associated with fertility and regeneration. She is known as the Lady of the Mountains and is the goddess of mining. Her stones are malachite and turquoise. As the Lady of the Sycamore, she is goddess of the tree. Another epithet for Hathor is the Golden One and she is also called Lady of the Vulva. As an important funerary goddess, she was the Mistress of the West. She was said to protect the deceased in the same way she protects the sun god Ra, when—in her aspect as Nut—she swallows him in the evening and holds him safe in her body as he travels through the night to be reborn in the morning. She has been seen as both the mother of Ra and the mother of Horus. She is also the wife of a different aspect of Horus as well as a consort of

Sobek. It is as a daughter of Ra that she is aligned with Sekhmet as the near destroyer of humankind. The ancient Egyptians felt that her fierce lioness aspect had to be pacified by beer. They drank copious amounts of it at her festivals in honor of the inebriation that returned her to her gentle, loving nature and saved the human race.

15. SET
SHADOW/ADVERSARIAL ALLY/TRICKSTER

Set is the embodiment of the darker aspects of our natures, which are often projected onto others. He is the scapegoat who carries the sins of the world upon his back and tricks us into meeting our fate in the outer world so that we may evolve forward to higher levels of consciousness. He is in truth both an adversary and an ally, hence his more dignified name is the Adversarial Ally. If we refuse to meet and own this part of ourselves in a conscious manner, our actions can turn into the evil we have no wish to embody.

Set is a complex and controversial character in the pantheon of Egypt. He is very old and was originally honored and respected—and feared—as a god of the desert, storms, and chaos and later as a god of foreigners. The ancient Egyptians knew that regardless of the tumult and confusion that surrounded him, Set was an integral part of life and a force that could not be removed. One must, rather, come to terms with him. Set and Horus were originally united and equal, as some temple images portray. Over time they became separated by politics, eventually becoming extremely combative. It was in these later times that Set was vilified and considered evil. In the prevailing myth, Set slew his brother Osiris and fought Osiris's son, Horus, for the rights of inheritance in a lengthy battle, which was finally decided by the gods in favor of Horus.

16. WADJET
LIFE-FORCE ENERGY/PURIFICATION/
DIVINE AWAKENER

Wadjet, the great cobra serpent, spirals her way into our lives. Her kundalini energy opens our chakras as this Divine Awakener purifies our motives and gives us the gift of humility. We can learn from wisdom or learn from woe, but Wadjet assures us that we will learn her lessons and take greater responsibility for our thoughts and actions in the world. She reminds us that it is not now or never, but now or later!

Wadjet is one of the oldest goddesses, her origins obscured in pre-dynastic Egypt. She is the sister of Nekhbet-Mother-Mut, with whom she shares guardianship of the Two Lands. The vulture and the cobra surmount the double crown worn by pharaohs, which symbolizes the joining of Upper and Lower Egypt, the south with the north, Earth with sky, and matter with spirit. Wadjet is called the Eye of Ra and from her place on the brow of pharaoh, she spits fire at his enemies. She was protector of all rulers of Egypt, and of childbirth and women. Although she is mostly associated with the cobra, in later times she has been seen in leonine and other forms. She is also closely related to the papyrus plant, which is the sacred plant of Lower Egypt.

17. SOTHIS
STAR CONSCIOUSNESS/GENEROSITY/
BODHISATTVA

Sothis is a pure channel for divine love and wisdom. She rises into the night sky and pours forth her spiritual essence, stellar energies, and compassionate wisdom upon all beings. Through her willingness to offer us these precious gifts and guidance we are elevated to a greater understanding of our own soul's purpose and the reasons we are here on Earth at this time. Sothis is the star of humanity, calling forth the best in each of us and inspiring us to step into our greater selves and offer our own unique gifts back to the world.

In earliest known times, Sothis had her own identity and importance as the herald of the inundation when she was first seen rising in the east on the first day of the New Year. Sothis is the Greek name for the star called Sopdet by the Egyptians. Over time she became closely identified with Isis in her personification as the brightest star in the sky, the Dog Star, Sirius. Isis/Sothis followed her husband, Osiris, who is associated with the constellation of Orion, into the Underworld for seventy days. Their reemergence in the night sky can also be seen as the restoration of Osiris, just as the earth is restored to life with coming of the flood each year. According to Robert Bauval, author of *The Orion Mystery,* the annual disappearance of Sothis and Orion from the night sky is the reason that the funerary rights lasted for seventy days.

Isis, as Sothis, helps the kings and mortals to ascend to the sky, just as she did with Horus and Osiris. As Isis is Great Mother of the Earth, Sothis is the Queen of the Sky.

18. KHONSU
LUNAR ENERGIES/DIVINE TIMING/
BLOOD MYSTERIES

Khonsu brings spiritual nourishment to our bodies and souls. He knows the exact timing in which we are ready to receive communion and "eat the flesh of the Gods" so that we may become as "one of them." Khonsu works on our behalf to fertilize our minds and hearts with the seeds of our own divinity. He engages the power of the moon to bring forth the healing rains that cleanse our old belief systems and he renews our DNA at a cellular level. He governs the tides of the oceans and human emotions. This Keeper of the Lunar Mysteries restores our souls to their very core.

Khonsu's representations have shifted in many directions over time, starting with references in the Pyramid Texts that portray him as "bloodthirsty" for consuming the other gods to assimilate their power. Later, as the son of Amun and Mut, he was part of the important triad of Thebes, portrayed with the side-lock of youth. Khonsu was also associated with Horus and shown as a protector and healer with a falcon head surmounted by the sun and crescent moon. He is most widely known as a lunar god who is closely linked with Thoth. As such, he is the measurer of time who determines the lifespan of humans. Still later he became associated with healing and the exorcising of demons, for which his fame spread beyond Egypt. At Kom Ombo he is depicted as the child of Sobek and Hathor. His name has been thought to mean "the king's placenta," "the traveler," and "he who traverses the sky."

19. AMUN-RA
SOLAR ENERGIES/
TRANSFIGURATION/ALCHEMICAL GOLD

Amun-Ra ushers spiritualized matter, dignity, and royalty into our true nature. The powerful light from the Solar Mysteries shines upon us and transfigures our consciousness. We turn ourselves toward the shining light of the sun and become spiritually mature beings who seek to embody shamanic consciousness in everyday life. Amun-Ra helps us to realize that everything we need to heal ourselves and our world is within our reach.

One of the most important gods in Egypt, Amun-Ra contains within himself diverse aspects that have combined together over millennia, resulting in the fusion of Amun, the invisible or hidden one, with Ra, the blazing and visible sun. He is considered the supreme god of the Egyptian pantheon, yet his nature is intrinsically mysterious and hidden. He was primarily revered as a great creator god, a solar god, and a fertility god. In the height of his veneration during the New Kingdom, he was believed to have created the cosmos through his thoughts. At the same time he was considered to be a self-generated ithyphallic symbol of strength and virility, and as such was related to the fertility god Min. The temple dedicated to the triad of Thebes—Amun, Mut, and Khonsu—is the largest religious-temple structure in the world.

20. PTAH
THE NEW AEON/IMAGINATION/
VISIONARY PROPHET

The great creator god Ptah has the power to imagine a new world and can open the mouth of creation to issue it forth. He is a prophet and a seer of the future aeons. He holds the potential of a Golden Age in his mind's eye. When we tap into his vision, he helps us harness his ability to speak things into being.

Ptah is said to have thought creation into being, whereas Thoth names the things of creation; they are closely aligned in this regard. Ptah is usually shown in anthropomorphic form with his limbs confined like those of a mummy. As such, he is often associated with both Osiris and Min, the ithyphallic fertility god. Amun, Ra, and Ptah together form a triad that some say formed all the gods. Their identity is hidden in Amun, visible in Ra, and embodied in Ptah.

This Lord of Ma'at, patron of truth and strength, Ptah was also the protector of craftsmen, the Great Fashioner who was worshipped by jewelers, craftsmen, and builders for his power to manifest anywhere in the vast realms between the Underworld and the farthest reaches of the sky. Ptah is usually shown wearing a blue skullcap and holding a scepter with the ankh, the djed, and the uas (or *was*) staffs combined. Ptah's once-magnificent temple complex at Memphis may well have been larger than Karnak and was primarily dedicated to the triad of Ptah, Sekhmet, and Nefertum (although a most exquisite chapel dedicated to Hathor is yet to be excavated there). The complex was called the Temple of the ka of Ptah, Hut-ka-Ptah, which in Greek was Aigyptos, quite possibly the source of the name Egypt.*

21. NUT AND GEB
WHOLENESS/CREATION OF SACRED
PURPOSE/DIVINE PARENTS

Nut and Geb represent the result of Ptah's dreaming of the universe, at least in terms of the perspective of human consciousness. Unified with passionate intent, they form a sacred union of wholeness and co-creation. They are our Divine Parents who help to initiate and birth us into our sacred purpose as we spiral around the great wheel of life, death, and rebirth on our shamanic path toward embodiment of the enlightened heart/mind. We are meant to awaken and remember our connection to the Divine so that we can become adult children of the gods and assume more responsibility in caring for our sacred planet Earth. We also inherit the powers of the ancient ones as we grow in their likeness.

Nut and Geb were born of Tefnut, the goddess of moisture and Shu, the god of air. Together they created the atmosphere that held the earth separate from the sky. Geb is the quintessential green god of fertility, the god of earth and vegetation, who is closely associated with his son, Osiris. His totem animal is a goose and he is sometimes called The Great Cackler. Nut is the vault of the sky and is related to both Hathor and Isis. Her body contains the firmament. When Nut swallows the sun each night, the hours during which it is invisible represent the hours of the Underworld journey of death. Each morning in the rosy red glow of dawn, she gives birth to the sun again in order to continue the cycle of birth, death, and resurrection. All of life pours forth from the union of Nut and Geb, including the gods Osiris, Isis, Horus, Set, and Nephthys—and, of course, Anubis.

---

*Wilkinson, *The Complete Gods and Goddesses of Ancient Egypt,* 124.

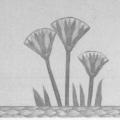

GLOSSARY OF TERMS

ab: The heart, considered by ancient Egyptians to be the seat of the soul and of our true intelligence. It is the place where the true self resides.

aeon: An indefinitely long period of time or age. Also can refer to a class of powers or beings that emanates from the Supreme Being.

akasha: The element of spirit, similar to what was originally named *ether* by Aristotle. It is the matrix of information that informs the other elements: earth, water, fire, and air.

akh: The "Shining One"; the illumined spiritual result of the merging of the ka and the ba. The akh is is said to be created at death, however it is also the result of the shamanic mysteries of death and rebirth. (See chapter 19, Amun-Ra.)

akh bird: The bird that represents the akh is a crested form of the illumined ba aspect of the akh, sometimes similar to a phoenix, but represented as a crested ibis. (See the definition of the word *ba*.) The crested ibis that usually represents the akh is also known as a hermit ibis. (Note that in *Shamanic Mysteries of Egypt*, Thoth holds the place of the Hermit in traditional tarot, and the sacred element of air is represented by the Sacred Crested Ibis.)

ankh: The Egyptian symbol of enduring life that also combines the masculine and feminine principles in the shape of a cross with a loop on the top.

Apis bull: Worshipped in ancient times as the "renewed life of Ptah," a Nile fertility god that was also known as the Bull of the Underworld and as such was associated with Osiris. These bulls were recognized by certain markings. When an existing one was replaced the previous one was killed and some flesh was eaten, while other parts were mummified.

atef crown: The tall conical crown, similar to the White Crown of Upper Egypt with two side feathers worn by Osiris. Sometimes there is a sun disk attached to or above it.

ba: The subtle body that is the soul of the individual, usually represented as a bird with the face of the person. (In-depth description occurs primarily in chapter 6.)

bennu bird: Considered the soul of Ra, this bird preceded the phoenix as the avian symbol of regeneration. By the New Kingdom it was represented by a grey heron sometimes depicted wearing the atef crown.

bodhisattva: A most compassionate and generous advanced soul who has fully incarnated and experienced all of life's lessons. Upon completion of these lessons these sacred star beings embrace both humanity and divinity, while offering back the light they have discovered along the way. They become guardians or spirit guides on our spiritual paths and stay with us until we complete our own journeys.

canopic jar: The ancient Egyptian vessels that contained certain organs of the deceased, which were placed there during the embalming process.

chakra: Etheric power centers in the human body, spiraling wheels of energy that encapsulate our experiences. They also function as portals and are associated with issues related to the elements.

communion: An ancient Egyptian ritual where bread and water or wine are offered to individuals ceremonially. The bread represents the body of the gods and the water or wine represents the blood of the gods. In this ritual the initiate is being invited to take on the incarnation and characteristics of the sacred neteru and to eat or become godlike.

diadem: Crown or certain other headdresses worn as a sign of royalty.

djed: A symbol representing the backbone of Osiris and the tree of life. Its presence indicates stability and it is one of the power symbols of

Ptah. The "Raising of the Djed" is a ritual symbolizing the resurrection of Osiris.

Djoser: Third Dynasty king who built the step pyramid at Sakkara, the oldest known pyramid structure.

draughts: An ancient spiritual/oracular game, similar to senet or checkers, which requires strategy for moving the pieces effectively. Thoth and Khonsu "gambled" using a divining tool similar to draughts in order to strategize the timing in which the neteru (Osiris, Isis, Set, Nephthys, and Horus) would be born onto this planet.

Duat (Dwat): The dimension known as the Underworld, the tomb/womb, which is the inner-world wherein we experience the deeper mysteries of death, physically and shamanically.

Enki: Sumerian moon god who sent help to the Underworld to assist Inanna to be born again and ascend back into the night sky as Venus.

Ereshkigal: The dark, or shadow sister of Inanna. Just as Inanna is the Queen of Heaven, Ereshkigal is the Queen of the Underworld.

Hatshepsut: A great female pharaoh who often presented herself dressed like a man and whose peaceful reign left a magnificent temple with carved reliefs of importing and trading rather than conquest. Hers was a controversial, if not violent, reign.

heka, Heka: Both an action and a neter, heka represents the magic and primeval power that existed since the time of creation itself; possibly the potent divine force that empowered the event. Personified as a god in Egypt (if you add a "t" it becomes the feminine form) and is associated with both Isis and Sekhmet (as in the use of heka in chapter 20, Ptah, and in the next entry, Heket).

Heket: The frog goddess of fertility, who may participate in the germination of sahu as she sparks the animation of life in the renewed body as well as in the newborn child. She is also a protector of women during childbirth.

Iktomi: Native American spider grandmother, the weaver and unweaver of creation.

Imhotep: The first named architect, designer of the step pyramid of the Old Kingdom pharaoh Djoser, was also a scribe, healer, teacher, and high priest whose fame eventually elevated him to godlike status.

Inanna: The ancient Sumerian Queen of Heaven who left her home in the upper worlds to travel to the Underworld to meet with her dark sister Ereshkigal. Many tales and mysteries surround both her descent and ascent.

ka: Our etheric double, the collective soul and energetic connection with our ancestors. It is the consciousness of the neteru that is woven into our very being, all the way into our DNA. (See primarily chapter 4, Khnum.)

Khemit: Ancient Egyptian name for Egypt, the Black Land with the fertile soil from the Nile.

koan: Usually related to Zen methods of teaching, it refers to a verse, question, or statement spoken to the initiate who then meditates on it so that the hidden meaning is revealed from within.

kundalini: Sanskrit term for the coiled snake that carries the life-force energy up from the base of the spine. Associated in these mysteries with Wadjet, the cobra goddess.

lotus: The plant symbol of Upper Egypt, representing creation and the beginning of life. It is associated with the gods Khepera and Nefertum. Some mystery schools believe that the lotus is a symbol for the Milky Way. Whether from the oozing muck at the bottom of the river or from the blazing firmament of the sky, it is a source of eternal life and exudes strength. Seeds have been found to be viable for a long as 50,000 years. There is conjecture that the blue lotus of ancient Egypt was used in ceremonies to help initiates achieve expanded states of consciousness.

Lower Egypt: The fertile Delta lands in the north of Egypt, also sometimes referred to as the Black Land. Because the Nile River runs south to north, the northern land is called Lower Egypt, and the southern part of the country is Upper Egypt. (See Upper Egypt.)

mammisi: These small temples are adjacent to a number of main temples, mostly built in the New Kingdom. They are birthing chambers that celebrate the birth of gods and pharaohs. The mammisi at the temple of Hathor at Dendera is most illustrative of the divine birthing process. Edfu, Philae, and Kom Ombo have other good examples.

mandala: Originating with Hindu theology, many forms of mandalas, both two and three dimensional, appear as sacred art. Tibetan

Buddhism also uses forms of the mandala to represent the universe. Here we speak of a circle drawing that depicts wholeness or the wheel of conscious awareness. (See chapter 10, Khepera, for further information.)

mantra: Sacred words of power that were usually realized through deep meditation, and passed on to others as a tool for learning and praying. It can be a word, a phrase, or a verse, and its intrinsic power is manifest through thought and/or voice and strengthened through repetition.

Medinet Habu: Mortuary temple of Ramses III on the West Bank across from Luxor.

menat: A tiered beaded necklace with a counterweight; a magical symbol of Hathor. When shaken, it produces the sound of Hathor coming out of the reeds and bulrushes by the Nile, where Horus was hidden. (During certain festivals it was shaken along with the sistrum.) It is a symbol of divine healing and protection and was sometimes buried with the dead.

Mitakuye Oyasin: Lakota words for honoring and sending prayers to "All My Relations."

multiplistic: Similar to multidimensional, it refers to someone who expresses a variety of attributes in many different ways. For example, Thoth speaks all the languages.

Nefertum: Originally associated with the sun god Ra, Nefertum is the protector of the Two Lands. His symbol is the fragrant blue lotus blossom, from which some say he was born. Later he was seen as the son of Ptah and Sekhmet, completing the powerful triad of Memphis. As the result of their union, he represents the fragrance of life.

negredo: The part of the alchemical process that takes place in darkness. Often seen as the journey of disintegration and death and the hidden mysteries that must be experienced in order for enlightenment, or spiritualization of matter (the prime material of alchemy), to occur. (See chapter 19, Amun-Ra.)

Neith: An ancient, primeval goddess worshipped as the creator of all, the mother of the sun, and the mother of Sobek. When seen with bow and arrows she is a goddess of war, yet she is also the patron of weaving and wears the symbol of a loom upon her head. The same symbol is often seen in tombs upon the chests of cobras, identifying her with the mummies to which she supplies the woven shrouds.

Nun: Primal waters from which creation sprung; common to all the creation myths of Egypt.

Oden: Norse god who put himself through what is known as "Oden's Ordeal." He hung himself from a great "world tree" for nine days seeking knowledge by communing with the dead until he achieved enlightenment. The day of his completion is celebrated as the Festival of the Discovery of the Runes.

Ogdoad: The eight primeval principles brought forth by Thoth in the creation myth held and expressed in the school of Hermopolis (Greek name for the place of the worship of Thoth).

Opening of the Mouth ceremony: An important ritual that animates or awakens the senses of the pharaoh, the deceased, a statue, or a temple. Initially a funerary ritual, it has gone through many permutations over time. Following the Opening of the Mouth, words take on their full power, and readily come into manifestation. (For further information and ceremony, see chapter 20, Ptah.)

palm frond: The symbol of everlasting life depicted by the years that Thoth gave to the pharaoh.

papyrus: A graceful Mediterranean aquatic sedge; the plant symbol of Lower Egypt, which is also connected to the sacred writings and hieroglyphs and the teachings of Thoth. It is also the plant from which the first paper was made; the word *papyrus* refers to the plant, the paper, and the document.

Persephone: The Greek goddess who was abducted by Pluto (Hades) into the Underworld. Her mother was Demeter, who made a deal with the gods to allow Persephone to live part of the year above the earth and part of the year in the Underworld with her husband.

plinth: In ancient Egypt it expresses the primeval mound of creation as a structure to rest or awaken upon. It is associated with Ma'at and she is usually seen upon a plinth, square pedestal with an angle at the front end. Today it can be any platform or pedestal that holds a vase or statue.

pranayama: In yoga, it is the practice of breathing that teaches us how to get power and energy from the breath in order to restore and maintain health, ultimately creating peace of mind. Many yoga and meditation teachers incorporate pranayama.

psychopomp: A guide for souls in their transitions through death. Anubis is the shamanic priest/deity of Egypt who is the Opener of the Way and fulfills this function. Many people, including nurses, hospice workers, shamans, and healers are drawn to help in this way, and can call on Anubis to guide and teach them these skills.

Pyramid Texts: The texts that were written on the walls of the "tombs" of the kings, and later the of the royalty and high priests, to guide them in their transitions between death and rebirth.

Ra Horakhty: Horus of the Horizon, the offspring that is born of the hieros-gamos, the sacred marriage of Ra and Osiris. He is usually shown as a hawk-headed man wearing a large sun disk surmounted with a cobra uraeus, although (as with many deities) he is represented in various forms at different times and places. Ra Horakhty expresses the current rule of the initiated sovereign, the realized divine human, be it on Earth or in the realm of the gods.

ren: The sacred power name of an individual. Your name has its own intrinsic power. In ancient Egypt, names were very important because they were considered to be the evidence, whether written or spoken, that a person lived. A person's *ren* is given at birth (both physical and shamanic) and lives as long as it is spoken. (For further information, see chapter 19, Amun-Ra.)

sahu: The transfigured, eternal spiritual body of the emergent human who has risen as Osiris and merged with Ra. Like the relationship between akasha and the elements, sahu is the matrix for the subtle bodies that were understood in ancient Egypt. It cannot be attained until the others are in place. The number of subtle bodies varies according to how deeply one delves into the literature.

Sakkara: Known as the step pyramid, this is the oldest known pyramid, built around 2700 BC. It was designed by Imhotep for the Pharaoh Djoser. Some say the name Sakkara, or Saqqara, is related to the word secret.

Sa Sekhem Sahu: A mantra expressing the power of heka, literally translated as Sa, the Breath of Life. Sekhem, the Power or Might, and Sahu, the realized or divine human. The best way to discover the meaning of these words is to meditate upon them in sacred ceremony and let their inner meaning be revealed to you from your inner, intuitive experience.

Sed festival: Festival of rejuvenation of the pharaoh, supposed to have been done after thirty years of rule to prove the pharaoh's physical and spiritual worthiness and power in order to continue to rule. These rites actually happened more often.

sekhem: Both the power of activation and the rod of power. Sekhem is also a symbol of authority. The word is related to Sekhmet, whose name means "power" or "mighty one."

senet: A spiritual/oracular board game played by ancient Egyptians. Its name means "passing." It is a game of life and death, similar to Hounds and Jackals and to checkers and draughts. It requires strategy in order to move the pieces appropriately. (See draughts.)

seraphim: A class of archangels found in both Jewish and Christian theology, referring to winged celestial beings who live very close to the sun and whose sounds are thought to be the celestial choir. They are made of pure light, are in direct communication with God, and their fiery nature expresses both purification and love.

Shakti: A Hindu goddess of many names who is the consort of Shiva and is the Divine Mother. She represents the vibrant feminine force.

shen: Symbol of eternity carried in the talons of Nekhbet, the vulture goddess. When it is stretched in length, it forms the cartouche, which holds the name of the pharaoh.

Shiva: The supreme god of the Hindu pantheon, he is the grounding part of the energy of Shakti, his consort, and the masculine power that holds her.

sistrum: This musical instrument, similar to a metal rattle, is shaped like an ankh. It is considered sacred to Hathor and additionally is seen with Bast, Bes, and Ihi. Besides using it in religious ceremonies, one shakes it to ward off unwanted energies and placate the neteru. It makes the sound of wind moving through the reeds, rattling the papyrus seeds.

Sophia: The divine feminine source or Mother of God or creation in Judeo-Christian and Mediterranean cultures, and seen here (on the cover of *Shamanic Mysteries of Egypt*) as the serpent that offers the fruit of wisdom to Adam and Even in the garden. The Greek meaning for Sophia is wisdom.

tarot: A body of arcane knowledge that is expressed through pictures, which reveal through symbolism the mysterious Arcanum (secret or hidden wisdom) in a similar manner as do the hieroglyphs, the sacred carvings of Egypt. Tarot comes to us in the form of an oracular tool of divination. It is usually presented as a deck of 78 cards, 22 of which constitute the "Major Arcana" or trump cards. It is the 22 Major Arcana (or akasha, the matrix of information sometimes referred to as spirit) plus the four suits, which are here presented as the elements (water, earth, fire and air, all derivatives of akasha) that make up the family of neteru we are introduced to in *Shamanic Mysteries of Egypt*.

Tefnut and Shu: The parents of Geb and Nut, these deities also represent the mist and the air, or the atmosphere between the earth and the sky. Tefnut is a leonine goddess resembling Sekhmet. Together they hold separate the yearning lovers, Earth (Geb) and Sky (Nut), so that creation can happen.

The Two Lands: See Upper Egypt.

uas (or was) staff: A scepter or wand of power that conveys dominion over the forces of death and darkness. One who carries it must have passed through and fully comprehended those shamanic rites. It is usually carried by gods, also carried by some awakened pharaohs.

Unas: A pharaoh from the Old Kingdom whose pyramid at Sakkara contained carved verses on the inner walls considered the first of the "Pyramid Texts." The rites recorded in the texts were those that initially inspired the work of *Shamanic Mysteries of Egypt*.

Upper Egypt: The Red lands, the desert lands in the south of Egypt. The first king, Narmer (Menes) founded the First Dynasty about 5,000 years ago, bringing the Two Lands, Upper and Lower Egypt, together and uniting Egypt. (See Lower Egypt.)

uraeus: Circlet crowning the head of pharaoh (and other awakened adepts) with the cobra raised on the brow.

Zep Tepi: The beginning of time and existence and the first Golden Age as expressed through the neteru. It may well have been the actual reign of Osiris on Earth. The words themselves mean First Time.

FOR FURTHER READING

Abbate, Francesco, ed. *Egyptian Art*. London: Peerage Books, 1972.

Almond, Jocelyn, and Keith Seddon. *An Egyptian Book of Shadows: Eight Seasonal Rites of Egyptian Paganism*. London: Thorsons, 1999.

Armour, Robert A. *Gods and Myths of Ancient Egypt*. Cairo, Egypt: The American University in Cairo Press, 1986.

Arrien, Angeles. *The Tarot Handbook: Practical Applications of Ancient Visual Symbols*. New York: Jeremy P. Tarcher/Putnam, 1997.

Assmann, Jan. *The Mind of Egypt*. New York: Metropolitan Books, 1996.

Bardon, Franz. *Initiation into Hermetics: A Practice of Magic*. Freiburg/Breisgau, West Germany: Verlag Hermann Bauer, 1956. Reprinted, Wuppertal, West Germany, 1981.

———. *The Key to the True Quabbalah*. Wuppertal, West Germany: Dieter Rüggeberg, 1971. Reprinted, 1982.

———. *The Practice of Magical Evocation*. Freiburg/Breisgau, West Germany: Verlag Hermann Bauer, 1956. Reprinted, Graz-Puntigam, Austria: Rudolf Pravica, 1967.

Barocas, Claudio. *Monuments of Civilization: Egypt*. New York: Grosset & Dunlap, 1972.

Barrett, Clive. *The Egyptian Gods and Goddesses: The Mythology and Beliefs of Ancient Egypt*. London: The Aquarian Press, 1992.

Bauval, Robert, and Adrian Gilbert. *The Orion Mystery: Unlocking the Secrets of the Pyramids*. Great Britain: William Heinemann Ltd., 1994.

————.*The Egypt Code.* New York: Random House, 2006

Blavatsky, H. P. *Isis Unveiled: A Master-Key to the Mysteries of Ancient and Modern Science and Theology.* 2 vols. Pasadena, Calif.: Theosophical University Press, 1976.

Bolen, Jean Shinoda. *Goddesses in Everywoman: A New Psychology of Women.* San Francisco: Harper & Row, 1984.

Brunton, Dr. Paul. *A Search in Secret Egypt.* New York: Samuel Weiser, Inc., 1935. Reprinted, 1977.

Budge, E. A. Wallis. *The Book of the Dead.* Great Britain: Kegan Paul, Trench, Trubner, 1899. Republished, London: Arkana, 1989.

————. *Dwellers of the Nile.* New York: Dover Press, 1977.

————. *The Egyptian Book of the Dead: The Papyrus of Ani.* New York: Dover Press, 1967.

————. *Egyptian Magic.* London: Kegan Paul, Trench, Trübner & Co. Ltd., 1899. Reprinted, 1975.

————. *The Gods of the Egyptians: Studies in Egyptian Mythology.* 2 vols. New York: Dover Publications, Inc., 1969.

Campbell, Joseph. *The Way of the Animal Powers, Vol. 1: Historical Atlas of World Mythology.* San Francisco, Calif.: Harper and Row, 1983.

Cannon Reed, Ellen. *Invocation of the Gods: Ancient Egyptian Magic for Today.* St. Paul, Minn.: Llewellyn Publications, 1992.

Carpiceci, Alberto Carlo. *Art and History of Egypt.* Italy: Centro Stampa Editoriale Bonechi, 1999.

Carson, Blanche M. *From Cairo to the Cataract.* Boston, Mass.: L.C. Page & Company, 1909.

Chaney, Earlyne. *Initiation in the Great Pyramid.* Upland, Calif.: Astara, Inc. 1987.

Clark, R. T. Rundle. *Myth and Symbol in Ancient Egypt.* London: Thames and Hudson, 1959.

Clark, Rosemary. *Sacred Magic of Ancient Egypt.* St. Paul, Minn.: Llewellyn Publications, 2003.

————. *The Sacred Traditions in Ancient Egypt: The Esoteric Wisdom Revealed.* St. Paul, Minn.: Llewellyn Publications, 2000.

Cott, Jonathan. *The Search for Omm Sety: A Story of Eternal Love.* United Kingdom: Rider, 1988. Republished, London: Arrow Books, 1989.

Crowley, Aleister. *Book of Thoth: A Short Essay on the Tarot of the Egyptians.* York Beach, Me.: Weiser Books, 1974.

Crowley Tarot. *The Crowley Tarot.* Akron Hajo Banzhaf, U.S. Games Systems, Inc. Translated from the German by Christine M. Grimm, 1995.

Davies, W. V. *Reading the Past: Egyptian Hieroglyph*. London: The British Museum Publications Ltd., 1987.

Dee, Jonathan. *Isis: Queen of Egyptian Magic*. New York: Sterling Publishing Company, 2003.

Dodson, Aidan. *The Hieroglyphs of Ancient Egypt*. United Kingdom: New Holland Publishers and Barnes and Noble, 2001.

Doreal. *The Emerald Tablets of Thoth-the-Atlantean: A Literal Translation and Interpretation of One of the Most Ancient and Secret of the Great Works of the Ancient Wisdom*. Nashville, Tenn.: Source Books, 1996.

Durbin-Robertson, Lawrence. *The Goddess of Chaldaea, Syria and Egypt*. Clonegal, Enniscorthy, Eire: Cesara Publications, 1975.

Eisler, Riane. *The Chalice and the Blade*. San Francisco: Harper & Row Publishers, 1988.

el-Din, Abdel Halim Nur. *The Role of Women in the Ancient Egyptian Society*. Cairo, Egypt: S.C.A. Press, 1995.

Ellis, Normandi. *Awakening Osiris: The Egyptian Book of the Dead*. Newburyport, Mass., and San Francisco: Phanes Press, an imprint of Red Wheel/Weiser, 1989.

———. *Dreams of Isis: A Woman's Spiritual Sojourn*. Wheaton, Ill.: Quest Books, 1995.

———. *Feasts of Light: Celebrations for the Seasons of Life*. Wheaton, Ill.: Quest Books, 1999.

el-Mallakh, Kamal, and Arnold Brackman. *The Gold of Tutankhamen*. New York: Newsweek Books, 1976.

El-Qhamid and Joseph Toledano. *Egyptian Erotica*. Astrolog Publishing House, 2004.

Erman, Adolf. *Life in Ancient Egypt*. London, Constable and Company, Ltd., 1894. Republished, New York: Dover Publications, 1971.

Fergus, Fleming, and Alan Lothian. *Myth and Mankind: The Way to Eternity: Egyptian Myth*. London: Duncan Baird Publishers, 1997.

Fletcher, Joann. *Egyptian Book of Living and Dying*. London: Duncan Baird Publishers, 2002.

Forrest, M. Isidora. *Isis Magic*. St. Paul, Minn.: Llewellyn, 2001.

Freke, Timothy, and Peter Gandy. *The Hermetica: The Lost Wisdom of the Pharoahs*. London: Judy Piatkus Publishers, 1997. Republished, New York: Penguin Putnam Inc., 1999.

Gardiner, Sir Alan. *Egyptian Grammar: Being an Introduction to the Study of Hieroglyphs*. London: Oxford Press, 1927. Reprinted, 1966.

Grant, Joan. *The Blue Faience Hippopotamus*. London: Methuen & Co. Ltd., 1984.

Greer, Mary K. *Women of the Golden Dawn*. Rochester, Vt.: Park Street Press, 1995.

Haich, Elizabeth. *Initiation*. London: George Allen & Unwin Ltd., 1965. Reprint, Redway, Calif.: Seed Center, 1974.

Halifax, Joan. *Shamanic Voices: A Survey of Visionary Narratives*. New York: E.P. Dutton, 1979.

Hall, Manly P. *An Encyclopedic Outline of Masonic, Hermetic, Qabbalistic and Rosicrucian Symbolical Philosophy: Being an Interpretation of the Secret Teachings Concealed Within the Ritual, Allegories and Mysteries of all Ages*. Los Angeles, Calif.: The Philosophical Research Society, Inc., 1968.

Hamilton-Paterson, James, and Carol Andrews. *Mummies: Death and Life in Ancient Egypt*. New York: The Viking Press and Penguin Books, 1979.

Hancock, Graham. *Fingerprints of the Gods: The Evidence of Earth's Lost Civilization*. New York: Crown Trade Paperbacks, 1995.

Hancock, Graham, and Robert Bauval. *The Message of the Sphinx*. New York: Crown, 1996.

Harner, Michael. *The Way of the Shaman*. New York: Bantam, 1982.

Hart, George. *The Legendary Past: Egyptian Myths*. Austin, Tex.: First University of Texas Press, 1990.

Hauck, Dennis William. *The Emerald Tablet: Alchemy of Personal Transformation*. New York: Penguin, 1999.

Hawass, Zahi. *Silent Images: Women in Pharaonic Egypt*. Cairo, Egypt: The American University in Cairo Press, 1998.

Heath, Maya. *The Egyptian Oracle*. Rochester, Vt.: Bear & Company, 1994.

Hope, Murry. *Practical Egyptian Magic*. New York: St. Martin's Press, 1984.

———. *The Way of Cartouche*. New York: St. Martin's Press, 1985.

Hornung, Erik, and Betsy M. Bryan, eds. *The Quest for Immortality: Treasures of Ancient Egypt*. Washington, D.C.: National Gallery of Art Publisher, 2002.

Houston, Jean. *The Passion of Isis and Osiris: A Union of Two Souls*. New York: Ballantine, 1995.

Ingerman, Sandra. *Soul Retrieval: Mending the Fragmented Self*, revised edition. San Francisco: HarperSanFrancisco, 2006.

Ions, Veronica. *Egyptian Mythology*. Middlesex, U.K.: Hamlyn House, 1968.

———. *Library of the World's Myths and Legends*. London; New York: The Hamlyn Publishing Group, 1965. Reprint, New York: Peter Bedrick Books, 1983.

Lamy, Lucie. *Egyptian Mysteries: New Light on Ancient Spiritual Knowledge.* New York: Crossroads, 1981.

Leadbeater, C. W. *Ancient Mystic Rites.* Wheaton, Ill.: The Theosophical Publishing House, 1986.

Lemesurier, Peter. *The Great Pyramid Decoded.* New York: Avon Books, 1977.

Lipton, Bruce. *The Biology of Belief: Unleashing The Power of Consciousness, Matter and Miracles.* Santa Cruz, N.M.: Mountain of Love Productions, 2005.

Macaulay, David. *Pyramid.* Boston, Mass.: Houghton Mifflin Company, 1975.

MacQuitty, William. *Island of Isis: Philae Temple of the Nile.* New York: Charles Scribner's Sons, 1976.

Manniche, Lise. *An Ancient Egyptian Herbal.* Austin: First University of Texas Press, 1989.

Masters, Robert. *The Goddess Sekmet: Psycho-Spiritual Exercises of the Fifth Way.* St. Paul, Minn.: Llewellyn Publications, 1990. Reprinted, Ashland, Ore.: White Cloud Press, 2002.

McDermott, Briget. *Decoding Egyptian Hieroglyphs.* Foreword by Joann Fletcher. San Francisco, Calif.: Chronicle Books, Duncan Baird Publishers, 2001.

Moss, Robert. *The Dreamer's Book of the Dead: A Soul Traveler's Guide to Death, Dying, and the Other Side.* Rochester, Vt.: Destiny Books, 2005.

Murray, Margaret. *Egyptian Religious Poetry.* London: John Murray, 1949.

Musaios. *The Lion Path: You Can Take it With You: A Manual of the Short Path to Regeneration for our Times.* Berkeley, Calif.: Golden Sceptre Publishing, 1985.

Narby, Jeremy. *The Cosmic Serpent—DNA and the Origins of Knowledge.* New York: Jeremy P. Tarcher/Putnam, 1999.

Naydler, Jeremy. *Shamanic Wisdom in the Pyramid Texts: The Mystical Tradition of Ancient Egypt.* Rochester, Vt.: Inner Traditions, 2005.

———. *Temple of the Cosmos: The Ancient Egyptian Experience of the Sacred.* Rochester, Vt.: Inner Traditions, 1996.

Nema. *Maat Magick: A Guide to Self-Initiation.* York Beach, Maine: Samuel Weiser, Inc., 1995.

Noble, Vicki. *Shakti Woman: Feeling Our Fire, Healing Our World—The New Feminine Shamanism.* New York: HarperCollins, 1991.

———. *Uncoiling the Snake: Ancient Patterns in Contemporary Women's Lives (A Snakepower Reader).* New York: HarperCollins, 1993.

Payne-Towler, Christine. *The Underground Stream: Esoteric Tarot Revealed.* Eugene, Ore.: Noreah Press, 1999.

Perkins, J. R. *The Emperor's Physician*. Chicago: Consolidated Book Publishers, 1944.

Plaskett, Norman. *The Ancient Egyptian Oracle: The Cards of Ra-Maat*. London: Carlton Books, 1998.

Pollack, Rachel. *The Shining Tribe Tarot*. St. Paul, Minn.: Llewellyn, 2001.

Redford, Donald B. *The Ancient Gods Speak: A Guide to Egyptian Religion*. New York: Oxford University Press, 2002.

Reed, Bika. *Rebel in the Soul: An Ancient Egyptian Dialogue Between a Man and His Destiny*. Rochester, Vt.: Inner Traditions, 1978. Reprinted, 1997.

Regula, deTraci. *The Mysteries of Isis: Her Workshop and Magick*. St. Paul, Minn.: Llewellyn, 1995.

Richardson, Alan, and B. Walker-John. *The Inner Guide to Egypt*. Bath, U.K.: Arcania Press, 1991.

Roberts, Alison. *Hathor Rising: The Power of the Goddess in Ancient Egypt*. Rochester, Vt.: Inner Traditions, 1995.

Robertson, Olivia. *The Call of Isis*. Clonegal, Eire: Cesara Publications, 1975.

Rose, Sharon. *The Path of the Priestess: A Guidebook for Awakening the Divine Feminine*. Rochester, Vt.: Inner Traditions, 2002.

Rossiter, Evelyn. *The Book of the Dead: Famous Egyptian Papyri*. Fribourg, Genéve: Productions Liber SA and Editions Minerva SA, 1984.

Salaman, Clement, Dorine van Oyen, William D. Wharton, and Jean-Pierre Mahé. *The Way of Hermes: New Translations of the Corpus Hermeticum and the Definitions of Hermes Trismegistus to Asclepius*. London: Gerald Duckworth & Co. Ltd., 1999. Republished, Rochester, Vt.: Inner Traditions, 2000.

Schuré, Édouard. *The Great Initiates: A Study of the Secret History of Religions*. West Nyack, N.Y.: St. George Books, 1961.

Schwaller de Lubicz, Isha. *Esoterism and Symbols*. Rochester, Vt.: Inner Traditions, 1985.

———. *Her-Bak: Egyptian Initiate*. Great Britian: Hodder & Stoughton, 1967. Republished, Rochester, Vt.: Inner Traditions, 1978.

———. *Her-Bak: The Living Face of Ancient Egypt*. Paris: Ernest Flammarion, 1955. Republished, Rochester, Vt.: Inner Traditions, 1978.

———. *The Opening of the Way*. Rochester, Vt.: Inner Traditions, 1981.

Schwaller de Lubicz, R. A. *Sacred Science: The King of Pharaonic Theocracy*. Translated by André and Goldian VanderBroeck. Rochester, Vt: Inner Traditions, 1982.

Seton-Williams, M. V. *Egyptian Legends and Stories*. New York: Barnes and Noble, 1988.

Shorter, Alan W. *The Egyptian Gods: A Handbook*. North Hollywood, Calif.: Newcastle Publishing, 1985.

Sjöö, Monica, and Barbara Mor. *The Great Cosmic Mother: Rediscovering the Religion of the Earth*. New York: Harper & Row, 1987.

Spence, Lewis. *Egypt*. London: Senate, 1994.

Sutherland, Joanna. *Egyptology: Search for the Tomb of Osiris*. Cambridge, Mass: Candlewick Press, 2004.

Temple, Robert K. G. *The Sirius Mystery: Was Earth Visited by Intelligent Beings from a Planet in the System of the Star of Sirius?* Rochester, Vt.: Destiny Books, 1987.

Three Initiates. *The Kybalion: Hermetic Philosophy*. Chicago: The Yogi Publication Society, 1912. Reprinted, 1940.

Veggi, Athon, and Alison Davidson. *The Book of Doors Divination Deck: An Alchemical Oracle From Ancient Egypt*. Rochester, Vt.: Destiny Books, 1995.

Villoldo, Alberto. *Shaman, Healer, Sage*. New York: Harmony Books, 2000.

Walker, Barbara G. *The Woman's Dictionary of Symbols and Sacred Objects*. San Francisco: Harper & Row, 1988.

———. *The Woman's Encyclopedia of Myths and Secrets*. San Francisco: Harper & Row, 1983.

West, John Anthony. *Ancient Egypt: the Meaning Behind the Magic*. Wheaton, Ill.: Quest Books, 1991.

———. *Serpent in the Sky: The Wisdom of Ancient Egypt*. Wheaton, Ill.: Quest Books, 1993.

———. *The Traveler's Key to Ancient Egypt: A Guide to the Sacred Places of Ancient Egypt*. New York: Alfred A. Knopf, 1988.

Wilkinson, Richard H. *The Complete Gods and Goddesses of Ancient Egypt*. Cairo, Egypt: The American University in Cairo Press, 2003.

———. *The Complete Temples of Ancient Egypt*. New York: Thames & Hudson Inc., 2000.

———. *Reading Egyptian Art: A Hieroglyphic Guide to Ancient Egyptian Painting and Sculpture*. New York: Thames and Hudson, Ltd., 1992.

Wolf, Fred Alan. *Mind into Matter: A New Alchemy of Science and Sprit*. Needham, Mass.: Moment Point Press, 2000.

Woolger, Jennifer Barker, and Roger J. Woolger. *The Goddess Within: A Guide to the Eternal Myths That Shape Women's Lives*. New York: Ballantine Books, 1987. Reprint, 1989.

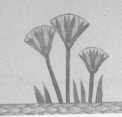

INDEX

ABOUT THE AUTHORS

NICKI SCULLY has been teaching healing, shamanic arts, and the Egyptian Mysteries since 1983. The techniques from her Alchemical Healing form are used internationally by thousands of practitioners. She is a lineage holder in the Hermetic tradition of Thoth and maintains the Lyceum of Shamanic Egypt. She was ordained by Lady Olivia Robertson, cofounder of the Fellowship of Isis, as a priestess of Hathor. During her first tour of Egypt with the Grateful Dead in 1978, Nicki experienced an epiphany on the top of the great pyramid and realized that her purpose in this life is to bring forth the hidden shamanic arts of Egypt. Drawing on the knowledge she has gained through decades of study and practice, she enlightens and uplifts all who study and travel with her.

In the late 1980s, Nicki founded Shamanic Journeys, Ltd., and has been guiding inner journeys and spiritual pilgrimages to Egypt, Peru, Greece, and other sacred sites. Nicki lives in Eugene, Oregon, where she maintains a comprehensive healing and shamanic consulting practice. She welcomes you to study with her at her beautiful garden center.

LINDA STAR WOLF is a gifted ritualist and ceremonial facilitator who weaves together the threads of ancient and contemporary healing methods that address current needs. She is founder of Venus Rising Institute for Shamanic Healing Arts and is creator of the Shamanic Breathwork™

Process. Star Wolf holds a Doctorate of Ministry from AIWP (Association for the Integration of the Whole Person) University and is a nationally certified addictions counselor. As a Shamanic Pastoral Counselor, spiritual midwife, and guide for souls in the transformational process, Star Wolf has an extensive background both personally and professionally in the mental health and spirituality arena, with experience ranging from addictions work and 12-step recovery, to psycho-spiritual and shamanic work. It is her particular passion to teach those who are ready to embody "Shamanic Consciousness in Everyday Life." She has led powerful transformational workshops in the U.S. and abroad since 1988 and has taught thousands of participants. She lives in a conscious community, Isis Cove, in the mountains of North Carolina.

ALSO BY NICKI SCULLY

Alchemical Healing
A Guide to Spiritual, Physical, and
Transformational Medicine
Bear & Company, 2003

Power Animal Meditations
Shamanic Journeys with Your Spirit Allies
Illustrated by Angela Werneke
Bear & Company, 2001

DVD AVAILABLE FROM NICKI SCULLY

Alchemical Healing
Experiences, Insights, and Empowerments
Produced by Sacred Mysteries

This interview covers many subjects related to Alchemical Healing, and provides two empowerments: The Fire Mist Shower empowerment that connects you to the Life Force Energy, and the Parabola Healing Ritual for people dealing with or supporting those with cancer.

CDs Available from Nicki Scully

The first three of the following CDs can function as audio illustrations for *Power Animal Meditations*.

Journey for Healing with Kuan Yin
Nicki Scully with music by Roland Barker and Jerry Garcia
Track one: "Journey for Healing with Kuan Yin"
Track two: Music only

Proceeds from the sale of this CD go toward the production and distribution of more of these CDs to be *given away* to people with AIDS, leukemia, or cancer, or to centers and practitioners working with those diseases. Donations are tax deductible.

Awakening the Cobra
Nicki Scully with music by Roland Barker
Track one: "Journey with the Cobra for Clearing the Chakras
and Awakening the Kundalini Energies"
Track two: Music only

Journey with Eagle & Elephant
Nicki Scully with music by Roland Barker
Track one: "Journey with Eagle & Elephant"
Track two: Music only

Tribal Alchemy
Three journeys are available on this CD: Renewal, Journey for Peace, and Animal Totems
Nicki Scully with music produced and arranged by Roland Barker

. . . And You Will Fly!
An Animal Circus Adventure (for children of all ages)
Written by Nicki Scully, Roland Barker, and Mark Hallert
Narrated by Nicki Scully
Music written and produced by Roland Barker

An Alchemical healing story produced as a radio play for children to be given away free to any child suffering from a potentially terminal disease, and to those hospitals and practitioners working with these children. Proceeds from the sale of this CD will go toward further production and distribution so that more can be given away. Donations are tax deductible.

To order, contact your local bookseller or
Nicki Scully
P.O. Box 5025
Eugene, OR 97405
www.shamanicjourneys.com
office@shamanicjourneys.com

CD Set Available from Linda Star Wolf

The Spiral
A two-CD set produced by
Linda Star Wolf and Soulfood

CD one: A musical journey of dreamy spiritual songs with a Native American flavor, six cuts.
CD two: "The Spiral Meditation," three guided meditations narrated by Star Wolf, accompanied by entrancing music and nature sounds.

To order contact
Venus Rising Institute for Shamanic Healing Arts
P.O. Box 486
Sylva, NC 28779
www.shamanicbreathwork.org
venusrising@shamanicbreathwork.org